ORIGINAL
FORD
MODEL A

Other titles available in the *Original* series are:

Original AC Ace & Cobra
by Rinsey Mills

Original Aston Martin DB4/5/6
by Robert Edwards

Original Austin Seven
by Rinsey Mills

Original Austin-Healey (100 & 3000)
by Anders Ditlev Clausager

Original Camaro 1972-1986
by Andy Kraushaar and Jason Scott

Original Citroën DS
by John Reynolds with Jan de Lange

Original Corvette 1953-1962
by Tom Falconer

Original Corvette 1963-1967
by Tom Falconer

Original Ducati Sport & Super Sport 1972-1986
by Ian Falloon

Original Ferrari V8
by Keith Bluemel

Original Ferrari V12 1965-1973
by Keith Bluemel

Original Harley-Davidson Panhead
by Greg Field

Original Honda CB750
by John Wyatt

Original Jaguar E-Type
by Philip Porter

Original Jaguar Mark I/II
by Nigel Thorley

Original Jaguar XJ
by Nigel Thorley

Original Jaguar XK
by Philip Porter

Original Land-Rover Series I
by James Taylor

Original Mercedes SL
by Laurence Meredith

Original MG T Series
by Anders Ditlev Clausager

Original MGA
by Anders Ditlev Clausager

Original MGB
by Anders Ditlev Clausager

Original Mini Cooper and Cooper S
by John Parnell

Original Morgan
by John Worrall and Liz Turner

Original Morris Minor
by Ray Newell

Original Mustang 1964½-1966
by Colin Date

Original Pontiac GTO 1964-1974
by Tom de Mauro

Original Porsche 356
by Laurence Meredith

Original Porsche 911
by Peter Morgan

Original Porsche 924/944/968
by Peter Morgan

Original Rolls-Royce & Bentley 1946-65
by James Taylor

Original Sprite & Midget
by Terry Horler

Original Triumph TR2/3/3A
by Bill Piggott

Original Triumph TR4/4A/5/6
by Bill Piggott

Original Triumph Stag
by James Taylor

Original Vincent
by J. P. Bickerstaff

Original VW Beetle
by Laurence Meredith

Original VW Bus
by Laurence Meredith

ORIGINAL
FORD
MODEL A

by Jim Schild

MOTORBOOKS

First published in 2003 by Motorbooks, an imprint of MBI Publishing Company, Galtier Plaza, 380 Jackson Street, Suite 200, St. Paul, MN 55101-3885 USA.

© Jim Schild, 2003

All rights reserved. With the exception of quoting brief passages for the purposes of review, no part of this publication may be reproduced without prior written permission from the Publisher.

The information in this book is true and complete to the best of our knowledge. All recommendations are made without guarantee on the part of the author or Publisher, who also disclaim any liability incurred in connection with the use of this data or specific details.

This publication has not been prepared, approved, or licensed by Ford Motor Company. We recognize that some words, model names, and designations mentioned herein are the property of the trademark holder. We use them for identification purposes only. This is not an official publication.

Motorbooks titles are also available at discounts in bulk quantity for industrial or sales-promotional use. For details write to the Special Sales Manager at MBI Publishing Company, Galtier Plaza, 380 Jackson Street, Suite 200, St. Paul, MN 55101-3885 USA.

ISBN-13: 978-0-7603-1252-0
ISBN-10: 0-7603-1252-4

On the front cover: The body of this 1931 40-B Deluxe Roadster is Brewster Green with black moldings and Apple Green stripe and wheels.

On the title page: The body of this 1931 45-B Standard Coupe is finished in Kewanee Green. This car is easily identified as a 1931 by the upper radiator shell and one-piece running board splash shields. *Kenneth Keeley*

On the frontispiece: This detail view of left-side door handle hardware on a 1929 Standard Fordor shows that by 1929 these handles all turn down at the ends.

On the Table of Contents page: This 1930 82-B closed cab pickup truck is finished in Blue Rock Green with Apple Green stripe and wheels. Note the black-painted radiator and headlight shells. The whitewalls and wood stakes in the truck bed are accessories.

On the back cover: This left front quarter view of a 1929 54-A Business Coupe shows the oval quarter windows used only that year. The lower body is Vagabond Green with Rock Moss Green moldings. *Kenneth Keeley*

Edited by Peter Bodensteiner
Designed by Chris Fayers

Printed in China

Contents

Acknowledgments 6
Introduction 7
Chapter 1: 1928 8
Chapter 2: 1929 32
Chapter 3: 1930 62
Chapter 4: 1931 88
Appendix 1: Related Clubs & Organizations 127
Appendix 2: Owners of Featured Cars 127
Index 128

Original Ford Model A

Acknowledgments

A book of this type cannot be produced without the cooperation, knowledge, and experience of many people. Although I have more than 40 years of experience with the Model A Ford, the value of this work has been greatly enhanced by the contributions of a number of other enthusiasts.

First, I have to thank the Model A Restorer's Club (MARC) and the Model A Ford Club of America (MAFCA) for allowing the use of the information published in the MARC/MAFCA Judging Standards. These standards are always the final reference authority for Model "A" Ford restoration. The value of the many years of research and work of the Judging Standards Committees cannot be overstated.

I must thank my friend Larry Hassel, who provided additional detail photography, and Model "A" News editor Ken Keeley, who provided photos from his files to cover additional body types. I also thank my wife, Myrna, who spent many hours proofreading and editing the text.

Last, but not least, I must recognize those Model A owners who put forth extra time and effort to assist me in producing useful photographs of their cars. These owners include Les Burton, Carle Garrett, Larry Hassel, Timothy Kelly, Bruce and Bunny Palmer, Jim Ruth, and H. Dave Weston.

Introduction

By 1925, Ford sales and production were going steadily downhill and Chevrolet sales were rising rapidly. Most of Ford's executives and advisors were arguing strongly against continuing the Model T. The Ford dealer network was going broke. The dealerships that did not close or leave the Ford Company were up in arms over Henry Ford's refusal to change policies and create a new car. Seven out of 10 Ford dealers were losing money and the ranks were demanding changes. Ford was no longer a leader in the industry. Customers everywhere protested the Model T's antiquated engineering and styling. The people wanted a more modern automobile; they wanted a speedometer, more speed, and a standard transmission.

By late 1926, Henry Ford had made a decision. He had given in to all of the pressures of his advisors, his dealers, and to Edsel, his son, who may have had the most influence though Henry would never admit it. As late as December 1926, Ford still declared there was no new car; however, development of the Model T's replacement was already underway.

The introduction of the New Ford in December 1927 was accompanied by what the Advertising Club of New York called "the most soundly coordinated advertising campaign in America's advertising history." Henry Ford used his considerable skill in publicity and promotion to make the announcement and introduction of the Model A one of his greatest accomplishments. The Model A was a world of difference from the previous Model T in styling, engineering, and operation. These improvements were well received by the automobile buying public, who placed more than 800,000 orders by the spring of 1928. The Model A Ford's success was proven with more than five million built by the end of production late in 1931.

With more than 40 colors, 50 body styles, and a significant styling change during its four-year production, the Model A Ford had something to offer for everyone. From the sporty roadsters and phaetons to stylish sedans, town cars, coupes, and trucks, the Model A covered every conceivable market need.

Today, the Ford Model A is one of the most popular collector cars in the world. It is estimated that more than 500,000 Model As still exist, and their restoration and enjoyment supports two major clubs with total membership of more than 23,000. Model A Ford owners drive and show their favorite cars at a variety of tours, shows, and events in all 50 U.S. states and in 30 foreign countries.

Original Ford Model A is a comprehensive and detailed guide to original factory specifications, equipment, colors, and trim for the 1928–1931 Model A. The purpose of this book is to provide precise and correct information on all models and years. Included are the running changes made during production with data not only on the common models but also the rarest. In addition to more than 40 years of experience with the Model A Ford, the author uses the information gathered from owners of original cars, factory literature, and the definitive data provided in the latest MARC/MAFCA Judging Standards to provide the most accurate reference available. (The most current MARC/MAFCA Judging Standards are the final, definitive authority for authenticity details beyond the scope of this book.)

Accompanying the authoritative text are 275 specially commissioned color photographs of authentic vehicles that are representative of the Model A Ford as it would have looked when new. Illustrations of body color and trim combinations and chassis parts provide a source of correct finishes and components that are found nowhere else. These photographs offer a view of the Model A that has never before been available. This book provides a valuable guide for collectors, restorers, buyers, and historians.

Original Ford Model A

Chapter 1
1928

The introduction of the new Ford Model A in November and December 1927 was without equal in size and scope. The president of the Advertising Club of New York recognized Ford's advertising and publicity program as "the most soundly coordinated advertising campaign in America's advertising history." By the time the public first saw Ford New Ford on December 2, almost 200,000 orders had already been received. Within the first few weeks that figure leapt to more than 400,000. Production could not keep pace. At a pace of barely more than 100 new cars per day, Ford built only a few more than 5,000 new cars in 1927. The company's financial losses for 1928 totaled $72,221,498.

The New Ford differed considerably from its predecessor in almost every way. Although the new engine was still a four-cylinder L-head design, the displacement was now 200.5 cubic inches compared to 176.7 cubic inches for the Model T. Brake horsepower was doubled to 40 at 2,200 rpm. The wheelbase was increased from 100.0 to 103.5

One of the first five body types available at the Model A introduction was the 35-A Phaeton. This four-door open car would have been called a touring car during the Model T era. The main body color is Arabian Sand Light with Copra Drab moldings and a French Gray stripe.

1928

This rear view of the 1928 35-A Phaeton shows the drum taillight on an A-13473 mounting bracket, early wheels, red steering wheel, and lack of outside door handles, which identify this car as an early 1928 model. The fender-mounted spare tires and wheels with covers and metal trunk are accessories.

inches. The front and rear suspension still used transverse springs, but the front and rear axles were of an entirely different design. The addition of hydraulic shock absorbers produced a superior ride and improved handling and safety. The Model A chassis used Alemite grease fittings rather than the oil cups used in the Model T.

Making the most of the updated chassis design and engineering of the New Ford required equally updated styling and construction. For 1928, Ford offered eight passenger and five commercial bodies. The passenger bodies were modern and low, with a clear family relationship to the Lincoln. The full-crown fenders and rounded nickel radiator shell design were almost identical to that of the Lincoln, which cost 10 to 15 times more than the Model A. The car also featured a new Ford script radiator emblem that copied the basic shape of the Lincoln design.

Chassis, Axles, and Wheels

The Model A frame has a ladder-type design with two tapered-channel side-members about 100 inches long with three cross-members. The frame is constructed of number 9 U.S.S.-gauge hot-rolled, open-hearth steel. The thickness is held between 0.140 and 0.160 inch with a tensile strength of 42,000 pounds per square inch. The three cross-members and four running board brackets are riveted to the side rails. The two forged front fender brackets are bolted to the frame side rails.

The front cross-member is a channel design and secures the front transverse spring in its center. The front cross-member also holds the front engine mount and the radiator, which is bolted to a pad at each side. The first design frame, A-5005-A, was used on very early 1928 cars. The front cross-member of this frame is of a riveted three-piece construction with a solid front engine mount. The A-design frame was used only on the first 200 cars and was replaced in December 1927 with the more familiar A-5005-B. A solid front engine mount identifies the front cross-member of this frame. This mount had ears that bolted directly to the front of the engine.

1928 Ford Model A Production

Model	Name	Weight	Price	Number Produced
35-A	Phaeton	2,140	$395	47,476
40-A	Roadster	2,106/2,161*	$385	82,206
45-A	Coupe	2,225/2,280*	$495	74,224
49-A	Special Coupe	2,225/2,280*	$495	(Combined w/Coupe)
50-A	Sport Coupe	2,250	$550	82,879
54-A	Business Coupe	2,225	$495	37,601
55-A	Tudor	2,340	$495	210,510
60-A	Fordor	2,386	$570	82,349
76-A	Open Cab Pickup	2,073	$395	23,972
79-A	Panel Delivery	2,416	$550	3,744
82-A	Closed Cab Pickup	2,215	$445	
	A Chassis	1,650	$325	
	AA Chassis	2,790	$460	
85-A	AA Panel Delivery	3,847	$850	2,486
88-A	AA Platform		$595	2,731
89-A	AA Express			4,087
188-A	AA Stake		$610	21,680

*With rumble seat. The 50-A Sport Coupe was equipped with a rumble seat as standard equipment.

The First Model A Ford

Although the Model A was ceremoniously presented to the public on December 2, 1927, the first Model A was actually not totally finished and delivered until much later. By August of 1927, Ford had produced prototypes of the Model A cars as manufacturing procedures were being finalized. The entire plant's operations and machinery had to be redesigned and new equipment had to be built. It was not until October 20, 1927, that the first complete Model A engine came off of the assembly line. Henry and Edsel Ford posed for photos with four members of Ford's senior engineering staff at the break-in stand and Henry personally stamped the first engine with the number A-1.

Engine number A-1 was carried to the new Rouge Assembly Plant on October 21 and installed into a chassis as the line production developed. The first car came out of the Rouge Plant with a 55-A Tudor sedan body and Henry Ford drove it off the line. Early production rates were very low, increasing slowly as operations were perfected. While line operations were being refined, the A-1 Tudor was delivered to the Ford Dearborn Laboratory for more testing and inspection.

When the Model A was formally introduced on December 2, 1927, Henry Ford's general secretary, Ernest G. Liebold, sent correspondence to Thomas Edison's personal assistant Mr. W. Meadowcroft, inquiring as to whether Mr. Edison would accept Mr. Ford's gift of Model A number one. Henry Ford had always admired Thomas Edison and had reserved ownership of this important car for Edison from the very beginning. Edison preferred a touring body, so the original Tudor body was removed. (While waiting for number one to be completed, Thomas Edison ceremoniously drove the first Model A built at the Kearny, New Jersey, assembly plant off the line on December 19, 1927.)

Due to production requirements for sales orders, the new Phaeton body was not produced and installed on chassis number one until May 31, 1928. While production was being delayed, further correspondence between Mr. Ford and Mr. Edison laid out details of the body according to Mr. Edison's preferences. The 35-A Standard Phaeton body was finished in dark green and was equipped with goatskin interior trim rather than the standard Spanish Brown artificial leather. The car was delivered with the early open-end bumpers that were used only on a very few early production models.

Thomas Edison used Model A number one, with periodic updates by Ford, until his death in October 1931. The car remained unlicensed and in the Edison family until 1943, when Edison's wife presented it to the Henry Ford Museum at Dearborn, Michigan. The car remains there on display, and restored to its original condition.

Although the Edison car is based on the first Model A built, it is believed that the first complete Model A delivered actually went to famous comedian and entertainer Will Rogers in December 1927.

This design was changed in November 1928 by eliminating the mounting ears and adding a flexible four-piece engine mount that was attached to the center of the cross-member channel. This design incorporated two small coil springs, providing a cushioning suspension for the engine. The A-5005-B frame also has mounting holes for the left-side parking brake rocker arm bracket on the left side-member. These were eliminated after the brake system was modified in June 1928.

The center cross-member is an inverted-channel design and incorporates mounts for the battery, battery cable, and stoplight switch. The center cross-member is also riveted to the frame side rails. On early 1928 cars, the center cross-member also provides stops and bracket mountings for the equalizing brake system.

The rear cross-member is riveted to the frame and also an inverted channel, but it has a high arch in the center that secures the rear transverse spring. The outer ends of the rear cross-member extend out from the frame rails and provide rear body mounting holes. The inside corners of the rear cross-member are gusseted to prevent twisting and flexing of the frame. The entire frame was painted with a gloss black pyroxilyn finish after final assembly. The black paint was not rubbed out nor was any attempt made to achieve a high-quality finish.

The front axle of the Model A (A-3010-C) is of I-beam construction and is suspended by a transverse-mounted semi-elliptic spring that is mounted to the center of the front cross-member with two U-bolts. Each end of the spring is attached to the front axle assembly by spring hangers with lubricated steel bushings. The front spring (A-5310-A) for all 1928 Model A body types has 10 leaves. Front and rear tread width of the Model A is 56 inches.

On the axle itself there was a 1-inch-long Ford script on the left front and right rear on the very early cars. This was changed by early 1928 to a smaller size script that was used through mid-1929. The only other change in the front axle assembly was in the design of the spindle-bolt locking pins. The first design, used through April 1929, has a large head with a small hex and is secured with a castellated nut. The spindle-bolt locking pin also serves as a steering stop for the spindle. The front axle finish is gloss black.

The front axle is held parallel by a wishbone-shaped radius rod attached to the bottom of the transmission bell housing by a ball-and-socket mounting. This ball-and-socket assembly consists of a two-piece mounting held in place with two special, slotted-head bolts, two spacers, and two small coil springs. This design lets the ball rotate easily in the socket, allowing the front suspension to articulate while still maintaining the stability of the front axle. Radius rod arms are welded, forged tubes. Early arms were a thin, tapered design that were welded at the top. In early 1928, these were changed to an inverted U forging that was welded at the bottom. This design was used through mid-1930.

The 1928 Ford Model A steering gear is a Ford-designed, seven-tooth, worm-and-sector unit. The design is unusual in that it incorporates a steering column that is welded to the sector housing. The New Ford steering gear was designed

1928

The front view of an early 1928 front axle and right brake backing plate. Note the Ford script on the front side of the axle. The brake drum has an accessory reinforcing band installed.

to reduce excessive feedback created when the balloon tires traveled on rough roads. Adjustments to this early design are accomplished by the use of shims for steering-shaft endplay and by an adjustment nut for sector-shaft endplay.

The gloss black–finished steering column housing also includes two nickel-plated rods, which control the hand throttle and ignition spark adjustment and a control tube for the lighting system and horn. The horn and light switch are mounted in the center of the red Fordite steering wheel and operated by a nickel-plated lever. The steering wheel was changed to a black rubber material very late in 1928. Some red wheels could have been used into early 1929.

The rear axle (A-1001) is a three-piece design that incorporates a welded banjo-style differential housing. Each axle housing is constructed of rolled, electrically welded steel with a $9^{11}/_{16}$-inch bell end. The housing is bolted to the differential housing with $10^{3}/_{8}$-inch hex-head screws and lock washers. The outer end of each housing supports the outer axle bearings and has an integral forged mounting for the rear spring perch and shock absorber mounting ball.

The rear spring has a transverse, semi-elliptic design, and all variations are identified by their distinctive high center arch. There are five variations of rear spring configuration depending upon the body type. The A-5560-C Roadster rear spring has seven leaves and noticeably less arch than the others. The A-5560-B rear spring has eight leaves and is used on the Phaeton, Coupe, and Sport Coupe. The Tudor used the A-5560-A 10-leaf rear spring. The 10-leaf A-5560-D rear spring is used on Fordors, while the A-5560-E 10-leaf spring is used on the Open and Closed Cab Pickups. Front and rear springs were finished in black. Each rear spring variation was originally identified by a letter on the face of one of the spring clamps.

The axles of the Model A are made of 1.128- to 1.130-inch-diameter heat-treated steel. The inner axle bearing is finished and is 1.493 to 1.494 inches in diameter. The differential gear is integral with the axle and is 3.428 inches in diameter. The outer end of each axle is tapered 1.5 inches per foot and is threaded and slotted for a key to attach the rear hub.

The differential gears of the Model A are spiral, bevel cut, and made from heat-treated forgings. The finished ring gear is 8.4 inches in diameter with a diametral pitch of 4.881 inches. The gear ratio of the Model A was initially 3.70:1 (10-37) through early 1929. In late 1928, a higher 3.54:1 ratio

Right: An inside view of the left rear axle housing, brake backing plate, and A-4751-AR rear radius rod and attachment on an early 1928 chassis. Note the L-shaped end on the early radius rod. Later rods have a Y-shaped end. Also note that there is no parking brake lever. *Larry Hassel*

Far right: The right rear A-1115-AR brake drum and hub assembly on an early 1928 chassis. This drum and hub may be used only with the early wheels. Note the distinctive taper to the front of the drum. *Larry Hassel*

Original Ford Model A

(11-39) was introduced to allow higher speeds and lower engine rpm. The differential gears are contained in a "banjo"-design housing.

The driveshaft torque tube is also a rolled steel tube. It attaches to the front of the differential housing with six safety-wired ⅜-inch screws. There were three torque tube designs used in 1928. The first design, used through mid-1928, has a 10-inch-long, 2-inch-diameter straight section behind the universal joint followed by an 18-inch tapered section. The second design was tapered over its entire length. This design was used from early 1928 through the end of production. The third design was introduced in March 1928 and was used alternately through the end of production. It has a 14-inch tapered section behind the universal joint. The front of the torque tube supports the front driveshaft bearing and the speedometer gear housing.

The outer ends of the rear axle housings are attached to the front of the torque tube housing by tube-type radius rods. The rear ends of the radius rods were attached to the axle housings with forged ends butt-welded to the oval tube. The earliest end design was essentially an L shape 2⅛ inches long with the top end higher than the radius rod tube. This design was used from the beginning of production through May 1928. The second design was still a forging but was a 7-inch-long Y-shaped design. This design was used through May 1930. The axle assembly, torque tube, and radius rods were all painted black after assembly.

One of the most important improvements the Model A offered over the Model T was the use of Houdaille hydraulic double-acting shock absorbers. Suspension damping of this type previously was found only on the most expensive cars. The company adopted hydraulic shock absorbers as a direct result of Henry Ford's experience driving one of the prototype cars. Upon accelerating across rough fields, ditches, and rocks, Ford said that the car rode too hard and dictated the installation of the shock absorbers, a significant improvement for a car in the Ford's price class.

Ford Houdaille shock absorbers were round and operated through the use of an arm that rotated on the center shaft. Each shock absorber unit has a filler plug on its upper radius and an adjustment screw in the center of the operating shaft. All 1928 shock absorber housings had a Ford script. This script was discontinued in January 1929. The car uses two different shock absorbers whose designs are essentially mirror images of one another: the right front and left rear are identical units of one construction, marked CW, while the left front and right rear are identical examples, marked AC, of the other. The letters indicate the motion of the shock. The shock absorber arms are connected to the axle housings

This is an early 1928 A-1015-AR 21-inch steel spoke wheel and ¹¹⁄₁₆-inch flat-top lug nuts. This wheel has a shallow hub depth to adapt to the early single-brake system and cannot be used with the later brake drums. The valve stem is fitted with the long nickel-plated Schrader dust cap.

by tubular links with adjustable spring-loaded plugs. These attach to a ball mounting on the front and rear axles. All shock absorbers were painted black.

Model A wheels have a welded steel-spoke design. The strength and durability of the new Ford wheels were emphasized as important features when the car was first introduced. The 1928 Model A is equipped with 21-inch drop-center rims with a distinctive rolled edge and 30 spokes. These wheels were manufactured by the Ford Motor Company to a proprietary design. All Ford wheels have a visible butt-welded seam where the rim was joined. The first design has a 1³⁄₁₆-inch-wide inner flange, used only with the early single-brake

1927 MODEL A ENGINE NUMBERS

MONTH	FIRST NUMBER	LAST NUMBER
October 20, 1927	1	137
November	138	971
December	972	5275

1928 MODEL A ENGINE NUMBERS

MONTH	FIRST NUMBER	LAST NUMBER
January	5276	17251
February	17252	36016
March	36017	67700
April	67701	109740
May	109741	165726
June	165727	224276
July	224277	295707
August	295708	384867
September	384868	473012
October	473013	585696
November	585697	697829
December	697830	810122

Note:
  Engine numbers include AA truck production. Except for a brief period from February to May 1928, all AA trucks were identified with an AA engine number prefix.
  The engine number indicates only when the engine was completed. Engine installation into the chassis at the assembly plant could have taken two weeks to four months. When the engine was installed in the chassis, the engine number was stamped on the top left side of the frame just ahead of the front body bolt hole.

1928

This is a driver's-side view of an early 1928 engine compartment. Note the square starter switch with pinned-on operating rod, Abel starter, and early Powerhouse generator with cadmium-plated rear cover and side-mounted cutout. The black-finish, Ford-designed, seven-tooth steering gear is the only one correct for a 1928 Ford.

system. In March 1928 it was replaced with the new dual-brake system and was totally phased out of production by August 1928. This wheel cannot be used with the updated brake system, as it will not seat properly against the brake drum. All 1928 Ford wheels were painted black at the factory.

The 1928 Ford wheels were equipped with Dill, Schrader, or Firestone valve stem components attached to the tire tubes. This assembly consists of a valve core, rim nut, bridge washer, valve cap, rim-nut bushing, and dust cap. Early dust caps were fluted and 2 9/16 to 3 inches tall. The valve stem was made of brass and was nickel plated. Five different types of valve stem equipment were used on the 1928 Model A.

Tires were made to Ford specifications but were manufactured by Firestone, Goodyear, BFGoodrich, and U.S. Rubber. The original tire size on the 1928 Ford was 4.50x21. All tires on a restored car should match. Since the spare was not usually installed at the factory, however, it may not match. All factory-installed tires were blackwall.

Hubcaps on the 1928 Ford are nickel-plated steel and 3 inches in diameter through August 1928 and 3 5/32 inches in diameter from mid-1928 through 1929. There were four different but similar designs used throughout 1928 with center indentations from 1 3/8 inches to 2 5/16 inches. The early hubcap used through June 1928 was marked with a Ford script with "Made in USA" stamped beneath it. This hubcap was used only on the early single-brake-system cars with the left-hand parking brake. The later 1928 hubcaps had a Ford script without the "Made in USA" legend.

Engine Assembly

The Ford Model A engine is a four-cylinder, L-head "cast en bloc" design. The bore is 3 7/8 inches and the stroke is 4 1/2 inches, producing a displacement of 200.5 cubic inches. It develops 40 horsepower at 2,200 rpm. The compression ratio is 4.22:1. Rather than the magneto and coil ignition of the Model T, the new unit was designed with a more conventional battery, generator, coil, and distributor system. The Model A was equipped with split-skirt aluminum three-ring pistons. These lightweight pistons contributed to the Model A's improved power and acceleration. The size and power of the Model A engine gave the car a distinct advantage in acceleration and speed over many other cars in its class.

The Model A Ford engine is painted Ford Engine Green and is clearly identified by the distinctive black Bakelite distributor housing with

Original Ford Model A

its two arms and solid brass sparkplug connectors. The intake and exhaust manifold assembly is mounted on the right side of the engine and is placed directly over the valve chamber cover. The carburetor is an updraft Zenith design that is painted black.

The water pump assembly is mounted on the front of the cylinder head. The two-bladed steel fan and pulley assembly attaches to the water pump shaft with a ⅝-inch castle nut.

The oil pan (A-6675) is black-painted steel, except for very early pans, which may have been cadmium plated. The early 1928 oil pan is equipped with a brass plug and a removable, round plate below the oil pump. This was intended to allow removal of sludge and was attached with four screws and lock washers. This plate was discontinued in October 1928. The early oil pan had no ribs on the sides to secure the inside tray.

The starter and generator are mounted on the right side of the engine. The early 1928 generator was known as the Powerhouse design and is shorter and of larger diameter than the later, more conventional type. The early 1928 starter is known as the Abel design and has a smaller-diameter shaft than that of later starters. The early starter switch is a rectangular design and is operated by an angled rod. This early starter was discontinued in October 1928 and was replaced with a more conventional Bendix design.

On the front of the engine is a cast-iron cover that includes the front engine mounting, front crankshaft seal, and timing pin. The cover is Ford Engine Green while the hex-head timing pin has a raven finish with a copper flat washer. This washer was used only in 1928. The 16 ⅜ raven-finish hex-head bolts securing the front cover have distinctive rounded heads and unfinished lock washers.

Transmission and Clutch

The Model A's three-speed sliding-gear transmission was another significant departure from the Model T. The New Ford transmission incorporated the standard H-pattern used by a majority of American manufacturers. The transmission case is made of cast iron with a Brinell hardness that must not exceed 228. The gears are made of heat-treated chrome-alloy steel. The main shaft runs on ball bearings, while the countershaft runs on roller bearings. The transmission case, top cover, flywheel, and clutch housings are painted Ford Engine Green.

The gearshift lever is Butler nickel plated and is topped with a black ball of hard Bakelite. The round ball with a ½-inch-wide band was used from the beginning of production through early 1928.

At this time, a mushroom-shaped black knob was adopted and used until the multiple-disc clutch was discontinued in November 1928. At that time, a round ball with a band was reinstated and used through the end of production. The Model A never featured a rubber boot around the gearshift lever.

The early 1928 Model A used a multiple dry-disc clutch, scaled down from the Lincoln design. This design used four driving discs and five driven discs. The driving discs were faced with an asbestos material and had teeth that mated with internal teeth on the flywheel. This clutch used a single 420-pound coil spring. A heavy-duty 455-pound spring was adopted for the AA truck in May 1928. The difference between A and AA clutches was eliminated when the new single-disc unit was adopted later in 1928. The multiple-disc flywheel, clutch, clutch housing, clutch and brake pedals, clutch-release shaft, collar, clutch-release fork and transmission housing, and main drive gear are unique and are not interchangeable individually with later single-disc components. Service problems (clogging and jamming of the discs) and high manufacturing costs caused the multiple-disc clutch to be discontinued in November 1928 and replaced with a more conventional single-plate design. This new clutch consisted of a pressure plate and cover assembly and a single 9-inch driven disc.

This front view of an early 1928 Model A shows the fluted headlight lenses and nickel-plated radiator shell with no raised area around the crank hole cover. The script outer front bumper clamps on this car are incorrect and should only be on the rear. The Motometer radiator cap is an accessory.

A detail of the crank hole cover on an early 1928 A-8200-AR nickel-plated radiator shell. After early 1929 the shell has a bell-shaped raised area around the cover. *Larry Hassel*

1928

The nickel-plated panel, red steering wheel, left-side parking brake lever, and recessed choke-rod handle identify this as the instrument panel of an early 1928 Phaeton. The marble shift lever ball is an accessory. The original ball was black Bakelite.

Cooling System and Radiator

The Model A cooling system brought another significant improvement over the Model T thermosyphon system. A centrifugal impeller water pump is attached to the front of the cylinder head. It is operated by a fan-mounted pulley and ⅝-inch V-belt running from the crankshaft pulley at 1½ times the crankshaft speed. The early 1928 cars were equipped with a gloss black-painted steel fan shroud attached to the radiator. The shroud was discontinued in February 1929.

The basic design of the Model A radiator for 1928 has 94 tubes, 106 long fins, and 11 short fins with a total cooling surface area of 360 square inches. The radiator uses fins and tubes to cool the 3-gallon system and operates without a thermostat. Ford, McCord, and Flintlock originally manufactured the radiators. Each type is identified by a different number of fins. The overflow pipe for 1928 ended at the bottom of the radiator. The radiator itself is attached to the frame with two ⅜-24 hex-head bolts, castle nuts, and black springs. The radiator base rests on a rubber or leather pad cut to match the lower mounting bracket. The 1929 Model A radiator shell is nickel-plated steel and has a vitreous blue–background Ford script badge attached to the top center. The Model A and AA commercial shell is painted black enamel and has the same badge with a blue background.

The coolant enters the engine through a black-painted, seamed steel lower pipe connected to the radiator and engine inlet by two 2¾-inch lengths of rubber hose. The hoses are attached with zinc or cadmium-plated clamps secured by 10-24x1⅛-inch slotted round-head screws and square nuts, with one screw for each clamp. The early water pipe has a bend closer to the radiator than later versions so it will clear the Powerhouse generator. The upper hose is 6½ inches long and connects the upper radiator inlet to the engine water outlet.

Original Model A radiator hoses were made by Firestone, Gates, and Goodyear and were black. The Firestone hose had a fine red spiral line, while the Goodyear and Gates hoses had a green spiral line. The red hose seen on some restored Model A Fords was actually a cheaper part sold by Gates as an aftermarket replacement and was not original equipment.

Fuel System

The Model A fuel system is one of its most distinctive and unique features. To keep the system simple, efficient, and reliable, Ford developed a fuel tank that accomplished three jobs. In addition to serving as the 10-gallon fuel tank, it serves as the upper cowl and as the base for the instrument panel inside the driver's compartment. The bottom of the tank also provides attachment for the steering column support and choke-rod grommet.

The design and engineering of this unit proved to be one of the most difficult jobs to accomplish during Model A development. The manufacture of this tank was particularly difficult because of the use of 18-U.S.S.-gauge terneplate steel. This material is difficult to weld and form. The deep draw pressing required of the design also created difficulties for Ford engineers.

The Model A fuel system operates on the gravity principle with fuel flowing directly from the bottom of the tank into the carburetor. A driver-operated fuel shut off is mounted under the tank inside the front compartment and a cast-iron sediment bowl mounts on the engine side of the firewall. The fuel flows through two terneplate seamed fuel lines.

The fuel gauge is integral with the tank. The face of the gauge is in the upper center of the instrument panel with the curved level indicator visible behind the glass lens. The early 1928 gauge had a vertical oval opening in the black face with centering marks. In mid-1928, this opening was changed to a horizontal oval opening with centering marks. The fuel gauge float pivots on the rear of the gauge unit allowing a steel rod and cork to read the fuel level in the tank.

Original Ford Model A

The Model A updraft carburetor was developed especially for the New Ford. The new design, built by Zenith, was one of the significant factors in the substantial horsepower increase of the Model A over the Model T. According to Henry Ford's well-known desire for production economy, the carburetor was held together with only one bolt.

The Zenith carburetor used on the Model A Ford is a single-throttle, dual-venturi updraft design made of cast iron and painted black. The driver's compartment is equipped with a single adjustment control that operates the choke and mixture control needle using a carburetor adjusting rod, commonly called a choke rod.

The choke rod on early 1928 Fords was mounted farther under the fuel tank than later versions due to a shorter rod. The early choke rod (A-9700-AR) has a smooth teardrop-shaped knob and is 22 inches long. This was changed to a 26-inch-long rod with a serrated edge knob (A-9700-B) in October 1928. All choke rods are cadmium plated with a polished aluminum knob.

Electrical System

The 1928 Model A Ford electrical system is of conventional design. The system consists of a 6-volt battery, generator, starter, single-point distributor, coil, ammeter, and wiring. The primary electrical system consists of the battery and starter. The battery is mounted under the left side of the frame and is grounded on the positive side by a lead-coated, multilayered strap attached to the frame's center cross-member. The negative battery cable is a 00 size multistrand cable, ⅝ inch in diameter, with a black woven fabric covering. It is 21½ inches long and is routed over the top of the starter-housing portion of the flywheel housing. It is insulated by a metal support and rubber bushing and is attached to the starter switch on the top of the starter.

The early 1928 starter is an Abel ball-bearing type with a ½-inch driveshaft. Three variations of this basic design were used through September 1928. The starter is painted black. The starter switch on the early 1928 Ford is rectangular with a rear negative cable terminal post. The switch could be either black enamel or cadmium plated. The earliest switch has an offset operating rod attached with a cotter pin and spring-loaded sleeve. There was also a second version of the rectangular switch used with a straight operating rod. The contact on the top of the starter does not allow the early rectangular switches to be used on later-type Bendix starters.

The early 1928 Ford is equipped with an unusual Powerhouse generator that is considerably shorter and of larger diameter than the later, more conventional-style generators. The Powerhouse generator has five brushes and has the cutout mounted on the side. It is painted black. The rear cover is cadmium-plated steel through early 1928 and black enamel thereafter. The cover is held in place with a heavy wire bail. Powerhouse generators have an adjusting arm attached to one of the front timing gear-cover bolts.

The charging system cutout is mounted on the side of the generator and serves as a switch to allow only one-way flow of current from the generator to the battery. The cutout is round and cadmium plated. It is attached to the generator with 10-32 slotted round-headed cadmium screws and unfinished lock washers. The 1928 cutout has a Ford script on the top center.

An ammeter mounted on the right side of the instrument panel monitors the charging system condition. The ammeter face has a black background with dull silver lettering. The ammeter bezel is bright nickel–plated brass. There was no Ford script on the face of the ammeter during Model A production.

The primary wiring system is connected to a black Bakelite two-piece terminal box mounted on the center of the engine side of the firewall. Until mid-1928, the terminal box had a Ford script between the top of the cover and the terminal studs. The terminal box cover is held in place by two brass one-sided wing nuts with a ball end.

The lighting system of the Model A Ford consists of the lighting switch mounted at the bottom of the steering column, the lighting switch and horn-switch handle in the center of the steering wheel, and the lighting wiring harness. The handle of the light control rod (A-3616-BR, actually a tube) controls the lighting system through a number of contacts in the light switch mounted on the bottom end of the steering column. The control tube also contains the wiring for the horn button, which is in the center of the steering wheel.

Here's a close-up view of an A-11805-AR early 1928 nickel-plated instrument panel. The oval speedometer is a Stewart Warner used through mid-1928. *Larry Hassel*

1928

The light switch body and cover (A-11654-B) are cadmium plated. The early switch had a knurled cover without a drain hole or bail. This cover was used until February 1928, when it was changed to the more common design with a drain hole and a bail to hold the cover in place. The drain hole should always face down. Model A switch bodies are always round rather than flat on the bottom. The early switch, used through mid-March 1928, has three positions: one for bright headlights, one for dim headlights, and "off." These positions were marked on the early switch. The main wiring harness, with an attached contact plate, fits into the bottom of the light switch with the wires exiting the switch housing.

The 1928 Ford is equipped with single-bulb headlamps with a bright and a dim filament. The headlight shells are parabolic in shape with nickel-plated steel construction. The lenses are flat with vertical, straight flutes. This basic design was used through January 1929. A small number of early fluted headlight lenses had a Ford script in an oval at the top center of the lens while later examples had the script in an oval at the bottom center. The headlight wiring is enclosed in nickel-plated flexible conduits.

The 1928 Ford has a single nickel-plated drum-style taillight (A-13405-AR) mounted on a forged, black-painted bracket on the left rear of the car. There are four variations, with each body style having a different mounting bracket. The taillight drum housing has "DUOLIGHT" stamped on the top. Commercial Model As have a black-painted (A-13404-R) rather than plated taillight housing. Some early housings may also have a Ford script. The lens is ruby with a steel "Stop" stencil mounted between the lens and the taillight door.

The Ford Model A ignition system consists of the distributor, coil, sparkplugs, ignition switch, and ignition cable. The distributor is an iron casting mounted on the top center of the head. The black Bakelite distributor cap is actually two pieces, the body (A-12105) and cap (A-12115). The distinctive Model A design has two arms, each with two studs for attaching the sparkplug connectors. The ignition cable attaches to a threaded opening in the distributor casting.

The sparkplugs are ⅞-inch Champion 3X with a copper asbestos gasket. The steel base of the spark plug is knurled around its perimeter. There are two hex-nut surfaces, as the original sparkplugs are capable of disassembly for cleaning. The original plugs have a black finish with a white insulator.

The ignition coil is mounted on the center of the engine side of the firewall. The original coil has a gloss black–painted steel body and a brown Bakelite base. Coils were made both with and without a Ford script. The script should never have an oval surrounding it. The coil bracket is spot-welded to the coil body and is attached to the firewall with two cadmium-plated, slotted round-head machine screws and lock washers.

The armored, flexible ignition cable (A-11575) is painted black. It passes through a rubber insulator in the terminal box and is threaded into the distributor. The cable makes contact with the end of the condenser mounted inside the distributor. The other end of the cable attaches to the ignition switch at the instrument panel inside the car. Through May 1928, the cable has a curved, solid end. This design was discontinued in June 1928, when a new cable with a short, straight end was introduced. The cable is held in place on top of the cylinder head by a clip attached to one of the center-head studs. The early clip for the curved-end cable is ¹⁵⁄₁₆ inch high. In mid-1928, this clip was changed to a ⁹⁄₁₆-inch height.

The ignition switch is mounted on the left side of the nickel-plated instrument panel. The 1928 model has a Ford-designed pop-out-type ignition switch. Through November 1928, the switch plate had the words "on" and "off" on the black-finish aluminum face. There is a bright nickel–plated ring holding the switch plate in place. All 1928 Fords were originally equipped with two ignition keys. There were also two keys (which may not necessarily match the ignition key) for each lock on the car.

The satin nickel–finished instrument panel (A-11805) also provides a mounting for the instrument panel lamp. For 1928, the bright nickel–plated lamp is mounted in the center of the panel. Turning and pushing in on the cap

Another view of the driver's side of a late 1928 engine compartment showing the Powerhouse generator, third type, with top-mounted cutout. This generator was used from October 1928 through July 1929. Note the correct black hoses with red stripe.

Original Ford Model A

Front view of an early 1928 Phaeton in Arabian Sand, Light. Note the early fluted headlight lenses and nickel-plated radiator shell. The fender-mounted spare wheels, mirrors, wind wings, and Motometer radiator cap are accessories.

operates the lamp. All instrument panel lamps have a 3 candlepower bulb.

Body and Fender Assembly

One of the most successful features of the Model A was the styling. The lines of the fenders, hood, and radiator shell closely followed those of the expensive Model L Lincoln. The fenders have a high crown and follow the shape and diameter of the tires. The bodies are significantly lower than those of the Model T. The Tudor, Coupe, Roadster, and Phaeton have a distinctive vertical coupe pillar that separates the hood and cowl from the rest of the body. The Fordor sedan has a different design that continues the lines of the body into the hood and cowl. All bodies are enhanced by distinctive window reveals and rounded side body moldings.

Like those of all other automobiles of the era, the Model A's fenders are actually considered to be part of the chassis. That is the reason that fenders were painted black enamel rather than given the lacquer finish found on the Model A bodies. The black enamel serves as a more durable finish. The fenders of the Model A were dipped at the factory so the finish on the top and bottom should be identical in quality.

Early 1928 Ford front fenders have a distinctive rounded inside rear skirt. This is clearly visible as a larger flat area at the rear of the fender along the hood shelf. This design was discontinued in December 1928, when a new design was introduced with a forged reinforcement at the outer edge where the fender bracket attaches. The edge of all fenders should be serrated, surrounding the rolled wire reinforcement built into the fender. There should be no welds or damage on the fender edges. All body styles use the same front fenders (A-16005 right and A-16006 left). The only variation is when service item fender-well equipment is used. In that case, an A-16035 right fender and A-16036 left fender are used.

The top of the inner edge of the front fenders is covered with a hood shelf (A-16713 right and A-16714 left) that attaches to the frame and fenders. It is secured by the same screws and nuts that hold the hood latches on each side. The hood shelf extends along each side of the frame between the cowl and the front frame horn. The hood shelf is also finished in black enamel.

1928

This left rear view of an early 1928 Phaeton shows the nickel-plated DUOLIGHT drum taillight and forged mounting bracket. Note that the bracket is attached to the body frame and not the fender. The metal trunk is an accessory.

A view of the left side of the hood clearly shows that the early 1928 hood louvers are not parallel with the hinge line. The louvers are all the same height and are parallel with the lower edge of the hood. This design was used through mid-1928.

A detailed view of a right-side fender-mounted spare tire support and rubber grommet. The A-1405-AR support was used on both right and left sides and is finished in black enamel. *Larry Hassel*

There is also a front splash-shield assembly (A-16527) that covers the void between the front frame horns below the radiator shell. It is black enamel like the fenders and is held in place by the same attaching screws that secure the front fenders to the frame.

Rear fenders are made in two basic variations. The Roadster, Coupe, and Pickup use the same A-16160 and A-16161 rear fenders. The Tudor, Phaeton, Fordor, and Panel Delivery use the A-16310 and A-16311 fenders. The primary difference between these fenders is their width. Early 1928 fenders will have a flat reinforcement plate on the inside lower edge. Later fenders have a ribbed plate. Early 1928 Coupe and Roadster rear fenders were narrower at the lower rear until April 1928. Original 1928 fenders will not have holes cut for the taillight attachment, as all taillight brackets for that year are forged iron and attach to the body sill or frame. Front and rear fender brackets on the 1928 Ford are made of forged iron, which allows them to be strong, yet flexible.

Rear fenders are insulated from the body with $3/16$-inch black welting. The original welting was made with a pyroxilyn-coated cloth wrapped around coiled heavy paper, which kept it straight and smooth. The same welting is also used between the inner edge of the front fender and the front edge of the splash shield.

Running board splash shields (A-16535 and A-16536) are made of stamped (pressed) steel. They attach to the top of the frame rails, the rear inner edge of the front fenders, and the front inner edge of the rear fenders. They are finished in black enamel like the fenders. The early 1928 splash shields are tapered front to rear on their top edge. They were originally attached to the body blocks with screws from the underside. The rear upper corner of the early shield has no hump as was used in the later design to clear the revised brake linkage. The splash shields and front fenders rest on a strip of $1\frac{1}{2}$-inch antisqueak webbing that lies on top of the frame.

Running boards for Model A passenger vehicles are steel with ribbed black rubber matting and zinc edge trim. The underside is finished in black enamel. Commercial vehicles and trucks have steel running boards with a stamped diamond pattern incorporating a stamped Ford script. These are painted entirely in black enamel. All 1928 Model As have a friction tape antisqueak strip between the running board and splash shield. Running boards are attached to the forged brackets with special acorn-head $5/16$-inch bolts, plus hex-head nuts and lock washers.

The body of the 1928 Ford was constructed entirely of steel, except for the Fordor. The wood in most body styles served only as reinforcement at lock pillars supporting the fabric roof and the interior trim. Fordors were made with considerably more wood structure, which makes this model heavier than the others. If the wood is deteriorated, it makes the Fordor more difficult to restore as it is relatively complicated to install.

There were eight basic passenger car body styles and five commercial body styles offered for the 1928 model year. Passenger models consisted of the Tudor, Roadster, Phaeton, Fordor, and four variations of coupes. Commercial styles were the Open Cab, Closed Cab, A Panel Delivery, AA Panel Delivery, and Deluxe Delivery. All but the Fordor have a distinctive curved, vertical coupe pillar between the cowl and the body.

The Model 35-A Standard Phaeton is a four-door, four-passenger open car equipped with snap-on side curtains and a folding top. The 1928 Phaeton was not equipped with outside door handles. The doors are operated by black-painted, nickel-plated knob-capped inside levers. When the side curtains are in place, it is necessary to reach inside a vent opening to open the doors. The windshield stanchions, which are body color after December 1927, are solidly mounted to the cowl. The windshield frame swings out from the bottom and is sealed with a flat rubber seal against the cowl

Original Ford Model A

Side view of an early 1928 Phaeton. The folding top is black, fine, long-short-grain artificial leather. The front door top pads, fender-mounted spare tires, and covers are accessories. Note that the upper rear of the early running board splash shields does not have a hump for the later brake system.

Rear view of an early 1928 35-A Phaeton showing the top folded. The one-piece rear bumper, metal trunk, and fender-mounted spare tires are accessories.

A detailed view of the inside of the right rear top framework on an early 1928 35-A Phaeton. All metal parts are painted black enamel. *Larry Hassel*

strip. Only a single driver's-side, hand-operated windshield wiper was available.

The 1928 Standard Phaeton was offered in six basic color combinations. The main body colors included Niagara Blue Light and Dark, Arabian Sand Light and Dark, Dawn Gray, and Gunmetal Blue. Contrasting or complementary colors were used for the moldings and striping. These colors may also have been available with the main body and molding colors switched.

Interior trim for the 1928 Phaeton was offered only in Spanish Brown colonial-grain artificial leather. Both front and rear seats are of plain, solid bench design with a single seam running laterally approximately one-third of the way back from the front of the seat. Door and quarter panels were in matching Spanish Brown colonial-grain cardboard. These cardboard panels are plain, flat, and trimmed with artificial-leather binding.

The folding top for the 1928 Phaeton was offered only in black, long-short-grain artificial leather. The bows are black steel and wood covered in black bow drill. The side curtains are made of the same black material as the top and have clear celluloid windows. The side curtains were stowed in a folding compartment under the rear floor. All 1928 Phaetons have black rubber floor mats. Early 1928 cars had a pyramid-pattern front rubber mat, but this was changed to a sunburst pattern with the introduction of the center parking brake handle in June 1928.

The Model 40-A Standard Roadster is a two-door, two-passenger open car equipped with snap-on side curtains and a folding top. The Roadster was available with either a rumble seat or a trunk. The 1928 Roadster was not equipped with outside

1928

Above: This view of the front compartment of a 1928 Phaeton shows the plain-panel Spanish Brown colonial-grain seat trim, left-side parking brake lever, and red steering wheel identifying this as an early 1928 model. The wind wings are accessories.

Above right: This is a detail of a right A-37328 top prop-rest and strap assembly. The unit screws into a socket inside the body structure. The straps keep the top assembly from moving when the car is in motion. *Larry Hassel*

Above far right: This A-35655-AR right interior door handle belongs to an early 1928 Phaeton. The knob is nickel plated. This type of handle was only used on early open cars without outside door handles. The trim is Spanish Brown colonial-grain artificial leather. *Larry Hassel*

door handles. Like the Phaeton, the doors are operated with a lever on the inside of the door. Also, like the Phaeton, the windshield is mounted on solid, body-color stanchions attached to the cowl with two 5/16-24 nickel-plated, slotted, oval-head screws on each side. The windshield frame also swings out from the bottom. Both the Roadster and the Phaeton have rubber seals on the bottom and sides of the windshield frame. Only a single, hand-operated driver's-side wiper was available.

The 1928 Standard Roadster was available in six basic exterior color schemes. Lower body colors were offered in Niagara Blue Light and Dark, Arabian Sand Light and Dark, Dawn Gray, and Gunmetal Blue with contrasting and complementary molding and stripe colors. Like the Phaeton, these colors may have been available with lower body and molding colors switched.

The interior trim of the Roadster was offered only in Spanish Brown colonial-grain artificial leather. The front seat and rumble seat cushions had a plain, solid design. The front seat has a single lateral seam one-third of the way from the front edge. The door and quarter panels are Spanish Brown colonial-grain cardboard, trimmed with matching artificial leather binding. The rumble seat for all 1928 cars is trimmed in Spanish Brown colonial-grain artificial-leather. Both the rumble seat cushion and backrest are plain with no pleats and only a perimeter welting.

The folding top for the early 1928 Roadster was made of a dark-cloth whipcord material with Spanish Brown colonial-grain artificial-leather binding. In June 1928 this was replaced with black, long-short-grain artificial leather with matching binding. The top frame is black-painted metal and wood covered with black bow drill. The side curtains were made of the same material as the top. They are stowed under the front seat. All 1928 Roadsters have rubber floor mats. Early 1928 cars had a pyramid pattern, but this was replaced with a sunburst pattern when the parking brake was moved to the center in June 1928.

The Model 45-A Standard Coupe is a two-passenger, two-door closed car with small stationary quarter windows. The body is steel, but the roof still has a soft fabric insert. The Standard Coupe was offered with either a rumble seat or a trunk. Like all 1928 Model A closed cars, the Coupe has a single electric windshield wiper on the driver's side only. The Owen-Dyneto Corporation made all closed-car electric wipers through November 1928.

The Standard Coupe was offered in five color schemes. Lower body colors were Niagara Blue Light and Dark, Arabian Sand Dark, Dawn Gray, and Gunmetal Blue. Belt moldings and reveals were in contrasting and complementary colors with appropriate stripe colors. The top insert and visor were covered in black, long-short-grain artificial leather.

The 1928 Standard Coupe was offered with only one interior trim scheme. The plain-panel front seat, quarters, and door panels are trimmed in gray cloth with a hairline stripe. The roof rail, header, and package tray are trimmed in plain gray cloth and the headlining is gray napped cotton. The cowl cardboard is gray colonial grain, and the metal garnish moldings are finished in gray. The window curtain is blue silk, and the front floor is covered with brown carpet. All interior hardware is nickel plated. The special-order rumble seat is trimmed in unpleated Spanish Brown colonial-grain artificial leather.

In June 1928, Ford replaced the Standard Coupe with the 49-A Special Coupe. The new car had artificial leather covering the rear of the roof down to the belt line. The black artificial leather on the rear center panel was installed with the grain running horizontally. Apart from the change in roof design, the Special Coupe was identical in appearance to the Standard Coupe and was offered in the same color combinations.

Original Ford Model A

The Special Coupe offered only a single interior trim scheme that differed from that of the Standard Coupe. The plain-panel seat, door panels, and quarters are trimmed in brown hairline stripe cloth. The roof rail, header, and package tray are in plain brown cloth, and the headlining is brown napped cotton. The cowl cardboard is Spanish Brown colonial-grain artificial leather with matching binding. The metal garnish moldings are Light Buff and the front carpet is brown. In late 1928, it was changed to a black rubber mat. Window curtains are brown silk. All interior hardware is nickel plated.

The Model 50-A Sport Coupe was the sportiest of the closed cars. It offered the smart styling of an open car and the comfort of a coupe. The Sport Coupe is a two-passenger, two-door closed car with a fabric roof styled to resemble a convertible coupe. It sported landau top irons and a fabric-covered visor. The Sport Coupe was equipped with a rumble seat and had the same body and wiper equipment as the Standard and Special Coupe.

The Sport Coupe was available in five standard color schemes. Lower body colors are Niagara Blue Light and Dark, Arabian Sand Dark, Dawn Gray, and Gunmetal Blue. Belt moldings, reveals, and stripe were in contrasting and complementary colors. The top and visor were covered in tan whipcord on the early 1928 cars, but this was changed in late 1928 to dark brown seal-grain artificial leather. The landau irons were finished in a matching paint with the center hinge area nickel plated.

Interior trim of the Sport Coupe was offered in two combinations. One is blue-checked cloth on the seat, door panels, and quarters, combined with tan cloth on the top quarters, bows, and headlining. The seat cushion and back are piped with eight pipes per cushion. Garnish moldings are gray, and the cowl cardboard is gray colonial grain. The front floor is covered with a brown carpet.

The Sport Coupe's interior headlining and roof bow trim differed according to the top material used. The early tan whipcord tops had a headlining of plain tan cloth with a multicolor weave. The later dark brown seal-grain tops had tan whipcord headlining.

The other combination is brown hairline-striped cloth on the seat, door panel, and quarters, coordinated with plain tan cloth on the top quarter, bows, and headlining. The seat has eight pipes as in the first combination. Garnish moldings are Light Buff and the cowl cardboard is two-tone, nut-brown pigskin. The floor was covered in brown carpet until late 1928, when it was changed to a black rubber mat for both combinations.

The Model 54-A Business Coupe was not one of the original models available when the New Ford was introduced. It was first offered in May 1928 and was designed for business people who needed an economical and comfortable car for

This 1928 40-A Roadster has a Dawn Gray body and Gunmetal Blue moldings. The stripe is French Gray. The top is tan whipcord, used only on early 1928 Roadsters. The car is posed in front of the original Ford factory at Greenfield Village. *Kenneth Keeley*

1928

Above: This view of a late 1928 55-A Tudor shows the distinctive coupe pillar used on most 1928–29 bodies. The car is finished in Dawn Gray lower body with Gunmetal Blue upper body back, moldings, and reveals. The stripe is Straw. *Kenneth Keeley*

Right: This is the left front door interior trim panel and door pocket of a late 1928 Tudor sedan. The door garnish molding is finished in Moulding Gray. The hardware is bright nickel plated. The window draft deflectors are accessories.

their daily work. The Business Coupe appears much the same as the Sport Coupe, but it does not have the landau irons. The 1928 Business Coupe was offered in the same five color combinations as the Coupe and Sport Coupe. The full top and visor was covered in black, long-short-grain artificial leather.

The 1928 Business Coupe was available in two interior trim combinations. One had blue-checked cloth on the seat, door panels, and rear quarter, coordinated with plain gray cloth on the top quarter, bows, and headlining. The cowl cardboard is gray colonial grain and the garnish moldings are gray paint.

The other combination for 1928 is Spanish Brown colonial-grain artificial leather on the seat, rear quarter, and door panel. The top quarter, bows, and headlining are plain gray cloth or black cloth with a fake twist. The cowl cardboard is the same brown artificial leather as the seat and the garnish moldings are Light Buff. The front floor in both combinations was brown carpet until late 1928, when it was changed to a black rubber mat.

The highest production and best-selling Model A body type is the Model 55-A Tudor sedan. This two-door, five-passenger closed car represents the Model A Ford in its truest form. The individual folding front seats and comfortable rear seat make this body type the most practical and economical transportation for families. The 1928 Tudor design has the same coupe pillar structure as the Coupe, Roadster, and Phaeton. The Tudor has a fabric roof insert and a covered visor. It has the same electric wiper as the coupes.

The Tudor was offered in five basic color combinations. Lower body colors are Niagara Blue Light and Dark, Arabian Sand Dark, Dawn Gray, and Gunmetal Blue. Belt moldings, reveals, upper body, and stripe are in contrasting and complementary colors. The 1928 Tudor's entire rear upper body came in one color and the lower body in another. Only the black finish was used on the entire body.

The 1928 Tudor was available in three interior trim combinations, all with wide-pleated seats front and rear. The first has gray cloth with wool-stripe seat sides and faces, door panels, and rear quarter. The header, back, and roof rail are plain gray cloth. The headlining is gray napped cotton cloth. The cowl cardboard and seat bottoms are gray colonial grain and the garnish moldings are painted gray. Curtains are blue silk.

The second interior combination has seats, door panels, and rear quarters trimmed in gray cloth with a silk stripe. The back, roof rail, and header are plain gray cloth. The headlining is gray napped cotton cloth. The cowl and seat bottom cardboards are gray colonial grain. Garnish moldings are painted gray, and the curtains are blue silk.

The third combination is blue hairline-striped seats, rear quarters, and door panels. The rear quarters, roof rail, and header are plain blue cloth. The cowl cardboard and seat bottoms are gray colonial grain. The garnish moldings are painted gray, and the curtains are blue silk. Carpets on all 1928 Tudors were brown until late 1928, when they were changed to a black rubber mat.

There was only one type of Fordor offered in the first year of Model A production. The stylish

Original Ford Model A

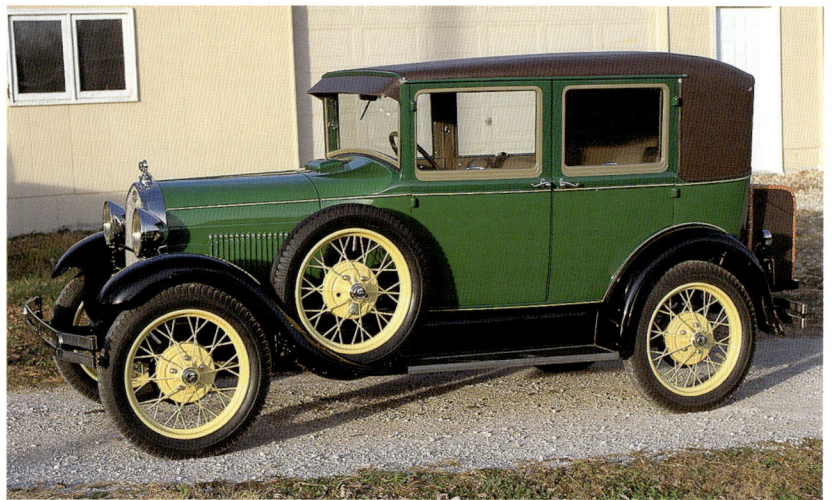
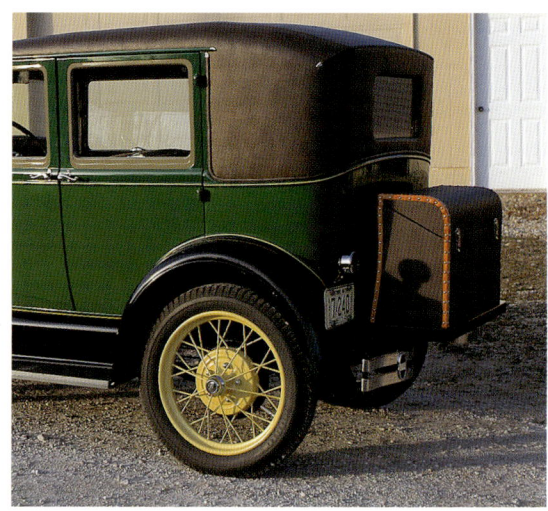
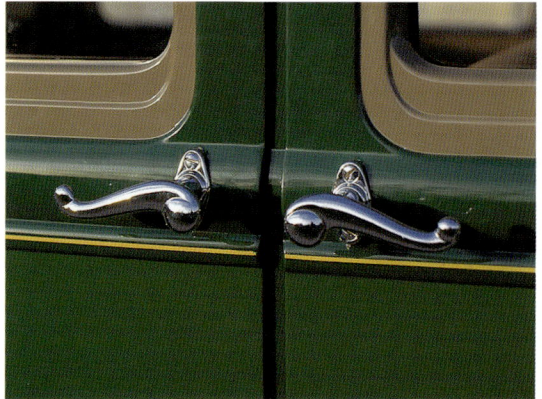

Top left: This 1928 60-A Fordor has a Balsam Green body with Valley Green moldings and Pembroke Gray window reveals. The stripe-colored wheels, trunk, and fender-mounted spare wheels are accessories. The stripe is Straw.

Top right: The top of this 1928 60-A Leatherback Fordor is covered with Seal Brown pebble-grain artificial leather. The trunk and colored wheels are accessories.

Above left: Exterior door handles on a 1928 60-A Fordor. The scroll-type handles on prototypes and some early cars were installed with the curved ends pointing up. The window reveals are Pembroke Gray and the stripe is Straw.

Above right: A close-up view of A-61205-AR and A-61206-AR outside door handles on a 1928 60-A Fordor. Door handles on later Fordors are mounted with the ends pointing down. The lower body color is Rose Beige with Seal Brown moldings and orange stripe.

Above: This 1928 60-A Fordor has a Rose Beige body with Seal Brown moldings and an orange stripe. Note the vent in the cowl, which was installed only in 1928 Fordors. This car also has the nonparallel hood louvers and fluted headlight lenses. The quail radiator cap is an accessory.

Left: Here's a close-up view of the driver's side cowl vent on a 1928 60-A Fordor body. The cowl vent was operated by a handle inside the car.

1928

Right: This is the front compartment of a Balsam Green 1928 60-A Fordor. The interior trim scheme is brown hairline-striped cloth. The red steering wheel and center-mounted squeeze-handle-type parking brake lever identify this as a late 1928 car.

Far right: A right-side view of the front compartment of a late 1928 60-A Fordor shows the inside operating handle of the cowl vent. The rubber boots on the shift and brake levers are accessories. Note the 1928-only mushroom-shaped gearshift ball.

Right: The inside trim panel of the driver's side front door of this 1928 60-A Fordor is trimmed in brown hairline-striped cloth. Note the chrome handle on the door garnish molding.

Far right: The rear compartment of a 1928 60-A Leatherback Fordor is trimmed in brown hairline-striped cloth. The rear floor is covered in brown square-weave carpet.

The front-passenger-side door panel of this 1928 60-A Fordor has a brown hairline-striped cloth and door pocket. The interior door hardware is bright nickel plated.

Model 60-A is a four-door, five-passenger car with closed rear quarters and a brown full, artificial-leather roof. The Fordor was a late arrival, introduced in May 1928. Although early photos of the 1928 Fordor prototype showed a body with a distinctive cowl side vent and a metal-frame celluloid visor, the original-style visor was eliminated in production cars and replaced with a standard, fabric-covered steel variety. The Fordor was promoted as a luxurious car and was equipped with decorative scroll door handles and a comfortable interior layout.

The 1928 Fordor was offered in four basic color schemes. The lower body colors are Balsam Green, Copra Drab, Rose Beige, and Andalusite Blue. Belt moldings, reveals, stripe, and upper body are in contrasting and complementary colors. The top is in Seal Brown artificial leather.

Original Ford Model A

Left: This early 1929 Town Car is finished in black. Eighty-nine Town Cars were built in late 1928 and have distinctive 1928 features such as a red steering wheel and drum taillight. The Town Car taillight was chrome rather than bright nickel as in the other models.

Below: The left rear quarter view of an early 1929 140-A Town Car clearly shows the black, coarse, long-short-grain genuine leather top. The red steering wheel identifies this as one of the 89 Town Cars made in late 1928.

There was only one interior trim scheme offered for the 60-A Fordor. The seat, back quarter, and header were in brown hairline-striped cloth and the headlining was brown napped cotton. The cowl cardboard was two-tone brown dash-grain and the garnish moldings were gray or Mocha Brown. The window curtains were brown silk and all interior hardware is finished in nickel plate. The floor covering was brown carpet front and rear until late 1928, when the front floor was changed to a black rubber mat like all other 1928 models.

The Model A chassis was also offered in a variety of commercial bodies. There were two versions of pickup, a Deluxe Delivery and a Panel Delivery. Except for the Deluxe Delivery, Model A commercial vehicles were equipped with a black-painted radiator, taillight, and headlight shells of the same design as the passenger car. All 1928 commercial vehicles were equipped with a standard left-side-mounted spare tire and fender well. All 1928 side-mounted spare tire brackets were painted black and were identical for both the left and right.

The Model 76-A Open Cab Pickup was created to offer the Ford economy and reliability to the commercial customer at the lowest possible price. The pickup was equipped with a 78-A body (bed) that was a direct carryover from the Model T. The A-16160 (RH) and A-16161-A (LH) rear fenders were the same ones used for the coupe and roadster. The pickup cab is equipped with a black, fine, long-short-grain artificial-leather fabric top on a black metal and wood frame. Although the top resembles that of the roadster, it is not foldable or removable. Standard equipment included side curtains in matching material. Like the other 1928 open cars, the pickup was not equipped with outside door handles.

This driver's-side close-up view of an early 1929 Town Car shows the distinctive chrome outside mirror used only on this model. The cowl design, cowl band, and cowl lights are the same as those used on the 1929 Town Sedans.

1928

1928 Body Color Schemes

35-A Standard Phaeton & 40-A Standard Roadster

Body	Belt, Quarter & Sill Molding	Stripe
Niagara Blue, Light	Duchess Blue	French Gray
Niagara Blue, Dark	Duchess Blue	French Gray
Arabian Sand, Light	Copra Drab	French Gray
Arabian Sand, Dark	Copra Drab	French Gray
Dawn Gray, Dark	Gunmetal Blue	French Gray
Gunmetal Blue	Dawn Gray, Dark	Straw

45-A Coupe, 49-A Special Coupe, 50-A Sport Coupe & 54-A Business Coupe

Body, Upper & Lower	Belt, Quarter & Sill Molding	Reveals	Stripe
Niagara Blue, Light	Duchess Blue	Duchess Blue	French Gray
Niagara Blue, Dark	Niagara Blue, Light		Duchess Blue
French Gray			
Arabian Sand, Dark	Copra Drab	French Gray	French Gray
Dawn Gray, Dark	Dawn Gray, Light	Dawn Gray, Light	Straw
Gunmetal Blue	Dawn Gray, Dark	Dawn Gray, Dark	French Gray

55-A Tudor

Body, Upper & Lower	Upper Body Back	Belt, Quarter & Sill Molding	Reveals	Stripe
Niagara Blue, Light	Niagara Blue, Dark	Duchess Blue	Duchess Blue	French Gray
Niagara Blue, Dark	Niagara Blue, Light	Niagara Blue, Light	Duchess Blue	French Gray
Arabian Sand, Dark	Copra Drab	Copra Drab	French Gray	French Gray
Dawn Gray, Dark	Gunmetal Blue	Dawn Gray, Dark	Dawn Gray, Dark	Straw
Gunmetal Blue	Black	Black	French Gray	French Gray

60-A Fordor

Lower Body	Upper Body	Belt, Quarter & Sill Molding	Reveals	Stripe
Balsam Green	Valley Green	Valley Green	Pembroke Gray	Old Ivory
Copra Drab	Seal Brown	Seal Brown	Copra Drab	French Gray*
Rose Beige	Seal Brown	Seal Brown	Rose Beige	Orange**
Andalusite Blue	Andalusite Blue	Andalusite Blue	Arabian Sand, Dark	Orange

*Dropped August 1928. **Available September 1928.

Right: This Owen-Dyneto electric windshield wiper is on an early 1929 140-A Town Car. The wiper body is finished in black enamel.

Below right: Another view of the driver's-side door of the early 1929 140-A Town Car. Note the scroll outside door handles and distinctive Town Car outside mirror. A removable black artificial-leather canopy roof covers the chauffeur's compartment. The canopy is stored under the driver's seat when not in use.

Left opposite: A special chrome T-shaped windshield crank-out control knob is on the upper dash rail of an early 1929 Town Car.

The 1928 Open Cab Pickup was offered in four basic color combinations. The upper and lower body colors are Rock Moss Green with no molding color, Rock Moss Green with black moldings, Commercial Gray (dropped in August 1928), and Gunmetal Blue (available in August 1928). All combinations have a French Gray stripe except the Commercial Gray, which has none.

The Open Cab Pickup was available with a single interior color scheme. The plain-panel seat, doors, quarters, and lock pillar are trimmed in Spanish Brown colonial-grain artificial leather. The garnish moldings are black, and the floor is covered with a black rubber mat. All interior hardware is nickel plated.

The 78-A pickup bed was also used with the 82-A closed-cab body. Although the front cowl section was identical to other Model A bodies, the doors and the rear of the cab were based on the similar body used on the 1927 Model T pickup. The Closed Cab Pickup came a little later in the model year and was not introduced until August 1928. The Closed Cab Pickup was available in the same standard exterior color combinations as the open-cab version. The roof and visor were covered in black, coarse, long-short-grain artificial leather.

The 1928 82-A closed-cab body was offered in only one interior trim scheme. It has a plain-panel seat, door panels, quarters, and header in Spanish Brown colonial-grain artificial leather. The roof lining is black duck. The garnish moldings are black, and the floor is covered in a black rubber mat.

In addition to the two versions of pickup, the Model A commercial line also included a Panel Delivery. The Model 79-A Panel Delivery was introduced in August 1928 and had bodies built by Budd Manufacturing. The Panel Delivery has a 57-inch-long, 50-inch-wide, 46.5-inch-high cargo space with center-opening double doors in the rear. Standard equipment included two folding front seats. The Panel Delivery was offered in the same four color combinations as the two pickup styles.

The interior trim of the Panel Delivery consists of two plain-panel seats, trim welt, door panels, and header of Spanish Brown colonial-grain artificial leather. The cowl cardboard is Spanish Brown. The roof lining is black duck. The front floor is covered with a black rubber mat.

AA Truck Chassis

In addition to the standard 103.5-inch wheelbase Model A passenger car chassis, Ford offered a 1½-ton, 131½-inch wheelbase commercial chassis designated the AA. The frame of the AA is made from $\frac{7}{32}$-inch steel channels that are 2½ inches

1928 Interior Trim Combinations

35-A Standard Phaeton & 40-A Standard Roadster
Trim Scheme Spanish Brown

Seats, Wind Cord, Quarters	Doors, Cowl, Lock Pillar	Floors	Hardware
Spanish Brown colonial-grain artificial leather	Spanish Brown colonial-grain artificial leather	Black rubber	Bright nickel

45-A Standard Coupe (Dropped June 1928)
Trim Scheme Gray

Seats, Wind Cord, Quarters	Doors, Lock Pillar	Floors	Headlining	Curtain	Cowl	Hardware	Moldings
Gray piped cloth with blue hairline stripe	Gray cloth with blue; hairlined stripe	Brown carpet	Gray napped cotton	Blue cloth	Gray colonial-grain cardboard	Bright nickel	Moulding Gray

49-A Special Coupe (Adopted July 1928)
Trim Scheme Brown hairline stripe

Seats, Wind Cord, Quarters	Doors, Lock Pillar	Floors	Headlining	Curtain	Cowl	Hardware	Moldings
Brown hairline-striped cloth	Brown hairline-striped cloth	Brown carpet (early) Black rubber (late)	Brown napped cotton	Brown cloth	Two-tone brown long-short-grain cardboard	Bright nickel	Moulding Gray

50-A Sport Coupe
Trim Scheme Blue check

Seats, Wind Cord, Quarters	Doors, Lock Pillar	Floors	Headlining	Cowl	Hardware	Moldings
Piped, blue-checked cloth	Blue-gray cloth	Brown carpet (early) Black rubber (late)	To match top option	Gray colonial-grain cardboard	Bright nickel	Moulding Gray

Trim Scheme Brown hairline stripe

Seats, Wind Cord, Quarters	Doors, Lock Pillar	Floors	Headlining	Cowl	Hardware	Moldings
Piped, brown hairline-striped cloth	Brown hairline-striped cloth	Brown carpet (early) Black rubber (late)	To match top option	Two-tone brown long-short-grain cardboard	Bright nickel	Moulding Gray

54-A Business Coupe
Trim Scheme Blue check

Seats, Wind Cord	Doors, Lock Pillar	Floors	Headlining	Cowl	Hardware	Moldings
Piped, blue-checked cloth	Blue-checked cloth	Brown carpet (early) Black rubber (late)	Plain gray cloth	Gray colonial-grain cardboard	Bright nickel	Moulding Gray

55-A Tudor
Trim Scheme Gray cloth with wool stripe

Piped Seats, Doors, Quarters	Back, Header	Floors	Headlining	Curtain	Cowl	Hardware	Moldings
Gray cloth with wool stripe	Plain gray cloth	Brown carpet (early) Black rubber (late)	Gray napped cotton	Blue cloth	Gray colonial-grain cardboard	Bright nickel	Moulding Gray

Trim Scheme Gray cloth with silk stripe

Piped Seats, Doors, Quarters	Back, Header	Floors	Headlining	Curtain	Cowl	Hardware	Moldings
Gray cloth with silk stripe	Plain gray cloth	Brown carpet (early) Black rubber (late)	Gray napped cotton	Blue cloth	Gray colonial-grain cardboard	Bright nickel	Moulding Gray

Trim Scheme Blue hairline stripe

Plain-panel Seats	Doors, Quarters, Seat Backs	Floors	Headlining	Curtain	Cowl	Hardware	Moldings
Blue hairline-striped cloth	Plain blue cloth	Brown carpet (early) Black rubber (late)	Blue napped cotton	Blue cloth	Blue-gray colonial-grain cardboard	Bright nickel	Moulding Gray

60-A Fordor
Trim Scheme Brown hairline stripe

Plain Seats, Doors, Quarters	Upper Quarters, Header	Rear Floor	Headlining	Curtain	Cowl	Hardware	Moldings
Brown hairline-stripe cloth	Plain brown cloth	Brown carpet / Front Floors Brown carpet (early) Black rubber (late)	Brown napped cotton	Brown cloth	Two-tone nut-brown pigskin-grain cardboard	Bright nickel	Mocha Brown

76-A Open Cab Commercial
Trim Scheme Black

Plain-panel Seats	Doors, Cowl, Pillars	Floor	Hardware
Black Arabian-grain artificial leather	Black Arabian-grain cardboard	Black rubber	Bright nickel

Trim Scheme Spanish Brown

Plain-panel Seats	Doors, Cowl, Pillars	Floor	Hardware
Spanish Brown colonial-grain artificial leather	Spanish Brown colonial-grain cardboard	Black rubber	Bright nickel

79-A, 85-A Panel Delivery
Trim Scheme Spanish Brown

Plain-panel Seats	Doors, Cowl, Header	Floor	Roof Lining	Hardware
Spanish Brown colonial-grain artificial leather	Spanish Brown colonial-grain cardboard	Black rubber	Black duck	Bright nickel

82-A Closed Cab Commercial
Trim Scheme Black

Plain-panel Seats	Doors, Cowl, Header, Pillars	Floor	Roof Lining	Hardware
Black Arabian-grain artificial leather	Black Arabian-grain cardboard	Black rubber	Black duck	Bright nickel

1928

Right: A Briggs body tag on the right lower cowl of a 140-A Town Car. Most Briggs- and Murray-built bodies did not have an outside body tag.

Far right: The DUOLIGHT drum taillight on the early 1929 Town Car was chrome plated rather than bright nickel, as it was on all other cars.

Right: The upholstery in the rear interior of an early 1929 Town Car is tan Bedford cord with tan broadcloth sidewalls and headlining. The carpet is Wilton wool.

Far right: The notebook and vanity mirror were installed in a covered compartment in the left rear armrest of the Town Car.

brake drums and backing plates. The front brakes are the same diameter as the Model A, but have a larger wheel stud configuration to mount the AA-1015-AR 20-inch steel-spoke wheels with semi-split rims and 30x5 high-pressure truck tires. These are equivalent to a modern 5.00x20 balloon size. The front spring is the AA-5310-AR with 12 leaves, which has the same width as the front spring on a Model A passenger car.

The 1928 AA chassis is equipped with an AA-400-AR worm-drive axle assembly similar to the design used on the Model TT trucks. Some of the parts are actually interchangeable with the TT axle. This axle was available in either a 7.25:1 or 5.17:1 gear ratio. It is supported on two cantilever 16-leaf AA-5560-B or 13-leaf AA-5560-C rear-spring assemblies attached to the axle housing by large bearing surfaces. The front of the spring is attached to the frame side rail with an AA-5775-A spring hanger bracket on each side.

The rear brake drums were 14-inch AA-1114-AR, but these were changed to AA-1114-BR when the separate parking brake system was adopted in June 1928. The mechanical brake system is similar in operation to that of the Model A, but some additional brackets and rocker shafts are necessary to accommodate the longer wheelbase. The rear wheels are the same AA-1015-AR as the front, but are mounted with 32x6 high-pressure truck tires. These are equivalent to a modern 6.50x20 balloon size. Both front and rear spoke wheels used the AA-1130-A cadmium-plated hubcap with Ford script. The 1928 steel truck wheels were equipped with Schrader or Dill straight, nickel-plated valve stems with 2⅜-inch

wide and 6 inches deep at their deepest point. The first frame variation was the 171 5/16-inch-long AA-5005-AR, which has a front cross-member with a solid engine mount and an arched rear cross-member similar in design to the one used on the Model A chassis.

The front axle of the 1928 AA is identical to that of the Model A, but uses a different spindle (AA-3105-AR) to accommodate the AA-1102-AR

Here is a left front quarter view of a 1928 AA with an 82-A closed cab and an aftermarket Railway Express body. The red-painted chassis and wheels are special-order commercial fleet items. This truck is equipped with the 1928-only AA-1015-AR 20-inch steel spoke wheels. *Kenneth Keeley*

Original Ford Model A

high-fluted dust covers similar to those used on passenger cars. Under the dust cover was the same nickel-plated valve cap with valve core removal tip as that used in passenger cars.

The AA truck chassis was equipped with the same engine and three-speed transmission configuration as the Model A, except that the multidisc clutch assembly had a heavier spring. This combination was identified with an "AA" engine number. This designation was dropped for a short time from February to May 1928. The only available variation for the truck chassis was the optional two-speed, dual-high auxiliary transmission, which mounted just behind the standard three-speed unit. A small rocker pedal on the floor in front of the driver's seat operates this unit.

The AA chassis was available in seven basic body configurations. Included were an open cab, a closed cab, and a cowl chassis. The open and closed cabs were available with the 88-A Platform or 188-A Stake body configurations. Also available was an 89-A Express body, which is similar to the 78-A pickup bed but longer. An 85-A Panel Delivery built by Budd was available too. Some of these models were not available until the spring or fall of 1928.

Above: Rear view of an early 1928 AA closed-cab Express body truck. The rear axle is a Ford-designed worm-gear type and was used through the end of 1929. The body is similar in appearance to the pickup body, but it is longer and wider. The wood racks are accessories.

Above: This early 1928 AA closed-cab Express truck was equipped with 20-inch wire-spoke wheels. The 1928 trucks had full-length running boards and splash shields. Bumpers were optional on all 1928 AA trucks. The red finish was not a standard 1928 color and would have been a special order.

The Ford script above the rear window of this 1928 closed cab was used only until February 1928. After July 1928 the rear window was centered on the panel.

Tools 1928 A chassis

Item	Part Number	Finish	Note
Oil can		Copper-plated steel	Only until May 1928, Ford script
Grease gun	A-17125	Dull nickel	Alemite
Tool bag	A-17005	Black top material	11x6½ inches (Closed)
Adjustable wrench			9½-inch
Sparkplug and head nutwrench	A-17017	Unfinished	
Pliers	A-17025	Unfinished	
Open-end wrench	A-17015		7/16x½ inch
Open-end wrench	A-17016		9/16x⅝ inch
Screwdriver		Unfinished/black	8 9/16 inch
Jack	A-17080, A-17080-A	Black	10½ inch
Jack handle	A-17081	Black	16 inch
Tire iron	A-17019	Unfinished/black	10 inch
Tire pump		Black	
Crank	A-17036, A-17036-A	Cadmium	
Crank	A-17036-B	Black	
Owner's manual		Tan	1928

Tools 1928 AA chassis

Identical to A except for AA starting crank, jack, jack handle and tire iron.

Starting crank 1928,		Unfinished/black	Socket for 1-inch lug nuts until May 1⅛-inch lug nuts after
Jack	AA-17080-A	Unfinished/black	1⅜-inch square top
Jack handle		Unfinished/black	24 inches long
Tire iron		Unfinished/black	16⅝ inches long

A side-mounted spare wheel and tire on an early 1928 AA Express-body truck. The AA-1015-AR, 20-inch steel-spoke wheels were only used in 1928. A spare tire would have been installed by the dealer and was not included with any Model A or AA from the factory.

A black-enamel DUOLIGHT drum taillight on an early 1928 AA truck. The taillight's body was stamped steel rather than brass, as were the nickel-and chrome-plated passenger car units.

The large 85-A Panel Delivery and the smaller A-chassis Panel Delivery were the first production panel bodies Ford offered. The body cargo compartment was 102⅜ inches long, 54½ inches wide, and 50 inches high, with two side-hinged, rear doors with windows. In addition to its practical cargo-carrying capacity, the Panel body offered a convenient space on each side for business advertising. The driver's compartment was equipped with two individual folding seats. The 85-A used the same A-79764-AR (RH) and A-79765-AR (LH) as the 79-A Panel Delivery. The rear AA-16438 (RH) and AA-16439 (LH) fenders were shared with the Stake and Express bodies.

The 89-A Express body was available with either a closed or open cab and was a variation of the TT Express body originally introduced in 1924. Although the Express was similar in appearance to the 78-A pickup body, it was considerably wider and longer. The stamped steel Express body had a cargo that was 48 inches wide, 86 inches long, and 12⅛ inches high. The overall width was 55 inches. The cargo floor was constructed of ⅞-inch-thick boards separated by steel batten strips. The Express body was equipped with a tailgate similar in design to that used on the pickup body. There was no Ford script on the Express-body tailgate.

The 1928 AA Panel Delivery and Express bodies were equipped with a spare tire mounted on the right-side running board behind the rear of the cab or door; the Platform and Stake bodies stowed the spare tire under the rear of the chassis. The body color and interior trim combinations for the AA chassis were identical to the corresponding models on the Model A chassis. A distinctive feature of the 1928 AA models was the use of full-length running board and rear fenders, which were not generally used in later years except on closed bodies.

Below: There were four types of jack used during 1928. From left to right they are: A-17080 Walker, A-17080 Walker with name tag, A-17080 Ajax, and the A-17080-A Walker, which was introduced in October 1928. The A-17080-A did not have the folding top.

Original Ford Model A

Chapter 2
1929

This early 1929 Canadian Roadster still has some late 1928 features, such as Arabian Sand body color, fluted headlight lenses, and a red steering wheel.

The beginning of 1929 saw the Ford Motor Company still struggling to increase Model A production while finally beginning to realize a profit. Ford worldwide sales figures for the 1929 model year were 1,967,741 cars and trucks. Profits for 1929 totaled $81,797,861. As it was with most manufacturers, calendar year changes were not as evident and important as they became in later years.

Improvements and changes to the Model A were evolutionary rather than dramatic. Because keeping up with production demands was paramount, it took Ford until the end of March to implement the changes that characterize a 1929 Ford. The majority of the changes made for 1929 reflected the unit losses realized on some of the early 1928 models. Factory cost sheets reported that as of March 1928 the company lost $318.79 per Tudor car and $335.84 per Phaeton. Since the company could not afford to produce models at a loss, it needed to implement production changes.

The changes implemented in March 1929 consisted of switching the headlight lenses from a fluted to a prism design and adopting a teacup-style taillight shell across the line. The Powerhouse generator was replaced with a cheaper and more common later type. There was also a new list of body colors and interior trim schemes that made most 1928 combinations obsolete. In late 1929, Ford, along with most other manufacturers, switched from nickel to chrome plating as chrome became more widely available.

Beginning in June 1929, the 55-A Tudor became the first Model A body type to adopt vacuum windshield wipers. The initial Trico C1B wipers were attached to the outside of the windshield frame and were equipped with 8½-inch Trico black enamel–painted blades. The original blades had five layers of rubber in gray, red, and black. The blades were attached by spring clip to the vacuum motor with a 6¼-inch

32

1929

The whitewall tires, door top covers, and trunk rack of this Canadian Roadster are accessories. This early 1929 car still has some distinctive 1928 features.

The front view of a 1929 Town Sedan shows the new prism-type headlight lenses and chrome radiator and headlight shells. The chrome outside door mirror and whitewall tires are accessories.

black enamel–painted arm. By September 1929, vacuum wipers were standard equipment on all Tudors and were integrated into the rest of the Model A line early in 1930.

Ford's big news for early 1929 was its release of several new models. By early February 1929, Ford had introduced the 140-A Town Car, 68-A Cabriolet, 155-A and 155-B Town Sedan, and 150-A Station Wagon. The Town Car, designed by LeBaron, was an open-front luxury model, intended for chauffeur-driven service. Its price of $1,400 placed it beyond the reach of most Ford customers and greatly reduced sales opportunities for Ford dealers.

The Cabriolet, on the other hand, was a more popular addition to the Model A line. It was promoted as a "deluxe sport coupe." The Cabriolet is what other manufacturers would call a convertible coupe, as its top and side window supports could be lowered.

The Town Sedan is a four-door, three-window design with the longest body in the Ford line. It was described as "long, low and straight, emphasized by the French roof quarters and belt molding." The Town Sedan was a deluxe four-door type with a higher level of interior trim appointments. For the first time, four-door bodies were made both by the Briggs and Murray body companies.

The new Ford Station Wagon was an innovative idea, as previous bodies of this type were offered only by aftermarket coachbuilders. The 1929 Ford was the first station wagon body built as a regular production-line offering. The wood bodies were actually assembled by Murray Body Company from subassemblies provided by Ford's Iron Mountain plant. By mid-1929 two more new models were introduced: the 165-A-B three-window Fordor (in May) and a leather-covered steel-back 60-C Fordor (in July).

Chassis, Axles, and Wheels

The frame was not changed significantly for 1929. The change to the flexible yoke-type front engine mounting had been made by the end of 1928 and the brake cross-shaft was changed to the solid design. Alterations in the center cross-member were made along with the elimination of the multipiece equalizer assembly used in 1928. These changes included the elimination of the small folded tabs that acted as stops for the equalizer arms. The holes used for mounting the equalizer shaft in the center cross-member supports were also eliminated.

In October 1929 the front cross-member was changed by the creation of a depression at the radiator mounting pads where previously there had been an embossed area. This change required the addition of two more rubber shims under the radiator mounting brackets. Longer A-20968 radiator-to-frame bolts were also required.

In late 1928, the forged battery support assembly was changed to a stamped design. Both designs had a square bottom plate with a single drain hole. In mid-1929, this support was redesigned to incorporate two drain holes. In both cases, the bottom plate is spot-welded to the supports. In September 1928, the battery cover was changed to a stamped design with built-in corners.

Following other changes for 1929, the running board brackets went from a forged to a stamped design in March. The new running board brackets were still riveted to the frame. The company continued to use forged fender brackets through the end of 1929.

Original Ford Model A

1929 Ford Model A Production

Model	Name	Weight	Price	Number Produced
35-A	Phaeton	2,235	$460	111,212
40-A	Roadster	2,106/2,147*	$450	209,518
45-A	Coupe	2,225/2,250*	$550	184,021
49-A	Special Coupe	2,225/2,250*	$550	(Combined with Coupe)
50-A	Sport Coupe	2,285	$550	138,828
54-A	Business Coupe	2,244	$525	38,687
55-A	Tudor	2,395	$525	80,245
60-A	Fordor	2,441	$625	
60-B	Fordor	2,441	$625	
60-C	Fordor	2,500	$625	173,357 (Combined)
68-A	Cabriolet	2,339	$670	17,764
135-A	Taxi-Cab	2,500	$800	5,401
140-A	Town Car		$1,400	1,102 (Note1)
150-A	Station Wagon	2,482	$695	4,959
155-A	Town Sedan (Murray)	2,517	$695	91,173, (A&B
155-B	Town Sedan (Briggs)	2,517	$695	combined)
165-A	Std. Fordor (Briggs)	2,497	$650	
165-B	Std. Fordor (Murray)	2,497	$650	
170-A	Std. Fordor (2W)	2,419	$625	
76-A	Open Cab Pickup	2,073	$445	
79-A	Panel Delivery	2,500	$615	
82-A	Closed Cab Pickup	2,215	$475	
130-A	Deluxe Delivery		$595	
	A Chassis	1,680	$365	(Note 2)
	AA Chassis	2,723	$540	(Note 2)
	AA Chassis w/cab	3,036		
85-A	AA Panel Delivery	3,847	$850	
88-A	AA Platform			
89-A	AA Express			
188-A	AA Stake			

Note:
Total includes 89 Town Cars built in 1928.
In June 1929, 28 York-Hoover 100-cubic-foot Mail bodies were ordered and installed on A Chassis. the same time, 306 August Schubert 200-cubic-foot Mail bodies were ordered and installed on AA Chassis.
*With rumble seat.

In February 1929, the Model A adopted the Gemmer-design hourglass, worm-and-two-tooth sector steering gear. This unit was a considerable improvement over the old Ford seven-tooth design and provided easier steering. This steering gear was used concurrently with the old gear through March 1930, when the seven-tooth gear was finally dropped. The new two-tooth design is easily identifiable by the clamps on the upper end of the housing.

The two-tooth steering gear was also easier to adjust than the old design. Rather than adding or removing shims, a mechanic could adjust this gear with an eccentric four-sector teeth mesh and a screw and locknut for steering shaft end-play. There is also a screw and locknut for sector shaft end play.

All types of steering gear housings were painted black, but the two-tooth's upper housing clamp has a cadmium finish with unfinished bolts, nuts, and lock washer. The springs and lower ends of the throttle and spark levers should be painted black, while the operating rods should be nickel plated. By early 1929, all steering wheels should be black rubber. The design is the same as the red wheel and both maintain the splined shaft design for the seven-tooth steering gear. The black rubber steering wheel for the two-tooth gear uses a keyed shaft.

There were no significant changes in the remainder of the chassis components. The 1929 Model A uses the same springs, axles, and radius rods as the 1928 models.

1929

A driver's-side view of the engine compartment of a 1929 Coupe. This car has the Ford-designed seven-tooth steering gear. Note the correct red stripe on the radiator hoses and the new-for-1929 generator.

Opposite: This 1929, 150-A Station Wagon has fluted headlight lenses and the body is finished in Manila Brown. The roof rack luggage carrier is an accessory.

The A-1015-BR wheels for the 1929 Ford are identical to those first used on the mid-1928 and later chassis and were still painted black from the factory on all models. Hubcaps are the identical steel, nickel-plated design through April 1929 when both nickel- and chrome-plated caps could have been used concurrently.

Engine Assembly

There were few changes in the engine for 1929. In January, Ford began to equip Model A engines with lighter, solid-skirt aluminum pistons. The new design was fitted with a nonexpanding steel insert anchored to the center of the piston head.

In March 1929, the rear main bearing cap was made thicker. The new cast-iron cap has mounting-bolt bosses that are $1\frac{1}{8}$ inches in height rather than $\frac{9}{16}$ inch, as in the earlier design. This change greatly increased the strength and rigidity of the cap. When restoring engines, it is a good idea to use these improved caps for added reliability.

1929 Model A Engine Numbers

Month	First Number	Last Number
January	810123	983136
February	983137	1127171
March	1127172	1298827
April	1298828	1478647
May	1478648	1663401
June	1663402	1854831
July	1854832	2045422
August	2045423	2243920
September	2243921	2396932
October	2936933	2571781
November	2571782	2678140
December	2678141	2742695

Note:
  Engine numbers include AA truck production. Except for a brief period from February to May 1928, all AA trucks were identified with a AA engine number prefix.
  The engine number indicates only when the engine was completed. Engine installation into the chassis at the assembly plant could have taken two weeks to four months. When the engine was installed in the chassis the engine number was stamped on the top left side of the frame just ahead of the front body bolt hole.

Original Ford Model A

The front view of a 1929 Town Sedan shows the new chrome radiator shell, prism headlight lenses, and oval center bumper clamp.

In May 1929, the A-6645 oil-return pipe on the A-6520 valve chamber cover was lowered and its length was increased. This change requires that the valve chamber cover and oil pipe be matched when accumulating engine parts for restoration. This change was made to lower the oil level in the valve chamber, reducing oil consumption. At about the same time, a $3/16$-inch oil hole was added to the rear of the valve chamber. This change permits the oil in the valve chamber to drain directly on the rear main bearing, increasing its lubrication. This modification should be made to earlier engines according to instructions in the Ford Service Bulletins.

In January 1929, the camshaft was changed from a five-bearing to a three-bearing design. The new camshafts may be used in the old engines. Valve guides were also reduced in length from $2\frac{3}{8}$ inches to $2\frac{1}{8}$ inches in July 1929 to help prevent sticking valves.

Transmission and Clutch

There were no significant changes in the transmission and clutch assembly for 1929. In December 1928, the front-mounted squeeze-lever-type parking brake handle was changed to a push-button type. In July 1929, the parking brake handle was moved to the side, which required the gearshift housing to be changed from the A-7222-BR with a front-mounted brake handle to the new A-7222-C design used through the end of production. All years and models use a handle that is Butler or unpolished nickel on the lower part and bright nickel on the grip.

In March 1929, two louvers were added to the A-7518-B clutch housing hand hole cover to aid breathing and help prevent pulling oil out of the rear main bearing.

In June 1929, the extension lug on the universal joint housing was eliminated and the holes

1929

in the caps were no longer unequally spaced. The old A-4520-BR cap assembly and A-4513-BR inner cap were replaced with the new A-4520-C outer cap and A-4513-A inner cap, which has equally spaced holes.

Cooling System and Radiator

The most noticeable change to the 1929 cooling system was the February 1929 elimination of the fan shroud. This was another change made purely for economic reasons because the shroud actually did improve cooling. The removal of the fan shroud brought the elimination of the shroud mountings in the radiator at about the same time. A small change was made in the water pump in April 1929 when the front bearing was eliminated. This change is visible by the lack of a front grease fitting on the water pump housing. This modification lasted until April 1930, when the front bearing was reinstated. The water pump rear packing nut remained a brass or bronze casting, as it was in 1928. The A-8291 outlet water pipe was altered to move the bend further to the rear when the company eliminated the Powerhouse generator in March 1929.

The only external change to the cooling system was the switch from nickel to chrome plating for the radiator shell, which was an industry-wide change. Chrome plating provides a more durable and brighter finish than nickel. This change was put into production during October to December 1929, when either finish might be found. The A-8212 Ford script radiator nameplate with vitreous blue background was carried over from 1928.

Fuel System

In January 1929, Ford adopted the practice of identifying the carburetor manufacturers with cast-in markings on the lower carburetor body. The design of the carburetor was similar but those made by Zenith were marked "Zenith 1" and those made by Holley were marked "Zenith 2." The carburetor body was still finished in black enamel as it was in 1928. The secondary venturi had been discontinued by June 1928, so by early 1929 the carburetor had reached the basic design configuration that would continue through mid-1931.

In April 1929, the A-9189 fuel shutoff valve located under the fuel tank was changed. The basic design remained identical to the 1928 valve, but the handle was changed from a butterfly-shaped forged type to a stamped steel design. Also changed in April 1929 was the A-9725 accelerator and throttle control linkage assembly. The A-9734-C main operating shaft was redesigned into a one-piece unit, which eliminated the previous separate accelerator control arm. The A-9732-A bell crank was still maintained as a forged part. As with most other 1929 changes, these alterations were intended to reduce the manufacturing cost of each car.

Electrical System

The most noticeable change to the 1929 Model A electrical system was the July replacement of the expensive, short Powerhouse generator. This large, five-brush unit was replaced with a more conventional three-brush, long generator. The new generator, first introduced in October 1928, was used concurrently with Powerhouse until the old design was phased out in July. The new generator was less expensive to produce and easier to service. The first version of this generator has ball bearings at both the front and rear and has the output terminal near the front of the unit. In January 1929, the generator pulley design was changed to a stamped steel construction with a smooth face that has no spokes. This design was used through 1929. All versions should have a glossy black enamel finish.

In early 1929, Ford adopted a new starter design with a ⅝-inch driveshaft to replace the old Abel design. This new unit became available in October 1928, but the old starter could still be found as late as mid-1929. In October 1928, the new rounded design A-11450-C starter switch

A detail of the chrome-plated 1929 headlight shells, front fender, and Fordor hood panel design on a 1929 Town Sedan. The black enamel–finished horn is mounted under the left side of the headlight bar.

Original Ford Model A

This 1929 40-A Roadster is finished in Andalusite Blue with black moldings and French Gray stripe. The spare tire cover is an accessory.

The Roadster has a black long-short-grain artificial-leather top. The chrome bars on the rear deck are top rests.

was introduced to replace the old rectangular switch used with the Abel starter. This new switch is used only with the new starter design, and it incorporates a new screw-type A-11470-C starter switch push rod.

In early 1929, the improved Twolight headlight assembly was adopted to replace the previous unit with fluted lenses. The lenses on the Twolight have a distinctive prism design and incorporate a separate, 3-candlepower parking lamp. The new headlight still has the Ford script in an oval at the bottom of the lens. This change required an alteration to the main light wiring harness to include another headlight wire. The rear light harness was also modified to accommodate the new A-13407 teacup-style taillight assembly. The wire was shortened to a point just to the back of the rear cross-member. There were no other significant changes to the remainder of the electrical system for 1929.

Body and Fender Assembly

The basic styling and body design of the 1929 Model A Ford does not differ from that of 1928. The big changes for 1929 were the addition of a number of new body styles and the introduction of new exterior color schemes and interior trim combinations. There were 12 new body types introduced for the 1929 model year, giving a total of 19 distinct bodies available on the New Ford chassis. Seven were variations of four-door sedans, one was the Station Wagon, one was the Cabriolet, and the remaining three were the very specialized Town Car, Deluxe Delivery, and Taxi Cab. In January 1929, fender well spare tire equipment was offered as an assembly-line option for the first time. Prior to this time, fender wells were only installed as a dealer service item. Spare tire wells were available on either the left or the right side. The 1929 running board splash shields may be immediately identified by the distinctive hump at the upper rear corner. This hump was added when the new brake system was adopted in mid-1928.

The Model 35-A Standard Phaeton for 1929 was very much like the 1928 body. The most visible change was the addition of outside door handles. The A-35626-AR open-car door handles are brass clad and nickel plated. They are mounted on a thin molded rubber pad. The previous inside lever was replaced with the nickel-plated A-35632-A handle, the same one used for a number of other Model A body styles. Both the inside and outside handles are mounted horizontally. A Ford Service Bulletin

1929

This early 1929 Canadian Roadster still uses the nickel-plated DUOLIGHT drum taillight from 1928. The trunk rack is an accessory.

This Canadian Roadster has a red steering wheel and Spanish Brown colonial-grain artificial-leather interior trim. The door panels and cowl are trimmed with matching cardboard.

A close-up view of the right windshield frame and cowl on a 1929 Roadster. The closed-end French Gray stripe was a carryover from 1928. The body color is Andalusite Blue with black moldings.

note for December 1928 listed the procedure for replacing the old system with the new outside handles. This directive means that some 1928 cars may have had the outside handles added at some time during their life.

Another visible outside change for 1929 production was the addition of windshield wind wings on the open cars. The wings were first offered as accessories in May 1928, but by 1929 they became standard on the Phaeton and Roadster. The brackets are nickel plated and mount to holes placed in the windshield supports. Instructions in the May 1928 Ford Service Bulletins detail the installation steps. The wind wings provide a bit of protection for the driver and front-seat passenger. They are adjustable and are secured inside the door frame when the side curtains are in place.

The 1929 Phaeton was offered in five basic color combinations. The main body colors included Bonnie Gray, Rose Beige, Balsam Green, Andalusite Blue, and Thorne Brown. Contrasting or complementary colors were used for the moldings and striping. Most of the 1929 open-car colors were darker than the colors available in 1928. Color changes always reflected market trends and fads for that particular year.

The 1929 Phaeton interior trim was offered in only one scheme of blue-gray colonial-grain artificial leather for the seats. Door, cowl, and quarter panels are finished in matching blue-gray colonial-grain cardboard. The cardboard panels are plain, flat, and trimmed with artificial-leather binding. Like the 1928 version, 1929 Phaeton front and rear seats have a single lateral seam approximately one-third of the way back from the front of the seat.

The folding top for the 1929 Phaeton was the same as the 1928 Phaeton top, finished in black, long-short-grain artificial leather. The bows are black steel and black bow-drill trimmed wood. The side curtains are made of the same material as the top deck and have clear celluloid side windows. Side curtains attach to forged posts that fit into sockets in each door panel. They are secured additionally by snaps in the sides of the body. The side curtains for the Phaeton are stowed in a hinged compartment under the rear floor. All 1929 Phaetons have black rubber floor mats with a spatter pattern.

The 1929 Model 40-A Standard Roadster is basically identical to the 1928 version, except like the Phaeton, nickel-plated outside door handles were added for 1929. The Roadster was also still available with either a trunk or rumble seat equipment.

By the beginning of 1929, the hand-operated windshield wiper had been replaced by electric equipment in both the Roadster and Phaeton.

Original Ford Model A

Above: The interior of this early 1929 Canadian Roadster is trimmed in the Spanish Brown colonial-grain artificial leather used in 1928 U.S.-built Roadsters. This car still has a red steering wheel.

Left: By early 1929 the Roadster steering wheel was black and the parking brake handle had been moved to the front of the gearshift lever. The interior trim is blue-gray colonial-grain artificial leather.

The new electric wipers, first introduced as optional equipment on open cars in April 1928, were made by the Owen-Dyneto Corporation and became standard equipment in November 1928. The earliest model was the OD-01, which was used through February 1929. Open-car wiper motors are painted gloss black and are secured to the windshield frame with steel clamps.

The 1929 Standard Roadster was offered in the same five basic color combinations as the Phaeton. The main body colors are Bonnie Gray, Rose Beige, Balsam Green, Andalusite Blue, and Thorne Brown with contrasting and complementary molding and stripe colors. All Model A striping should be $\frac{1}{8}$-inch to $\frac{3}{32}$-inch wide. On 1929 open cars, the stripe was not closed at the front of the belt molding as it was in 1928.

The interior trim of the Roadster was the same blue-gray colonial artificial-grain leather as used on the Phaeton. The door and cowl panels were plain and the seat has the same lateral seam as the 1928 equipment. One difference from 1928 was that the rumble seat for 1929 did not match the front seat. The rumble seat and side cardboard panels were trimmed in the same Spanish Brown colonial-grain artificial leather as the 1928 models. The rumble seat back and cushion were plain with only a perimeter welting.

The folding top of the 40-A Roadster is trimmed in black, long-short-grain artificial leather with matching side curtains. The top frame is black-painted metal and black bow-drill covered wood. The side curtains are stowed under the front seat. The 1929 Roadsters have a floor mat of black spatter- or sunburst-pattern rubber.

At the beginning of 1929, the 45-A Standard Coupe was not being built and the 49-A Special Coupe was still the only hard roof coupe being offered. The 49-A Special Coupe was identical to the Standard Coupe except that its artificial-leather roof covering extends all the way down to the body moldings. The 49-A was built through July 1929, when production of the 45-A Standard Coupe was resumed.

Both the Standard Coupe and Special Coupe were offered initially in four color schemes. In April 1929, one of the original colors was dropped and two new ones were added to the line. The original 1929 coupe color combinations are Bonnie Gray, Vagabond Green, Rose Beige, and Andalusite Blue. In April 1929, Bonnie Gray was dropped and Thorne Brown and Mountain Brown were added. In all combinations complementary or contrasting colors were used for the moldings and striping.

The 1929 Special Coupe was continued with the same brown hairline-striped interior trim

The Canadian bumper clamps are smooth finish with no inset panels or Ford script. These smooth clamps were used from June 1928 to August 1930 on Canadian-built cars.

1929

Top right: This detail of the windshield frame on an early 1929 Canadian Roadster shows the Robertson screws used only on Canadian-built cars. The finish is Arabian Sand with Copra Drab moldings. The wind wings are accessories.

Top far right: The left outside door handle on an early 1929 Canadian-built Roadster. The door-top armrest is an accessory that protects the door from wear and the driver's arm from heat.

Right: A detail of Sparton horn and cadmium-plated horn and headlight wire conduits on an early 1929 Canadian Roadster. Rubber grommets are used to seal the wires from the radiator shell.

Far right: This Canadian headlight lens is slightly different from the U.S. version and incorporates the 1928-style flutes with a prism on the top.

A 1929 Standard Coupe finished in Vagabond Green with Rock Moss Green moldings and Straw stripe. The roof and visor are covered with black, coarse, long-short-grain artificial leather. The turn signals are safety additions for modern touring.

Original Ford Model A

A front view of a 1929 Special Coupe. The 49-A has a black, artificial-leather roof and was built only from July 1928 to July 1929. This car has a Vagabond Green body with Rock Moss Green moldings. The stone guard, wind wings, mascot, whitewall tires, and fender-mounted spares are accessories.

Far left: The front compartment of a 1929 Standard Coupe with brown-checked interior trim. The seat sides and door panels are trimmed with plain brown cloth. The turn signal is a more modern safety addition.

Left: The left front door on a 1929 Standard Coupe. The door panel is trimmed in plain brown cloth to match the brown-checked interior trim scheme. The door hardware is plated in bright nickel.

scheme as it had in 1928. When production of the Standard Coupe was resumed in July 1929, a new interior trim scheme was adopted. The new trim combination consisted of a plain-panel seat of brown-check cloth; and doors, quarter panels, header, and seatback covered in plain brown cloth. The headlining was trimmed in brown napped cotton cloth. Garnish moldings for the brown-checked trim scheme were finished in Light Buff. Window curtains were brown cloth.

In October 1929 a new optional interior trim scheme was adopted for the Standard Coupe. On special order, an owner could get the seat, doors, seatback, and quarters trimmed in blue-gray colonial-grain artificial leather. The headlining was gray napped cotton and the window curtains were blue cloth. The rumble seat area for all 1929 coupes was trimmed in Spanish Brown colonial-grain artificial leather.

The Model 50-A Sport Coupe was another direct carryover from 1928. The body design was identical with the only differences being in interior trim combinations. The Sport Coupe was offered in the same exterior color schemes as the

1929

Right: This early 1929 50-A Sport Coupe is finished in Vagabond Green with Rock Moss Green moldings and Straw stripe. The top and visor are covered with tan whipcord fabric, a carryover from 1928. This material was only used through February 1929. Note the body-color landau irons.

Below: The rear-quarter view of a Vagabond Green 1929 Sport Coupe illustrates the square rumble seat step plates on the right rear bumper and fender.

Right: A close-up view of a tan whipcord fabric roof on a 1929 50-A Sport Coupe. Note the hide-em welting and chrome tips on the valance seam on the rear of the top.

Above: The front view of a 1929 50-A Sport Coupe shows chrome-plated radiator and headlight shells. The body is finished in Andalusite Blue. The Motometer and whitewall tires are accessories.

43

Original Ford Model A

This 1929 50-A Sport Coupe is finished in Andalusite Blue. The top is the 1928-type tan whipcord material used through February 1929. The door window draft deflectors, whitewall tires, and fender-mounted spare tires are accessories.

Standard and Special Coupes. In early 1929, the Sport Coupe top was trimmed in the same dark brown seal-grain artificial leather as the late 1928 cars. In early or mid-1929, this material was changed to a light brown seal-grain artificial leather. In April 1929 a new brown two-tone diagonal-grain artificial-leather material was offered.

The Sport Coupe interior was offered in two schemes. The first was brown hairline stripe seats with the door panels, quarters, and seatbacks in plain brown cloth. The seats for 1929 are plain panel with a lap seam. The cowl is trimmed in two-tone nut-brown pigskin-grained cardboard. The headlining was changed from tan whipcord to brown mock twist early in 1929 to correspond with the change in top material.

The second interior trim scheme featured brown-checked cloth on the plain-panel seats and plain brown cloth on the doors, quarters, and seatbacks. The cowl was finished with two-tone dash-grain cardboard. Sport Coupes have a black rubber floor mat with either interior trim combination. Both brown interior trim schemes have Light Buff–painted garnish moldings.

There were a number of changes and additions to the 54-A Business Coupe offerings for 1929. The most distinguishable change was the addition of an oval window in the fabric top quarters. There were also three interior trim schemes rather than the two offered in 1928.

The 1929 Business Coupe was offered in the same exterior body color combinations as the Standard, Special, and Sport Coupe. The top was covered in the same long-short-grain artificial leather as the 1928 Business Coupe. By late 1928, the rear window was larger than the original version. The exterior of the rear window frame is a bright polished aluminum casting.

The left rear view of a 1929 Sport Coupe shows nickel-plated DUOLIGHT drum taillight and A-13471-AR forged support bracket. The trunk, trunk rack, and whitewall tires are accessories.

A close-up view of the rear quarter of the tan whipcord top used on a 1929 Sport Coupe. Note the landau iron arms finished in body color.

1929

Right: The seats of this 1929 50-A Sport Coupe are trimmed in piped brown-checked cloth with the seat sides and door panels in plain brown cloth. The floor is covered with a black rubber mat.

Far right: Detail of a 1929 21-inch front wheel and tire. The wheel is the later A-1015-BR adopted when the new six-brake system was introduced in mid-1928. Note the nickel-plated fluted valve stem dust cover. The whitewall tire is an accessory.

Right: Rumble seat cushions in a 1929 50-A Sport Coupe are trimmed in plain-panel Spanish Brown colonial-grain artificial leather. This material is a carryover from 1928 open cars.

Far right: Note the Ford script marking on the front of the 1929 axle and the cadmium-plated brake adjusting wedge nut and black enamel tubular shock absorber link.

Left front quarter view of a 1929 54-A Business Coupe shows the oval quarter windows used only that year. The lower body is Vagabond Green with Rock Moss Green moldings. The stripe is Straw. The top is covered with black long-short-grain artificial leather. *Kenneth Keeley*

Original Ford Model A

A side view of a 1929 55-A Tudor sedan finished in Andalusite Blue with a French Gray stripe. The moldings and rear upper back should be black.

The 1929 Business Coupe was offered in three interior trim combinations. The first is the same Spanish Brown artificial-leather as in 1928. The brown artificial leather trim scheme was dropped in August 1929. The second trim combination has a plain-panel seat, door panels, seatback, and rear quarters in a granite gray cloth with a white stripe. The seat cushion had a lap seam. The early 1929 door panels had a gray broad lace strip across the top of the door panel. The inside of the top and top quarters had a gray plain cloth or gray mock twist cloth. The garnish moldings were finished in Moulding Gray. The cowl is covered with a gray colonial-grain cardboard.

The third interior trim combination, available optionally on special order beginning in October 1929, had a plain seat panel, door panels, quarters, and seat back of blue-gray colonial-grain artificial leather. The seat cushion had a lap seam. The cowl was covered with a blue-gray colonial-grain cardboard. Garnish moldings were painted Moulding gray.

The Model 55-A Tudor sedan was still the most popular Model A for 1929 with more than 500,000 built. The basic body design with the distinctive coupe pillar is identical to the 1928 Tudor with differences only in body color combinations and interior trim schemes. For 1928, the upper body back was usually a separate color, while in 1929, the upper body back was the same color as the belt, quarter, and sill moldings. While for 1928 the Tudor offered a choice of three interior trim combinations, 1929 Tudors had only one trim scheme available at a time, with a change made midyear.

There were four body color schemes offered on the 55-A Tudor through April 1929. Lower and upper body colors are Bonnie Gray, Vagabond

Green, Rose Beige, and Andalusite Blue. Complementary and contrasting moldings and stripes enhanced these colors. In April 1929, Bonnie Gray was dropped and replaced with Mountain Brown and Thorne Brown also with contrasting and complementary stripes and moldings.

The 1929 Tudor was offered in only two interior trim schemes. The first had the plain panel seats trimmed in blue hairline cloth, while the door panels, quarters, seat sides and backs, and header were in plain blue cloth. The headlining was blue napped cotton and the cowl and seat bottoms were finished in blue-gray colonial-grain cardboard. Window curtains were blue cloth. Garnish moldings were painted Moulding Gray. This combination was dropped in July 1929.

The steel trunk rack of this 1929 Tudor sedan is an accessory. The A-16311-AR and A-16310-AR rear fenders are also used on the Standard Phaeton, Standard Fordor, Town Car, Deluxe Delivery and Panel Delivery, and Town Sedan. The sedan is finished in Andalusite Blue.

1929

Right side view of the front compartment of a 1929 Tudor. The interior trim is blue hairline-striped cloth with plain blue cloth on the seat sides, door panels, and quarters. The garnish moldings are painted Moulding Gray. This early 1929 car has the push-button front parking brake handle.

The right-side engine compartment detail of this 1929 Tudor shows correct Zenith carburetor and cast-iron fuel sediment bowl. The Air-Maze air filter is an accessory.

The black enamel TR-C1A Trico vacuum wiper motor (top) first used on the 1929 Tudor and later adopted for most closed bodies. The black enamel 8½-inch Trico four-layer blade and 6½-inch arm were used with this wiper. Note the Trico logo visible on the arm and blade.

The second interior combination, adopted in July 1929, was with the plain panel seats trimmed in brown-checked cloth and the door panels, seat sides and backs, quarters, and header finished in plain brown cloth. The headlining was brown napped cotton and window curtains were brown cloth. The cowl and seat bottoms were trimmed in two-tone brown dash-grain cardboard. Garnish moldings were painted Light Buff.

The stylish Briggs-built 60-A Fordor was carried over basically unchanged from 1928, but a new version with a black pebble-grain artificial-leather top was also offered. This new model is known as the 60-B and is essentially the same as the 60-A except for the top material. Additionally, there was a steel-back version of the two-window Fordor identified as the 60-C. For 1929, there were also another six Fordor variations with bodies built by both Briggs and Murray.

The 60-A two-window Fordor for early 1929 carried over the same body color schemes as 1928. Interior trim for the 60-A has the seats, door panels, lower quarters, and lower pillars trimmed in brown hairline cloth. The upper quarters, upper pillars, roof side rails, and header are in plain brown cloth. The headlining is brown napped cotton cloth. The cowl is two-tone nut-brown pigskin-grain cardboard.

The 1929 60-B Fordor with black artificial-leather roof and 60-C with steel roof were offered in six body color combinations. The lower body was finished in Bonnie Gray, Vagabond Green, Rose Beige, Andalusite Blue, Thorne Brown, and Bramble Brown. The upper body, belt, quarters, reveals, and stripe were finished in contrasting and complementary colors. The 1929 60-C steel-back two-window Fordor was the first Model A closed body to have an uncovered steel windshield visor.

The 78-A Open Cab and 82-A Closed Cab Pickup truck bodies were carried over without change from 1928, except for the change from Spanish Brown to black Arabian-grain artificial-leather interior trim materials. The 1929 78-A open-cab body continued without outside door handles. All trucks were still equipped with black enamel–painted headlight, taillight, and radiator shells as they were in 1928.

The only other change was the addition of four body color schemes to the commercial line. For 1929, the commercial bodies had the same combinations as in 1928, plus new ones with the lower body in L'anse Green Dark and L'anse Green both with black moldings and a combination with Gunmetal Blue in the same variations. Contrasting stripes were standard with both combinations.

The 79-A Panel Delivery was also continued for 1929 basically unchanged except for the new interior and exterior trim schemes. New for 1929 was the 130-A Deluxe Delivery. Introduced in February 1929, the Deluxe Delivery body is similar to the Tudor, but the rear-quarter window area is longer. This body style is what some manufacturers would call a sedan delivery. The Deluxe Delivery body is equipped with a single, hinged rear door rather than the double doors of the Panel Delivery. The rear door was equipped with a nickel-plated, locking T handle, and there were two folding individual front seats.

The Deluxe Delivery exterior trim schemes were passenger car rather than commercial color combinations. The lower body was available in Bonnie Gray, Vagabond Green, Rose Beige, and Andalusite Blue with contrasting and complementary molding and stripe colors. The Deluxe Delivery was also offered with the rear quarter panel painted a different color to be used for advertising purposes, in colors contrasting the lower body colors. The radiator, headlight, and taillight shells were nickel-plated passenger-car parts.

Original Ford Model A

A 1929 76-A Open Cab Pickup. Note the black-painted radiator and headlight shells. The body is finished in Rock Moss Green with no molding or stripe color.

Below: Rear-quarter view of 1929 Open Cab Pickup. The black artificial leather top is not foldable or removable. The wood bed rails are accessories.

Above left: The interior trim scheme of this 1929 Open Cab Pickup is blue-gray artificial leather on the seats and matching blue-gray cardboard on the door panels and cowl.

Left: The interior view detail of the nonfolding top on a 1929 Open Cab Pickup. The top frame is black enamel stamped steel. Note the 1928 style-inside door handle that was used on all 1928 to early 1930 open-cab bodies.

The interior trim of the Deluxe Delivery had seats and headlining in Spanish Brown colonial-grain artificial leather. Door panels, windshield header, cowl, and seat bottoms were trimmed with Spanish Brown colonial-grain cardboard. Interior hardware was identical to that of standard passenger cars. A special interior light and switch was mounted above the windshield on the header panel. In August 1929, an accessory package tray was offered for the Deluxe Delivery. This kit provided a vertical screen mounted just behind the driver's compartment and placed a flat horizontal tray (A-132905) on the body rails that reached all the way to the rear door opening.

Early in 1929, two unusual new models became part of Ford's line. Both had been developed late in 1928 but are identified as 1929 models. The first was the 135-A Taxi-Cab and the

1929

A 1929 135-A Taxi-Cab finished in Duchess Blue with Medium Cream upper back and reveals, with black moldings and cream stripe. The Taxi-Cab is the only Fordor with a coupe-pillar body design.

Rear view of a 135-A 1929 Taxi-Cab. All Taxi-Cabs used the 1928 style DUOLIGHT drum nickel-plated taillight and forged mounting bracket.

Above: The wiper on this 135-A 1929 Taxi-Cab is an outside-mount electric type. The windshield frame is finished in Medium Cream.

Right: Front compartment of a 1929 Taxi-Cab with the seat trimmed in gray sharkskin genuine leather. This is an original interior. Note the standard taximeter on the right side of the front compartment.

second was the 140-A Town Car. Both models were relatively expensive to develop, high in price, and unsuccessful in the market.

The Taxi-Cab was the only Model A four-door design that incorporated the distinctive coupe pillar and exposed fuel tank used on the Coupe and Tudor sedan. Initial Ford advertising illustrations as early as December 1927 showed a four-door sedan that looked very much like the 135-A Taxi-Cab except for the Taxi-Cab's longer rear body and quarter windows. The Taxi-Cab was developed to satisfy the statute requirements of cities such as New York that required any car used as a taxi to be capable of accommodating four passengers. Ford also wanted to compete with outside body builders who had been offering bodies and conversions on the Model A chassis since early 1928.

Briggs Manufacturing Company began delivering the first of 2,500 Taxi-Cab bodies Ford ordered by early December 1928. There was a single front seat mounted in front of a division partition. The right front compartment was open and designed to carry luggage. A taximeter was installed in the front compartment. The Taxi-Cab was equipped with larger 4.75x21-inch tires to compensate for the extra weight of passenger work.

The 135-A Taxi-Cab was available in two standard body color combinations for 1929. The upper and lower body were finished in either Balsam Green or Duchess Blue, each with black belt moldings, Medium Cream upper back and reveals, and a cream stripe. The Taxi-Cab was also available in 10 other optional color combinations. Of course, fleet orders of any other required colors could be accommodated.

Original Ford Model A

Far left: Right front door panel of a 1929 Taxi-Cab. The door panel is trimmed with gray sharkskin artificial leather. This is an original interior.

Left: Rear compartment of a 1929 Taxicab. The seat is trimmed with piped gray mohair, but the quarters, door panels, and headlining are gray sharkskin artificial leather like the front.

The Taxi-Cab was available in only one interior trim scheme due to the special design and purpose of the car. The plain-panel front seat was trimmed in gray sharkskin genuine leather and the door panels, partition, headlining, and header were trimmed in dark gray sharkskin artificial leather. The cowl was gray sharkskin cardboard. The rear compartment main and folding seat were trimmed in gray mohair. Window curtains were gray cloth. Front and rear garnish moldings were gray. The front floor mat was black rubber, and the rear floor was covered with a gray rubber mat. In February 1929 it was changed to black rubber.

The most expensive Model A was the 140-A Town Car. Town Car production began late in 1928, but the car was officially introduced in January 1929. The body was described as "a LeBaron town car body." Although designed by LeBaron, the body was actually built by Briggs Manufacturing. The Town Car body featured the same smooth cowl, hood, and body design used for the other Fordors and the Cabriolet. The new $1,400 car was first available only through Lincoln dealers, but Ford later expanded the distribution to the Ford showrooms.

The Town Car is in every way a custom type of design normally available only on the most expensive large chassis. Ford wanted the Model A Town Car to appeal to the person who did not have to prove his or her wealth and still wanted a correct car for daily business. The smaller size was especially attractive to women. It was also attractive to the European markets where smaller streets were the norm. The Town Car had standard nickel-plated cowl band and cowl lights.

This 1929 right-hand-drive 140-A was one of 89 Town Cars built in late 1928. This car has fluted headlight lenses and the late-1928-style center bumper medallion.

1929

Right: This 1929 Town Car is the only right-hand-drive Town Car known to exist. Note the distinctive red alignment stripe with notch to mark the valve stem location on the spare tire. The roof is covered with black genuine Landau leather.

Far right: This view of the right side of the 1929 Town Car shows the distinctive A-17716 chrome Town Car outside mirror and electric windshield wiper.

Right: The seat and door panels of this 1929 Town Car are trimmed with black, fine, long-short-grain genuine leather. Note the round clutch and brake pedals and center accelerator pedal used only on right-hand-drive cars.

Far right: This close-up view of the rear quarter of a Madras Carbuncle 1929 Town Car shows the drum taillight and Casino Red stripe on the black moldings. The roof is covered in genuine leather.

Right: This special chrome A-17716 outside mirror assembly was used only on the Town Car.

Far right: The left rear door panel of a 1929 Town Car. The trim is tan Bedford cord, and the hardware and garnish moldings are painted Mocha Brown.

Original Ford Model A

A 1929 Town Car with chauffeur's canopy in place over the driver's compartment. The center front fog lamp is an accessory.

The 140-A Town Car was available in five body color schemes. The lower body and reveals were finished in Brewster Green, Thorne Brown, black, Mulberry Maroon, or Madras Carbuncle. The upper body and moldings were finished in black in all combinations. The stripe was in a contrasting color for all combinations. Madras Carbuncle and Mulberry Maroon were exclusive colors reserved only for the Town Car. The Town Car top was covered in black, coarse long-short-grain artificial leather. The removable chauffeur's canopy was made of the same material. The inside of the chauffeur's top was lined with black duck.

The Town Car was available in a single interior trim scheme. The front driver's compartment, including the seat door panels, is finished in black, fine, long-short-grain genuine leather. The floor is covered with a conventional design spatter-pattern black rubber mat. The cowl is trimmed with black, fine-grain artificial leather. The rear seat is trimmed in tan Bedford cord, and the door panels, back, headliner, quarters, and partition were trimmed in tan broadcloth. The rear floor is covered with a tan Wilton wool carpet. Window curtains are copper-tone silk. Rear compartment hardware is finished in painted Mocha Brown

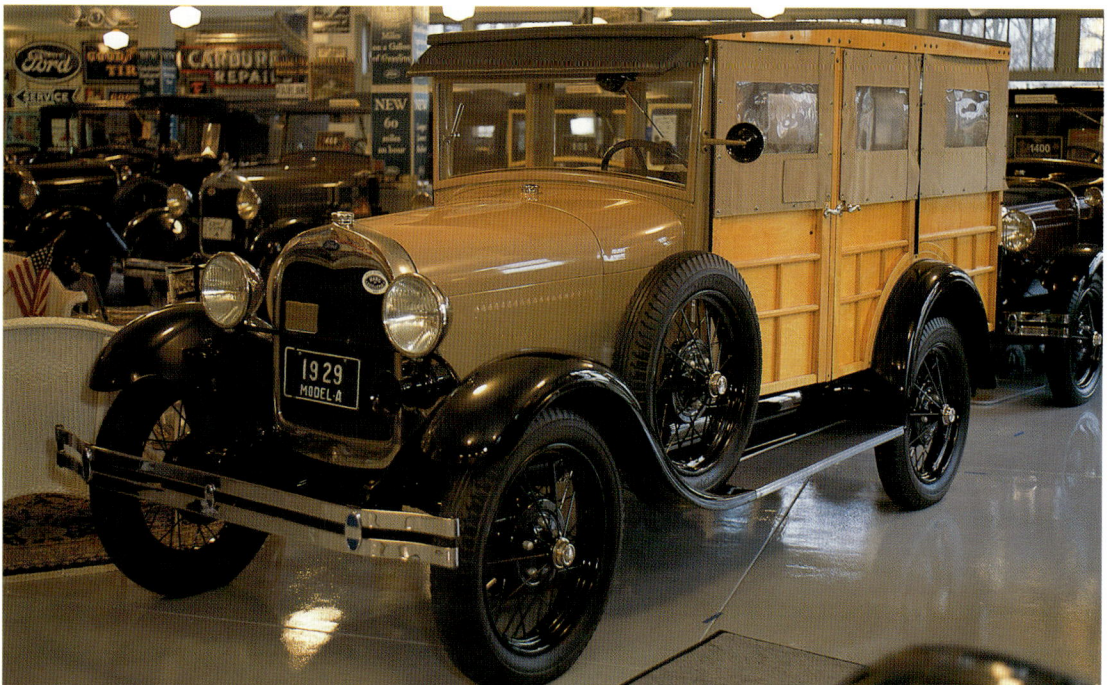

This 1929 150-A Station Wagon is finished in Manila Brown with natural maple and birch varnished wood finish. The side curtains are rubber interlined tan fabric with clear celluloid window inserts.

1929

Right: This side view of the wood body structure of a 1929 Station Wagon shows the side curtains removed. The framing is hard maple and the paneling is birch plywood.

Far right: A detail of a wood door frame and paneling and exterior door handles on a 1929 150-A Station Wagon. The cover on the side curtain is for extending the driver's arm for signaling.

Right: Here is the distinctive outside commercial mirror used on the driver's-side door of the 150-A Station Wagon. The mirror bracket is painted body color, which in this case is Manila Brown.

Far right: This photograph shows the left rear quarter of a 150-A 1929 Station Wagon with side curtains in place. The windows were made of clear celluloid and sewn in between the fabric layers.

rather than plated as in all other body types. Front compartment hardware was Butler chrome.

Another important addition to the 1929 Ford line was the 150-A Station Wagon. This model was significant in that it represents the first time that any manufacturer offered a mass-produced factory station wagon. Until 1929, Ford station wagon and wood-bodied utility vehicles were equipped with bodies made by outside builders. Initially, the bodies were designed by Ford Engineering and produced by Murray Body Company.

The Model A Station Wagon was equipped with a maple-framed body that was paneled with cross-grained exterior birch plywood. The interior roof has visible basswood slats. Seating arrangements consisted of a bench front seat, two removable center seats, and a removable bench rear seat. There were no roll-up windows, and side curtains provided the only weather protection. When not in use, the side curtains were stowed in a steel compartment under the rear floor. Side fender-mounted spare tire equipment was standard.

Standard body finish on the Station Wagon is Manila Brown with no stripe. This medium-tan color was used only on the 1929–31 Station Wagon and was selected to match the tone of the wood

Right: The seat of this 1929 Station Wagon is trimmed in blue-gray colonial-grain artificial leather, and the cowl is matching cardboard. The floor is covered with a black rubber mat.

Far right: The interior view of a right rear door and roof structure of a 1929 Station Wagon. The black enamel reinforcement brackets are stamped steel.

Original Ford Model A

Above: Detail of left front inside door hardware on a 1929 155-B Briggs Town Sedan. The garnish molding is mahogany woodgrain and the trim is green mohair.

Left: The body of this 1929 155-B Briggs Town Sedan is finished in Vagabond Green with Rock Moss Green moldings and Straw stripe. The Town Sedan is identified by its chrome cowl band and cowl lights.

finish. All wood framing and panels were finished in a clear high-gloss spar varnish, leaving the wood's natural color visible. Black paint was used on all structural steel brackets and mounting hardware.

Although the Station Wagon was officially considered a commercial vehicle, it was still equipped with the nickel-plated radiator and headlight shells of the passenger cars rather than the normal black paint used on trucks. The top and windshield visor were covered with coarse, black, long-short-grain artificial leather.

Interior door handles were A35632-B one-piece lever type and were nickel plated and mounted to visible black-painted door latches. Outside door handles were A-25205/A-25206 nickel-plated brass clad. There was a single, commercial-type black-painted A-17741-A mirror bracket and A-17730 mirror mounted on the upper driver's door body pillar.

There was only one interior trim scheme offered on the Station Wagon. The plain-panel seats were trimmed in blue-gray colonial-grain artificial leather. The cowl and windshield header are blue-gray colonial-grain cardboard. Side curtains are made of a tan rubber interlined fabric with clear celluloid inserts. Floors were covered with a black rubber mat front and rear.

In May 1929, there were four new variations of three-window Fordor sedans in addition to the Briggs-built two-window carryover from 1928. The new bodies used the same distinctive hood and no coupe-pillar cowl design as the other Fordor, but these were built by Murray Body Corporation in addition to Briggs. There are essentially two different body configurations called the Standard Fordor and the Town Sedan.

The bodies were basically the same, but the Briggs bodies have side windows with a distinctive square look and the Murray cars have a more rounded appearance to the window shape. Inside, the door pulls on the Murray bodies were die-cast zinc fastened to the garnish moldings, while the Briggs bodies had the pulls of stamped steel spot-welded to the moldings. There are also differences in the door openings. Murray Fordors have front and rear doors of the same width, while Briggs bodies have front doors that are about 1 inch wider than the rear doors. Each body builder's example of Fordor was identified by a different model number suffix—"A" for the Murray and "B" for the Briggs.

Below: Left side view of a Vagabond Green 1929 155-B Town Sedan. The trunk rack, trunk, whitewall tires, and chrome outside mirror are accessories.

1929

Above: Rear quarter view of a 1929 Briggs Town Sedan. The whitewall tires, spare tire cover, chrome trunk rack, and trunk are accessories.

Above right: Close-up view of chrome cowl light and cowl band on a 1929 Briggs Town Sedan. The lower body is Vagabond Green and the stripe is Straw.

Right: The front compartment of this 1929 Briggs Town Sedan is trimmed in piped green mohair on the seats and plain-panel green mohair on the door panels and quarters.

Far right: The left front door panel on a 1929 Briggs Town Sedan is trimmed in green mohair. The garnish moldings are painted mahogany woodgrain with a chrome pull handle.

The 1929 Town Sedan 155-A and 155-B were the luxury or deluxe versions of the new three-window Fordors. Both models differed from the Standard Fordor in having three rather than two interior trim schemes, side and center armrests in the rear compartment, and woodgrain garnish moldings. The Town Sedan also has standard cowl lights and a nickel-plated cowl band that were not used with the Standard Fordors.

The 165-A and 165-B Standard Fordor body is identical to the Town Sedan in design and construction but differs in appointments and finish. All four bodies are important in that they are the first use of the basic body design that would be adopted for 1930. The doors and other structural body components of the Briggs or Murray Fordor are interchangeable with the corresponding bodies for 1930 and early 1931. Parts are generally not interchangeable between Briggs and Murray bodies.

The exterior color combinations of both the Standard Fordor and Town Sedan are the same, with seven basic schemes available. The lower body and reveals were finished in Bonnie Gray, Vagabond Green, Bramble Brown, Rose Beige, Andalusite Blue, Dawn Gray, and Ford Maroon. The moldings, upper body, and stripe were finished in contrasting and complementary colors.

Original Ford Model A

A 1929 Standard Fordor finished in Ford Maroon and black with a vermilion stripe. The body is identical to the Town Sedan but without deluxe trim, chrome cowl lights, and cowl band. The fender-mounted spare tire is an accessory.

Far left: Detail view of Briggs and Murray body tags used on the Model A bodies. These tags would be stamped with a body-style number and body serial number from the coach builder.

Left: Detail view of left-side door handle hardware on a 1929 Standard Fordor. By 1929 the handles all turn down at the ends.

The interior trim of the 155-A and 155-B Town Sedan was offered in three basic combinations. The first, available only in the 155-A Murray Body, has the seats in gray-checked cloth with the seatback, quarters, door panels, and header in plain gray cloth. The headlining is trimmed in gray napped cotton with gray silk window shades. The cowl is trimmed with two-tone brown dash-grain cardboard. The floor covering is brown carpet, which is also used to trim the bottom edges of the door panels and rear quarters. There is also a gray twisted robe cord on the back of the front seat.

The next trim scheme, available in both Briggs and Murray bodies, has the seats, front seatback, quarters, header, and door panels trimmed in brown mohair. The headlining is brown napped cotton and the window curtains are brown silk. The cowl is trimmed with two-tone brown dash-grain cardboard. The floor covering is brown carpet, also used on the lower doors and lower rear quarters. There is also a brown twisted robe cord attached to the rear of the front seat.

The third trim scheme has the seats, front seat back, quarters, door panels, and header finished in green mohair. The headlining is green napped cotton and the window curtains are green silk. The cowl is two-tone green dash-grain cardboard. The floor covering, lower door, and lower rear quarter panels are trimmed in brown carpet. There is a green twisted robe cord attached to the rear of the front seat.

All three 1929 Town Sedan interior trim schemes had front and rear seats piped with 10 pipes in the front and 11 in the rear. The 1929 Fordor and Town Sedans had scroll-type interior hardware, but the design used in the Briggs bodies differed from that of the Murray bodies. The handles and escutcheons used on the Briggs Fordor and Town Sedan were the same ones used

1929 Interior Trim Combinations

35-A Standard Phaeton & 40-A Standard Roadster
Trim Scheme Blue-gray

Seats, Wind Cord, Quarters	Doors, Cowl, Lock Pillar	Floor	Hardware
Blue-gray colonial-grain artificial leather	Blue-gray colonial grain cardboard	Black rubber	Bright nickel

45-A Standard Coupe (Adopted July 1929)
Trim Scheme Brown check

Seat	Doors, Quarters, Header	Floor	Headlining	Curtain	Cowl	Hardware	Moldings
Brown check cloth	Plain brown cloth	Black rubber	Brown napped cotton	Brown cloth	Two-tone brown dash-grain cardboard	Bright nickel	Light Buff

45-A Standard Coupe (Special order after October 1929)
Trim Scheme Blue-gray artificial leather

Seat, Quarters, Doors, Header	Floors	Headlining	Curtain	Cowl	Hardware	Moldings
Blue-gray colonia-grain artificial leather	Black rubber	Gray napped cloth	Blue cloth	Blue-gray colonial-grain cardboard	Bright nickel	Moulding Gray

49-A Special Coupe (Dropped June 1929)
Trim Scheme Brown hairline stripe

Seat	Doors, Quarters, Header	Floor	Headlining	Curtain	Cowl	Hardware	Moldings
Brown hairline-striped cloth	Plain brown cloth	Black rubber	Brown napped cotton	Brown cloth	Two-tone nut-brown pigskin-grain cardboard	Bright nickel	Moulding Gray

50-A Sport Coupe (Dropped July 1929)
Trim Scheme Brown hairline stripe

Seat	Doors, Quarters	Floor	Headlining	Cowl	Hardware	Moldings
Brown hairline-stiped cloth	Plain brown cloth	Black rubber	To match top option	Two-tone nut-brown pigskin-grain cardboard	Bright nickel	Moulding Gray

50-A Sport Coupe (Adopted July 1929)
Trim Scheme Brown check

Seat	Doors, Quarters	Floor	Headlining	Cowl	Hardware	Moldings
Brown-checked cloth	Plain brown cloth	Black rubber	To match top option	Two-tone brown dash-grain cardboard	Bright nickel	Light Buff

54-A Business Coupe (Dropped August 1929)
Trim Scheme Brown artificial leather

Seat, Rear Quarters, Doors, wind cord, package tray	Top Quarters & Sides, inside top, rails	Floor	Headlining	Cowl	Hardware	Moldings
Spanish Brown colonial-grain artificial leather	Plain gray cloth or black mock twist	Black rubber	Plain gray cloth or black mock twist	Spanish Brown colonial grain artificial-leather	Bright nickel	Moulding Gray

54-A Business Coupe
Trim Scheme Gray cloth with stripe

Seat, Rear Quarters, Doors, Wind cord, package tray	Top Quarters & Sides, inside top, rails	Floor	Headlining	Cowl	Hardware	Moldings
Granite gray with white stripe	Plain gray cloth or black mock twist	Black rubber	Plain gray cloth or black mock twist	Gray colonial-grain artificial leather	Bright nickel	Moulding Gray

54-A Business Coupe (Special order after October 1929)
Trim Scheme Blue-gray artificial leather

Seat, Rear Quarters, Doors, Wind Cord, Package Tray	Top Quarters & Sides, Inside Top, Rails	Floor	Headlining	Cowl	Hardware	Moldings
Blue-gray colonial-grain artificial leather	Plain gray cloth or black mock twist	Black rubber	Plain gray cloth or black mock twist	Blue-gray colonial-grain cardboard	Bright nickel	Moulding Gray

55-A Tudor (Dropped July 1929)
Trim Scheme Blue hairline stripe

Seats	Doors, Quarters, Header	Floors	Headlining	Curtain	Cowl	Hardware	Moldings
Blue hairline-striped cloth	Plain blue cloth	Black rubber	Blue napped cotton	Blue cloth	Blue-gray colonial-grain cardboard	Bright nickel	Moulding Gray

55-A Tudor (Adopted July 1929)
Trim Scheme Brown check

Seats	Doors, Quarters, Header	Floors	Headlining	Curtain	Cowl	Hardware	Moldings
Brown check cloth	Plain brown cloth	Black rubber	Brown napped cotton	Brown cloth	Two-tone brown dash-grain cardboard	Bright nickel	Light Buff

60-B & 60-C Fordor
Trim Scheme Brown hairline stripe

Seats	Seat back, sides, quarters, side rails	Floors	Headlining	Curtain	Cowl	Hardware	Moldings
Plain panel with lap seam Brown hairline stripe cloth	Plain brown cloth	Black rubber	Brown napped cotton	Brown cloth	Two-tone nut brown pigskin-grain cardboard	Bright nickel	Mocha Brown

68-A Cabriolet
Trim Scheme Gray check

Seat	Doors, Quarters, Seat back	Floor	Headlining, Top Inside	Cowl	Hardware	Moldings
Piped, gray-checked cloth	Plain gray cloth	Black rubber	Gray drab mock twist & Gray drab cloth (late)	Two-tone brown dash-grain cardboard	Butler nickel	Moulding Gray

1929 INTERIOR TRIM COMBINATIONS (CONTINUED)

140-A Town Car
TRIM SCHEME Tan Bedford cord

FRONT COMPARTMENT SEAT, DOORS	REAR COMPARTMENT SEAT	REAR COMPARTMENT DOORS, QUARTERS	FLOOR	HEADLINING, REAR	CURTAINS	COWL	HARDWARE	MOLDINGS
Black fine long-short-grain genuine leather	Tan broadcloth	Tan Bedford cord	Rubber	Tan broadcloth	Copper-tone silk	Black fine long-short-grain artificial leather	Butler nickel ?Brown (rear)	Mocha/walnut (rear)

165-A Fordor
TRIM SCHEME Brown hairline cloth

SEATS	DOORS, QUARTERS, SEAT BACK	FLOORS	HEADLINING	CURTAIN	COWL	HARDWARE	MOLDINGS
Brown hairline-striped cloth	Plain brown cloth	Black rubber	Brown napped cotton	Brown cloth	Two-tone brown dash-grain cardboard	Bright nickel	Mocha Brown

165-A, B Fordor
TRIM SCHEME Brown check

SEATS	DOORS, QUARTERS, SEAT BACK	FLOORS	HEADLINING	CURTAIN	COWL	HARDWARE	MOLDINGS
Brown-checked cloth	Plain brown cloth	Black rubber	Brown napped cotton	Brown cloth	Two-tone brown dash-grain cardboard	Bright nickel	Mocha Brown

170-A Fordor
TRIM SCHEME Brown check

SEATS	DOORS, QUARTERS, SEAT BACK	FLOORS	HEADLINING	CURTAIN	COWL	HARDWARE	MOLDINGS
Brown-checked cloth	Plain brown cloth	Black rubber	Brown napped cotton	Brown cloth	Two-tone brown dash-grain cardboard	Bright nickel	Mocha Brown

155-A Town Sedan (Murray)
TRIM SCHEME Gray check

SEAT	DOORS, QUARTERS, SEAT BACK	FLOORS	HEADLINING	CURTAIN	COWL	HARDWARE
Piped, gray-checked cloth	Plain gray cloth	Brown carpet	Gray napped cotton	Gray silk	Two-tone brown dash-grain cardboard	Butler nickel

155-A, -B Town Sedan
TRIM SCHEME Brown mohair

SEATS, DOORS, QUARTERS, HEADER, SEAT BACK, PILLARS	FLOORS	HEADLINING	CURTAIN	COWL	HARDWARE	MOLDINGS
Piped, brown mohair	Brown carpet	Green napped cotton	Brown silk	Two-tone green dash-grain cardboard	Butler nickel	Mocha Brown

155-A, -B Town Sedan
TRIM SCHEME Green mohair

SEATS, DOORS, QUARTERS, HEADER, SEAT BACK, PILLARS	FLOORS	HEADLINING	CURTAIN	COWL	HARDWARE	MOLDINGS
Piped, green mohair	Brown carpet	Green napped cotton	Green silk	Two-tone green dash-grain cardboard	Butler nickel	Mocha Brown

76-A Open Cab Commercial
TRIM SCHEME Spanish Brown

PLAIN-PANEL SEATS	DOORS, COWL, PILLAR	FLOOR	HARDWARE
Spanish Brown colonial-grain artificial leather	Spanish Brown colonial-grain cardboard	Black rubber	Bright nickel

79-A, 85-A Panel Delivery
TRIM SCHEME Spanish Brown

PLAIN-PANEL SEATS	DOORS, COWL, HEADER	FLOOR	ROOF LINING	HARDWARE
Spanish Brown colonial-grain artificial leather	Spanish Brown colonial-grain cardboard	Black rubber	Black duck	Bright nickel

82-A Closed Cab Commercial
TRIM SCHEME Spanish Brown

PLAIN-PANEL SEATS	DOORS, COWL, HEADER, PILLARS	FLOOR	ROOF LINING	HARDWARE
Spanish Brown colonial-grain artificial leather	Spanish Brown colonial-grain cardboard	Black rubber	Black duck	Bright nickel

130-A Deluxe Delivery
TRIM SCHEME Spanish Brown

PLAIN-PANEL SEATS	DOORS, COWL, HEADER	FLOOR	HARDWARE
Spanish Brown colonial-grain artificial leather	Spanish Brown colonial-grain cardboard	Black rubber	Bright nickel

for the 1929 Town Car and Cabriolet. The handles and escutcheons used on the Murray bodies were used on the 1929 to early 1931 Murray-bodied Fordors and Town Sedans and the early 1930 Cabriolets.

The interior of the 1929 three-window Standard Fordor was trimmed in two schemes. The first, available only with the 165-A, has the seats trimmed in brown hairline-striped cloth. The seats are plain with a single lateral lap seam. The door panels, front seatback, quarters, and header are finished in plain brown cloth. The headlining is brown napped cotton and the window curtain is brown cloth. The cowl is two-tone brown dash-grain cardboard. The Standard Fordor floor covering is a black rubber mat.

1929 Body Color Schemes

35-A Standard Roadster & 40-A Standard Phaeton

Body	Belt, Quarter & Sill Molding	Stripe
Bonnie Gray	Chelsea Blue	Straw (Dropped May 1929)
Rose Beige	Seal Brown	Orange
Balsam Green	Valley Green	Medium Cream
Andalusite Blue	Black	French Gray
Thorne Brown	Black	Gold (Available October 1929)

45-A Coupe, 49-A Special Coupe, 50-A Sport Coupe & 54-A Business Coupe

Body, Upper & Lower	Belt, Quarter & Sill Molding	Reveals	Stripe
Bonnie Gray	Chelsea Blue	Chelsea Blue	Straw (Through April 1929)
Vagabond Green	Rock Moss Green	Rock Moss Green	Straw (Through April 1929)
Rose Beige	Seal Brown	Seal Brown	Orange (Through April 1929)
Andalusite Blue	Black	Niagara Blue, Light	French Gray (Through April 1929)
Vagabond Green	Rock Moss Green	Vagabond Green	Straw (After April 1929)
Rose Beige	Seal Brown	Rose Beige	Orange (After April 1929)
Mountain Brown	Thorne Brown	Mountain Brown	Straw (Available October 1929)
Thorne Brown	Black	Thorne Brown	Gold (Available October 1929)

55-A Tudor

Body, Upper & Lower	Upper Back & Moldings	Reveals	Stripe
Bonnie Gray	Chelsea Blue	Chelsea Blue	Straw (Through April 1929)
Vagabond Green	Rock Moss Green	Rock Moss Green	Straw (Through April 1929)
Rose Beige	Seal Brown	Seal Brown	Orange (Through April 1929)
Andalusite Blue	Black	Niagara Blue, Light	French Gray (Through April 1929)
Vagabond Green	Rock Moss Green	Vagabond Green	Straw (After April 1929)
Rose Beige	Seal Brown	Rose Beige	Orange (After April 1929)
Andalusite Blue	Black	Andalusite Blue	French Gray (After April 1929)
Mountain Brown	Thorne Brown	Mountain Brown	Straw (Available October 1929)
Thorne Brown	Black	Thorne Brown	Gold (Available October 1929)

60-B, -C, 170-A Fordor

Lower Body	Upper Body, Belt & Quarter	Reveals & Sill Molding	Stripe
Bonnie Gray	Chelsea Blue	Bonnie Gray	Straw (Dropped May 1929)
Vagabond Green	Rock Moss Green	Vagabond Green	Straw
Rose Beige	Seal Brown	Rose Beige	Orange (Sill molding Seal Brown)
Andalusite Blue	Andalusite Blue	Niagara Blue	French Gray (Sill molding Andalusite Blue)
Thorne Brown	Black	Black	Gold
Bramble Brown	Thorne Brown	Bramble Brown	Cream (Stripe may be Orange for January 1929)

155-A, -B, Standard Fordor & 165-A, -B Town Sedan

Lower Body	Upper Body, Belt, Quarter & Sill	Reveals	Stripe
Bonnie Gray	Chelsea Blue	Bonnie Gray	Straw (Dropped May 1929)
Vagabond Green	Rock Moss Green	Vagabond Green	Straw
Bramble Brown	Thorne Brown	Bramble Brown	Cream
Rose Beige	Seal Brown	Rose Beige	Orange
Andalusite Blue	Andalusite Blue	Niagara Blue, Light	French Gray
Dawn Gray	Black	Dawn Gray	French Gray
Ford Maroon	Black	Ford Maroon	Vermillion

68-A Cabriolet

Lower Body & Reveals	Upper Body, Deck, Belt, Quarter & Sill Moldings	Stripe
Cigarette Cream	Seal Brown	Orange
Bronson Yellow	Seal Brown	Orange (Available October 1929)
Andalusite Blue	Black	French Gray (Available July 1929)
Thorne Brown	Black	Gold (Available July 1929)
Mountain Brown	Thorne Brown	Straw (Available July 1929)

140-A Town Car

Lower Body & Reveals	Upper Body, Belt, Quarter & Sill Molding	Stripe
Brewster Green	Black	Serpent Green
Thorne Brown	Black	Orange (Also Gold or Silver)
Black	Black	Gold
Mulberry Maroon	Black	Coach Vermillion (Dropped January 1929)
Madras Carbuncle	Black	Casino Red (Available January 1929)

135-A Taxi-Cab

Upper & Lower Body Reveals	Belt	Upper Back & Reveals	Belt Stripe
Balsam Green Balsam Green	Black	Medium Cream	Cream
Duchess Blue Duchess Blue	Black	Medium Cream	Cream

There were also optional colors available, which were: Rock Moss Green, Commercial Drab, L'anse Green, Gunmetal Blue, Bonnie Gray, Vagabond Green, Rose Beige, Andalusite Blue, Chelsea Blue, and Seal Brown

130-A Deluxe Delivery

Lower Body	Belt, Quarter Molding & Upper Back	Reveals & Ad Panel	Stripe
Bonnie Gray	Chelsea Blue	Chelsea Blue	Straw
Vagabond Green	Rock Moss Green	Rock Moss Green	Straw
Rose Beige	Seal Brown	Seal Brown	Orange
Andalusite Blue	Black	Niagara Blue, Light	French Gray

Commercial, Open & Closed Cab

Body, Upper, Lower & Reveals	Belt & Quarter Molding	Stripe
Rock Moss Green	Rock Moss Green	French Gray
Rock Moss Green	Black	French Gray
Commercial Drab	Commercial Drab	Straw
Commercial Drab	Black	Straw
L'anse Green, Dark	L'anse Green, Dark	Straw
L'anse Green, Dark	Black	Straw
Gunmetal Blue	Gunmetal Blue	French Gray
Gunmetal Blue	Black	French Gray

The second trim scheme, available on both the 165-A and -B, has the seat trimmed in brown-checked cloth. The seat has a plain panel with a single lateral lap seam. The front seatback, quarters, door panels, and header are plain brown cloth. The headlining is brown napped cotton, and the window curtain is brown cloth. The cowl is trimmed in two-tone brown dash-grain cardboard. The floor covering is a black rubber mat.

A new Fordor style was introduced in July 1929. It was promoted as the "improved Fordor." The new two-window Standard Fordor had a steel back with no rear quarter windows. This new design replaced the previous carryover designs of the 60-A, -B, and -C. This new model is known as the 170-A and was designed and built by Briggs. This body design was available only as a Standard Fordor and was not offered with deluxe appointments.

The 170-A Standard Fordor was available in six color combinations. The lower body was finished in Bonnie Gray, Vagabond Green, Rose Beige, Andalusite Blue, Thorne Brown, and Bramble Brown. The upper body, belt moldings, quarters, and stripe were in contrasting and complementary colors.

The 170-A was offered in only one interior trim combination. The seats are plain panel with a single lateral seam and trimmed in brown-checked cloth. The front seatback, quarters, door panels, and header are in plain brown cloth. The headlining is brown napped cotton and the window curtains are in brown cloth. The cowl is two-tone brown dash-grain cardboard. The floors are covered with a black rubber mat.

One of the more exciting new models for 1929 was the sporty Model 68-A Cabriolet. This two-door convertible body is what other manufacturers might call a convertible coupe. The Cabriolet was one of the early 1929 introductory models and was shown at the Ford New York exhibition at their New York showroom on Broadway in January 1929. The preproduction car shown at the Auto Show was finished in an uncharacteristic color combination with a dark body and lighter moldings. The design was referred to as a "deluxe sport coupe" and was a distinct addition to the Ford line.

The Cabriolet body was produced by Briggs Body Corporation and completely assembled prior to being shipped to the Ford assembly plants. The folding top assembly includes a folding rear upper door frame and attached landau irons. The door window frames were different from any other Ford body and were finished in chrome metal. The cowl and hood design were the same as that used on the Fordors, but the body did not have the coupe pillar of the Tudor and Coupe.

When the Cabriolet was first introduced it was offered in only one body color scheme: Cigarette Cream lower body with Seal Brown upper body, molding, and rear deck. The stripe was orange. Later in 1929, additional color combinations were available with the lower body in Bronson Yellow, Andalusite Blue, Thorne Brown, and Mountain Brown. The moldings, upper body, rear deck, and stripe were in contrasting and complementary colors.

The folding top was trimmed in olive tan drab rubber interlined fabric. The functional landau irons were nickel plated. The landau iron spacers on the rear of the top were made of black Bakelite-type material and covered with long-grain black top material. The inside of the top was trimmed in gray mock twist through mid-1929 and gray drab cloth in late 1929.

The 68-A Cabriolet was available in only one interior trim scheme. The piped (12-10) seat was trimmed in gray-checked cloth while the door panels, quarters, and seatback were trimmed with plain gray cloth. The cowl was two-tone brown dash grain cardboard. Interior hardware for the Cabriolet was the deluxe type.

AA Truck Chassis

The 131½-inch wheelbase AA truck chassis continued mostly unchanged into early 1929. The first change came in February 1929 when the 20-inch steel-spoke wheels were replaced with Ford-designed AA-1015-B 20-inch disk-type wheels having six vent holes. These are relatively flat-appearing discs and are quite different from the later Budd wheels. The new wheels were still equipped with cadmium-plated split snap rings to hold the tires in place and the same straight valve

The three designs of jacks used during the 1929 model year. From left to right they are: A-17080-A Ajax, A-17080-A Walker, and A-17080-B1 Ajax. They are all painted black and all three used the A-17081-A 20-inch-long jack handle.

Tools 1929 A chassis

Item	Part Number	Finish	Note
Grease gun	A-17125	Dull nickel	Alemite
Tool bag	A-17005	Black top material	11x6½ inches (Closed)
Adjustable wrench			9½ inches
Sparkplug and head nutwrench	A-17017	Black	
Pliers	A-17025	Unfinished/black	
Open-end wrench	A-17015		7/16x½
Open-end wrench	A-17016		9/16x/8
Screwdriver		Unfinished/black	8 9/16 inch
Jack	A-17080-A, Ajax/Walker	Black	9½ inch
Jack handle	A-17081-A	Black	20 inch
Tire iron	A-17019	Unfinished/black	10 inch
Tire pump		Black	
Crank	A-17036-B	Black	
Owner's manual		Tan	1929

Tools 1929 AA chassis

Identical to A except for AA starting crank, jack, jack handle, and tire iron.

Starting crank		Unfinished/black	Socket for 1⅛-inch lug nuts
Jack	AA-17080-A	Unfinished/black	1⅜-inch square top
Jack handle		Unfinished/black	24 inches long
Tire iron		Unfinished/black	16⅝ inches long

1929

Left front quarter view of a 1929 AA 85-A Panel Delivery. This truck is equipped with the AA-1015-BR Ford-designed 20-inch disc wheels with cadmium-plated snap rings. Six vent holes and a flatter disc differentiates these from the later Budd truck wheels. *Kenneth Keeley*

stems as the 1928 spoke wheels. This new wheel also incorporated a new three-tiered zinc- or cadmium-plated AA-1130-BR hubcap that fits over the axle nut and was held in place by the wheel. Front tires were still 30x5 as they were in 1928.

An important change came in October 1929 when the new Warner T8-1 heavy-duty four-speed transmission was adopted to replace the existing three-speed car transmission. The new transmission was another example of Ford Motor Company replacing a Ford-made part with a better system from another manufacturer. Warner specialized in building transmissions for cars and trucks and could do a much better job of engineering and building a unit to meet commercial requirements.

The AA four-speed offered more strength, and lower gear ratios allowed the truck owner to carry more weight. This increased flexibility greatly increased the sales advantages of the Ford truck over its competitors. The overall low gear ratio with the standard 7.14:1 rear axle was 45.69:1.

The presence of the four-speed transmission is easy to determine because the shift lever is painted black rather than plated nickel as on the three-speed levers. The four-speed shift lever also has a small AA-7215 latch trigger mounted just under the shift ball that operates the reverse lock-out. The small lever must be pulled up to enable engagement of reverse. The right-side mounted A-2780-F parking brake lever was still nickel plated and the same as the passenger car lever. The four-speed transmission also requires the use of an AA-82245 floor plate to accommodate the larger transmission housing and shift lever. This plate is painted gloss black and has a raised center section.

Sometime during early 1929 a new bevel gear rear axle was used concurrently with the standard worm-gear drive. This rarely seen axle had a banjo housing design similar to that of the Model A passenger cars, but it was much larger. This axle used AA-4010-C housings and had gear ratios of 7.16:1 and 5.11:1.

Two additional AA body types became available in February 1929. Both were basically additions to the standard 88-A Platform body. The first was the 134-A stock rack body. This variation had taller 48-inch racks consisting of a single front rack, one-piece sides, and a two-section tailgate.

The second variation was the 134-B grain-side option, which consisted of 20½-inch-high hardwood sides that provided an enclosed cargo volume 73.5 inches wide by 68 inches long. All 1929 Platform-based bodies were still equipped with long running boards, splash shields, and rear fenders. The Panel Delivery and Express bodies were direct carryovers from 1928.

Chapter 3
1930

During the opening weeks of 1930, Ford introduced the first significant styling improvements on the Model A. Almost every detail of the body and fender design was changed. The higher and deeper radiator, higher and longer hood line, and streamlined moldings that swept toward the rear of car were the distinctive features of the 1930 Ford. The appearance of a longer, lower car was enhanced by the use of smaller wheels and larger tires, which also gave the car a heavier image. Fenders were more sweeping in their line and the running board splash shields were brought closer to the bodylines for a more modern appearance.

One of Ford's important innovations on the 1930 Model A was the use of rustless steel, or Allegheny Metal as it was known. This stainless steel was used in the new radiator shell, headlight shells, hubcaps, cowl strip, and taillight shells. Most parts that had previously been chrome or nickel plated were now made from this new material. The new finish was of great interest to buyers, as it would not crack, tarnish, or rust in normal

This 1930 Standard Roadster is finished in Brewster Green with an Apple Green stripe. The whitewall tires, cowl lights, quail radiator cap, and running board step plates are accessories.

1930

The whitewall tires, running board step plates, right taillight, and spare tire guard of the 1930 40-B Standard Roadster are accessories.

use. The stamped rustless steel radiator shell now had a flatter front and a more massive appearance, which immediately identifies a 1930 Ford.

The new design innovations were not lost on the public. Almost 10 million people viewed the new Ford during the first five days of its introduction across the country. Public acceptance of the new car motivated $58 million worth of new orders in the car's first week. Company president Edsel B. Ford pointed out that this increased business was evenly distributed over the entire country, which indicated nationwide approval.

Early in 1930, the company adopted Trico vacuum windshield wipers across the entire line. As with most other changes in the evolution of the Model A, vacuum wipers were used because of the lower cost and simpler design than the electric versions used in Model A closed bodies. The standard hand-operated wipers on open cars were also replaced with the more simply operated vacuum units. Hand-operated wipers were still being used on all commercial bodies well into April 1930.

Ford added six new models to the Model A body-style line in 1930. One of the most innovative was the 180-A Deluxe Phaeton. This model, which would be called a Convertible Victoria by most other manufacturers, was a custom-styled car at its best. The Deluxe Phaeton was unlike any other Model A and brought a definite air of luxury with its two-door, four-passenger Phaeton body and genuine leather interior trim.

Adding deluxe versions of existing body styles created two more of the new models. The company produced the 40-B Deluxe Roadster and 45-B Deluxe Coupe by adding more luxurious trim packages to the existing standard models. The Deluxe Roadster had a redesigned top frame and windshield combined with a more luxurious interior trim scheme and top material. The Deluxe Coupe offered a more attractive interior trim scheme. Both combined these improvements with cowl lights, different exterior colors, and a broader range of trim combinations. In some cases, the addition of standard fender-mounted spare tires added an air of luxury to an otherwise standard car.

There was also a new 170-B Deluxe Two-Window Fordor, which featured improved interior trim combinations and armrests over the standard "blindback" Fordor design. Another very innovative model introduced much later in the year was the 190-A Victoria Coupe. This design combined the sportiness of a coupe with the passenger comfort and room of a Tudor Sedan. It was the first Model A to introduce the new 1931 styling updates.

Although the new styling features were introduced to the passenger car line at the beginning of 1930, trucks and commercial vehicles maintained the 1929 styling and body components through June 1930. A transition period followed during which remaining old-style bodies were fitted with a combination of 1929 and 1930 components.

Chassis, Axles, and Wheels

The Model A's basic A-5005-C frame was not changed from 1929. There were small changes in items such as the stoplight switch and parking brake operating shaft. In September 1929, the raised portion of the radiator mounting on the front cross-member had been changed to a depressed flat area. This change was due to the new radiator mounting and remained unchanged through the end of production. In December 1929, a radiator drain hole was added to the left front of the front cross-member.

In April 1930, the emergency brake cross-shaft was changed from a tubular to a solid design. Brackets mounted to the inside of the frame rail supported the old-design shaft. The new shaft projected through the frame side members, thus holes and a pocket were incorporated into the frame construction before the new shaft was introduced.

Ford supplemented the new body designs with a new steering wheel. The 1928–29 wheel has a thinner rim and a dish to the spokes. The A-3600-CR, or A-3600-D, 1930 wheel has flatter spokes and a heavier appearance. It is constructed of black resin-coated soybean composition or a solid black resin with a satin finish. The steering wheel was never painted. The new steering wheel also required a new light switch design that appeared flatter than the old switch and lever. The new horn button was black Bakelite rather than nickel plated as in 1928–29. In February 1930, the steering column was lengthened 1 inch to provide more clearance between the wheel and the driver's seat.

Bumpers were new for 1930. Still chrome plated as in 1928–29, the new bumpers were flatter, with a subtle curve across their length, rather than a flat section between the bumper mounts with the ends angled backward as in the previous design. The new front bumpers were 62⅞ inches-wide, but in August 1930 a shorter 60-inch-wide bumper was released. The rear bumperettes or fender guards had a similar design. Bumper clamps were identical to the 1929 style except that a stainless-clad style was used as a production option.

The wheels were smaller for 1930, reduced to 19 inches from 21 inches in 1928 and 1929. The rolled rim of the 21-inch wheels was eliminated and replaced with a more conventional straight-bead rim adopted from a Kelsey Hayes design. The tire size was increased from 4.50 to 4.75, which provided an improved ride quality and lower appearance for the new cars. Original equipment tires were manufactured by Firestone, BFGoodrich, Goodyear, and U.S. Rubber.

1930 Ford Model A Production

Model	Name	Weight	Price	Number Produced
35-B	Phaeton	2,212	$440	16,479
180-A	Deluxe Phaeton	2,285	$625	3,946
40-B	Roadster	2,155	$435	112,901
40-B Dlx.	Deluxe Roadster	2,230	$520	11,313
45-B	Coupe	2,250	$500	232,564
45-B Dlx.	Deluxe Coupe	2,250	$545	29,777
50-B	Sport Coupe	2,285	$530	72,572
55-B	Tudor	2,395	$500	376,271
68-B	Cabriolet	2,339	$645	25,868
140-B	Town Car	2,525	$1,200	96
150-B	Station Wagon	2,500	$650	3,510
155-C	Town Sedan (Murray)	2,495	$640	
155-D	Town Sedan (Briggs)	2,495	$640	104,435 (Combined)
165-C	Std. Fordor (Murray)	2,462	$600	
165-D	Std. Fordor (Briggs)	2,462	$600	41,133 (Combined)
170-B	Std. Fordor (2W)	2,488	$600	5,279
170-B Dlx.	Deluxe Fordor (2W)	2,488	$640	12,854
190-A	Victoria Coupe	2,375	$580	6,447
76-B	Open Cab Pickup	2,073		3,429
79-B	Panel Delivery	2,500		8,282
82-B	Closed Cab Pickup	2,215		
130-B	Deluxe Delivery	2,282		
295-A	Town Car Delivery			3
	A Chassis/cab	1,680		
	AA 131 Chassis/Cab	2,723	$510	
	AA 157 Chassis/Cab	3,492	$545	
85-B	AA Panel Delivery	3,904	$780	2,781
88-B	AA-131 Platform	3,631/3,728		
89-B	AA Express	3,422		
185-A	AA-157 Platform	4,400		
186-A	AA-157 Stake	4,442		
188-B	AA-131 Stake	3,673/3,837		

1930 Model A Engine Numbers

Month	First Number	Last Number
January	2742696	2826649
February	2826650	2940776
March	2940777	3114465
April	3114466	3304703
May	3304704	3509306
June	3509307	3702547
July	3702548	3771362
August	3771363	3883888
September	3883889	4005973
October	4005974	4093995
November	4093996	4177733
December	4177734	4237500

Note:
Engine numbers include AA truck production. Except for a brief period from February to May 1928, all AA trucks were identified with an AA engine number prefix.

The engine number indicates only when the engine was completed. Engine installation into the chassis at the assembly plant could have taken two weeks to four months. When the engine was installed in the chassis, the engine number was stamped on the top left side of the frame just ahead of the front body bolt hole.

1930

Rear view of a 1930 45-B Standard Coupe. The new modernized bodylines and straight-through moldings are evident. The lower body and reveal color is Kewanee Green with upper body and moldings in Elkpoint Green. The stripe is Apple Green.

Chicle Drab and Copra Drab 1930 55-B Standard Tudor sedan. The flatter bumper and 19-inch wheels are clearly visible.

65

The new 19-inch wheels were equipped with new design valve stem equipment. Although Dill and Schrader were still the major manufacturers of the brass valve stems, they were also made by Firestone and Bridgeport Brass Works. The stems were now shortened to 2⅜ inches from 2 13/16 to 2⅝ inches tall and were equipped with short 1 1/16-inch-high grooved dust covers that were open on top, allowing the stem and cap to protrude. There were two basic designs of dust covers, each dull nickel plated with ⅞-inch hexagonal bases.

Wheels on standard models were still finished only in black until June 1930, when colors were offered as an accessory option. Colored wheels were standard on all deluxe body styles. Wheel colors were limited to available stripe colors, and various standard colors were adopted at different times throughout the year.

The new A-1015-D wheels also needed new hubcaps. The former 3 5/32-inch-diameter, deep-drawn design was replaced with a stainless 4⅛-inch-diameter cap that had a flatter profile. In July 1930, the original one-piece design A-1130-D hubcaps were replaced with a steel, stainless-clad cap more resistant to dents.

Engine Assembly

The company made few mechanical improvements or changes to the engine in 1930. In March 1930, the rear main bearing cap oil drainpipe was increased from 5/16 inch to ⅜ inch. This change allowed the oil to drain more quickly from the main bearing into the oil pan tray. This change also decreased the chance for rear main bearing leakage. Timing gear cover lock washers were changed from unfinished to raven finish in mid-1930. The remainder of the engine is almost identical in appearance to that of late 1929.

The A-5095-A rear engine mount plate was changed to a new design with clipped corners for 1930. The bolts and castellated nuts holding the rear engine mounts were unfinished until mid-1930 when they were changed to a raven finish.

In April 1930, the A-9725 throttle control assembly was changed to a design with a one-piece throttle pedal and carburetor control lever. The previous design had the carburetor control portion of the lever attached with a pin to the shaft. The spring was now a tapered design rather than cylindrical. This change, like most others of 1929 and 1930, made the part simpler and less expensive to produce. The lever was still constructed of forged iron.

Another small change to the 1930 engine configuration was the new cylinder head coolant outlet connection. Because of the taller radiator, the new A-8250-B outlet is 6 inches tall and ⅞ inch longer than the old unit. The upper radiator hose was also made longer to accommodate the new parts. Upper and lower radiator hose clamps remained identical to the old system.

Transmission and Clutch

There were no significant changes to the transmission and clutch components for 1930. The transmission top cover had already been changed in 1929 to the A-7222-C design with the parking brake lever on the right side.

Cooling System and Radiator

The most significant change to the Model A cooling system for 1930 was the change in radiator design in accordance with the new styling. The new A-8005-B radiator was taller and narrower than the 1928–29 unit. The new radiator has 102 tubes and 120 long and 12 short fins. There were no longer variations between manufacturers as there were in 1928–29. The radiator has a total cooling surface area of 374 square inches but maintains the same 3-gallon cooling system capacity as the earlier design. In April 1930, a new radiator upper splash plate was adopted, which prevented excess coolant loss from the top of the radiator neck. This modification may be made to earlier radiators to improve performance.

The new A-8100-C radiator cap is flatter and has finer knurling than the 1928–29 cap. The cap is made of stainless steel and now attaches with a bayonet-type fitting rather than being threaded, as was the earlier cap. There were five variations of the new radiator cap, which depended upon the manufacturer—Eaton or Welker-Hoops—and whether the vehicle was an early or late model. These variations are shown more clearly in the *MARC/MAFCA Judging Standards* cooling system chapter.

One of the most obvious identifying features of the 1930 Ford is the new stainless steel A-8200-C radiator shell. The basic shell stamping is a single piece with a black-painted steel panel insert in the lower section. The same blue background vitreous enamel A-8212-B nameplate used in 1928 and 1929 is used for 1930. The shell is attached to the radiator with unfinished 3/16x½-inch binding-head slotted screws with thick square nuts. In mid-1930, the bolt was changed to a raven finish and the nut was cadmium plated for the remainder of Model A production. The ⅝-inch-wide fabric hood lacing was attached to the shell with small black-enamel steel rivets with the heads facing outward. The 1930 A-8200-D commercial radiator shell was of the same design as the passenger car unit but was made of magnetic steel and painted black enamel. It uses the same nameplate as the standard passenger car unit.

1930

Right-side detail of the engine compartment on a 1930 Standard Roadster shows the deeper firewall design and correct Zenith carburetor. Note the Ford patent data plate above the vacuum line fitting on the firewall. The heat deflector under the distributor is an accessory that protects the condenser.

This 1930 engine block has a side cover and oil return pipe. The block, side cover, and cylinder head are Ford Engine Green, and the oil return pipe is black enamel. The side cover bolts are natural finish, and the head nuts are cadmium plated.

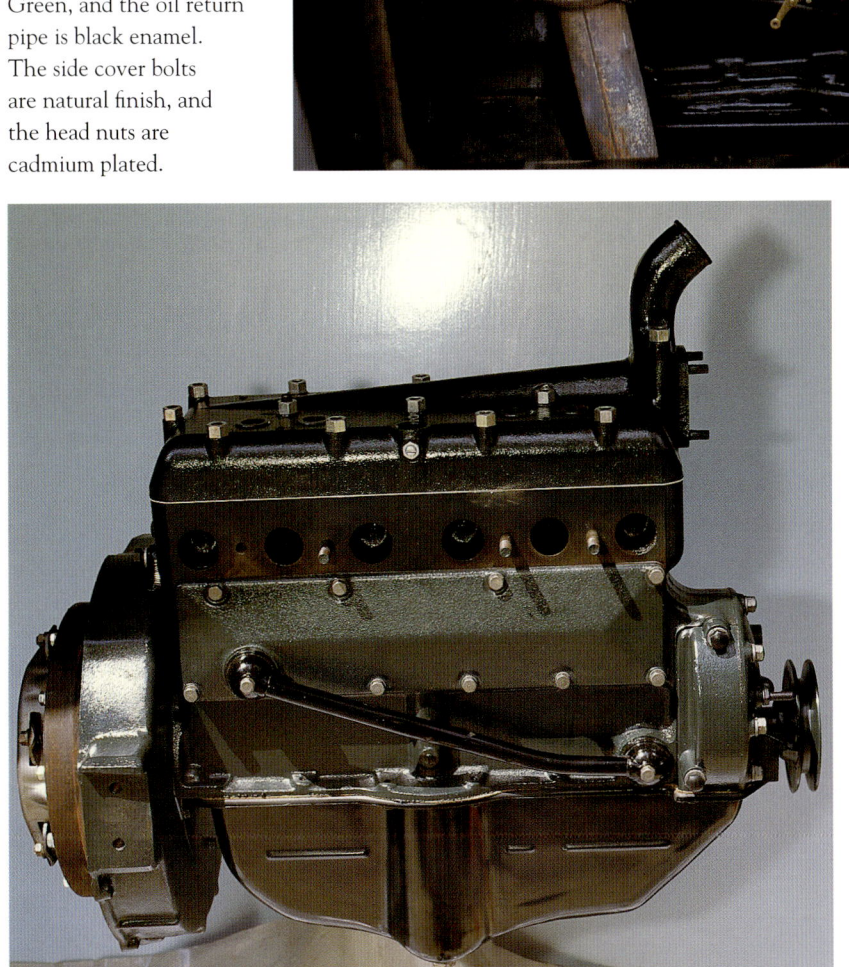

Fuel System

The most important change to the 1930 fuel system was the new A-9002-AR cowl tank unit necessitated by the styling and body changes. The tank uses a new design A-9030-C filler cap. Like the radiator cap, the new fuel filler cap was changed from a screw-on to a bayonet-type cap. Caps were made by Eaton, Welker-Hoops, and Stant and were of one-piece or two-piece construction. All caps were made of stainless steel and were equipped with a gasket.

The new cowl tank still maintained the early design instrument panel with oval speedometer through June 1930. In July, the new horizontal ribbed instrument panel design was adopted. This new A-11805-B panel was made of either brass or steel and finished in bright or Butler nickel plating. A new A-17255-D round-face speedometer was used for the new panel, which no longer had a dash light in the center. The dash light was now mounted on a small bracket under the edge of the upper dash rail.

The Zenith 1 and Zenith 2 carburetors were left essentially unchanged for 1930 except that early in

Original Ford Model A

The rear view of a 1930 Standard Roadster showing the folded convertible top and hold-down straps. The whitewall tires, spare tire guard, and right taillight are accessories.

The top hold-down straps and top prop rest on a 1930 Standard Roadster. The top boot is an accessory for 1930.

the year, the brass fittings were changed to steel. This was a cost-saving alteration, as were many others of the time. In mid-1930, the vacuum fitting in the intake manifold was moved from 3 inches to 2½ inches above the carburetor mounting flange. The vacuum fitting hole was blocked with a brass or steel oval-head slotted plug on cars equipped with an electric wiper. This plug could be either unfinished or painted Ford Engine Green.

From mid-1929, either a glass bowl or cast-iron firewall-mounted sediment bulb could be used. The A-9155 cast-iron bulb was painted black and had a brass nut with a lead washer between the nut and the casting. There were four types of sediment bulbs, but any of them are acceptable in all the years that the firewall-mounted unit was used.

Electrical System

The most noticeable change to the electrical system for 1930 was the new stainless steel "Twolite" headlamp design. The new lamps were more rounded and hemispherical in the back compared to the parabolic-shaped 1928–29 units. The lenses are identical to those used in the older lights and still have a Ford script in oval at the bottom. Cars without cowl lights have a two-bulb reflector, while those with cowl lights have one headlight bulb. The cowl lights also serve as parking lights.

Cowl lights were also redesigned to match the styling of the headlights, of which they look like a miniature version. The new cowl light brackets are designed to mount just behind the stainless steel cowl band and have a support arm that rides over the band.

Taillights for 1930 have the same "Duolamp" teacup style as those used on late 1929 cars, but 1930 shells are made of stainless or "rustless" steel. The lens design for 1930 has two colors. The stoplight portion is amber and the taillight portion is ruby. The rear lamp body for commercial vehicles was black-painted steel but had the same lens and lens door as the passenger light. All 1930 Model A Fords were equipped with only a left-side rear light. Rear lights on the Phaeton, Roadster, Tudor, Town Car, Deluxe Delivery, Coupes, and Fordors were mounted on the stamped, black-painted A-13471-B lamp bracket. This bracket was bolted to the left rear fender, instead of the body as with the earlier 1928-style forged brackets.

In February 1930, the engine compartment terminal-box-to-generator-wire conduit was changed from a raven finish metal tube to a woven fabric material. This change was made to reduce costs, because the metal conduit and attaching hardware were more expensive to produce and finish than the fabric design. The change in the wiring conduit was accompanied with a change in the firewall conduit clip. The old style A-14576 clip was changed to the A-14577-A clip identical to the one used on the water outlet. Both clips are painted black.

1930

Right: The rearview mirror bracket, bevel glass mirror, and Trico vacuum windshield wiper on a 1930 Standard Roadster.

Far right: The 1929-style instrument panel with oval speedometer of this Roadster identifies it as an early 1930 car. The 1930 steering wheel is flatter and has a heavier rim than the 1928–29 wheel.

The windshield frame of this 1930 Standard Roadster should be painted body color rather than chrome plated. The Standard Roadster windshield frame is 1½ inches higher than the Deluxe frame.

The A-35626-B outside door handle for a 1930 40-B Standard Roadster is the same handle used on the 35-B Standard Phaeton. Open cars have a thin rubber pad under the handle mounting flange.

Body and Fender Assembly

The styling advances of the 1930 Model A were considerable and contributed greatly to increased sales. Bodies were lower, longer, and wider for the most part, and the fenders were more sweeping. This produced a more modern and substantial appearance. Body moldings now continued gracefully from the radiator to the rear of the body, coordinating all of the styling elements. The new rich colors and stainless metal trim brought a definite air of quality to the new Ford.

The new body design also brought about a more harmonious variety of body types. The Fordors, Cabriolets, and the rest of the model line now shared the same cowl and hood design. Of course, this styling improvement was also more economical. Most Ford bodies were still of all-steel construction except for the Fordors, Cabriolet, and Victoria, which had wood sills and more structural body wood framework.

Starting in June 1930, commercial vehicles used the A-175014-BR front body assembly, which included a special upper dash rail that allowed aftermarket bodies such as the Mail Truck and Huckster to be mounted flush with the rear of the cowl. This front body assembly was used on both the A and AA commercial chassis. The vertical sides of the door opening now had no provision for door hinges.

All body styles used the standard A-16005 (RH) and A-16006 (LH) front fenders. The only variation was when fender well equipment was specified. An identifying feature of 1930 front fenders is the attached front splash shield section, which is spot-welded to the fender. The splash shield front section bolts to the A-16050-R (RH) and A-16051-R (LH) splash shield rear sections. The rear section of the splash shield is also attached to each respective running board. The running boards now have a pyramid-pattern rubber matting rather than the ribbed design of the 1928–29 boards.

Apparently this design was meant to make assembly easier, but it was actually a more expensive construction method. All front fenders and splash shields were dipped in black Japan enamel. Front fenders no longer used the separate hood shelf from 1928–29. Hood clips were now attached directly to the top of the hood. The two slotted oval-head front fender screws were attached directly through the top of the fender, which had a raised stamped rim around the screw's hole.

The rear fenders were also new with styling to match that of the front fenders. The same right and left rear fenders were used for the 40-B, 45-B, 50-B, 68-B, and 78-A. The other right and left rear fenders were used for the 35-B, 55-B, 79-B, 130-B, 140-B, 150-B, 155-C, 155-D, 165-C, 165-D, 170-B, 190-A, 225-A, and 295-A. All rear fenders were dipped in black Japan enamel so the finish should be the same on both outer and underside surfaces.

There were 17 passenger car bodies offered for 1930, but only five of them were totally new. They were the Deluxe Phaeton, Deluxe Roadster, Deluxe Coupe, Two-Window Deluxe Fordor, and Victoria. There were also six commercial bodies for 1930. Commercial bodies did not adopt the new styling until June 1930.

The Model 35-B Standard Phaeton is a four-door, four-passenger open car equipped with snap-on side curtains and a folding fabric top. The new Phaeton body now had lower, wider styling. The 1930 Standard Phaeton body had a more modern appearance than the previous design. It no longer had a coupe pillar, and body moldings now ran straight through from the radiator and around the rear of the body. The 2-inch-wider doors were operated by nickel-plated outside door handles.

In addition to being hinged at the top and swinging out at the bottom for ventilation, the new windshield frame also folds at the stanchion mounting. The windshield stanchions are made of rustless steel. The windshield frame is painted on the Standard Phaeton and seals against the stanchions with a flat rubber seal. All 1930 open cars are equipped with a standard electric windshield wiper.

The 1930 Standard Phaeton was offered in seven basic body color combinations. The main body colors consisted of Thorne Brown, Kewanee Green, Copra Drab, Chicle Drab, Andalusite Blue, Lombard Blue, and black. Contrasting and complementary colors were used for the moldings and striping.

Interior trim for the 1930 Phaeton was offered in only one trim scheme. The piped seats, quarters, and wind cord were trimmed in black-brown, two-tone Cobra cross-grain artificial leather. The door panels, cowl, and rear lower lock pillars are finished with black-brown, two-tone Cobra cross-grain cardboard. Interior hardware is bright nickel plated.

The folding top for the 1930 Standard Phaeton was trimmed with black, fine, long-short-grain artificial leather. The bows are black steel and black bow-drill-covered wood. The standard side curtains are made of the same material as the top and have clear celluloid windows. The side curtains are stowed in a covered compartment under the rear floor. All 1930 Standard Phaetons have black rubber spatter-pattern floor mats front and rear.

The Model 180-A Deluxe Phaeton, introduced in June 1930, was an entirely new model for 1930. This distinctive car was an unusual and luxurious design that was unlike any body style made by any other manufacturer. The Deluxe Phaeton was a two-door, four-passenger open car with a folding fabric top.

In addition to the distinctive body design, the Deluxe Phaeton was equipped with a chrome-plated windshield frame and stanchions that were 1½ inches shorter than those of the standard open cars. The stanchions and windshield still folded down flat against the cowl. Cowl lights and a stainless cowl band were standard equipment.

The Deluxe Phaeton also had standard windshield windwings, a standard fender-well-mounted spare tire, and a standard full-length rear bumper and trunk rack. In late 1930, the Deluxe Phaeton was equipped with a steering column lowering block to make the most of the lower body.

The Deluxe Phaeton was available in 11 standard color schemes, some of which were only available on the line's deluxe models. The main body was offered in Washington Blue, black, Brewster Green, Stone Brown, Thorne Brown, Kewanee Green, Chicle Drab, Andalusite Blue, Lombard Blue, Ford Maroon, and Bronson Yellow. Moldings and stripe were finished in contrasting and complementary colors. Colored wheels matching the stripe were standard on the Deluxe Phaeton.

The Deluxe Phaeton was offered in only one interior trim scheme. The piped seat faces, welting, top of armrest, front backrest sides, and windcord are trimmed with two-tone tan Bedouin-grain genuine leather. The seat sides, door panels, quarters, seat bottoms, and cowl are trimmed with two-tone tan Bedouin-grain artificial leather. The front and rear floor are covered with brown carpet. The rear floor is depressed to give additional legroom in the rear compartment.

The Deluxe Phaeton's folding top was made of tan olive-drab rubber interlined fabric lined with tan drab cloth. The Deluxe Phaeton top is 1½ inches lower than the Standard Phaeton top because of the lower windshield stanchions. The Deluxe top frame is also a different design with natural finish wood bows and chrome-plated frame. The rear bow supports are mounted higher than the standard top and give a distinctive appearance to the entire top. The side curtains are made of the same tan fabric as the top. They are stowed in a special compartment behind the back cushion of the rear seat.

The Model 40-B Standard Roadster is a two-door, two-passenger open car equipped with a folding top and snap-on side curtains. The Roadster was available with either a rumble seat or a trunk. The 1930 Roadster has outside nickel-plated door handles and remote inside door handles. The windshield stanchions are nickel plated and the windshield folds down on the cowl like the Phaeton. The windshield frame is painted body color.

The 1930 Standard Roadster was offered in seven standard body color schemes. The main body was finished in Thorne Brown, Kewanee Green, Copra Drab, Chicle Drab, Andalusite Blue, Lombard Blue, and black. The moldings and striping were finished in contrasting and complementary colors.

The interior trim of the Standard Roadster was offered in one trim scheme. The piped seat, seatback frame, and seat sides are trimmed in black-brown, two-tone Cobra cross-grain artificial leather. Door panels and cowl are trimmed with black-brown, two-tone Cobra cross-grain cardboard. The rumble seat cushion is also piped and finished in the same material. The rumble seat compartment is trimmed in the same material as the front compartment.

1930

Above: The front compartment of a 1930 Standard Roadster. The seat is piped black Cobra cross-grain artificial leather. The door panels are matching cardboard. The floor is covered with a black rubber mat. Note the parking brake lever to the right of the shift lever for 1930.

Right: The rumble seat compartment of a 1930 40-B Standard Roadster. The seat cushions are trimmed in piped black Cobra cross-grain artificial leather. The top boot is an accessory.

The folding top is made of black, fine, long-short-grain artificial leather and lined with black drill cloth. The top frame is painted and the wood bows are covered with black bow-drill cloth. The side curtains are made of the same material as the top and are stowed under the front seat. All 1930 Standard Roadsters have black rubber spatter-pattern floor mats in both the front and rumble seat compartments.

The 40-B Deluxe Roadster, introduced in August 1930, uses the same basic body shell as the standard Roadster but with the lowered, chrome-plated windshield stanchions and frame of the Deluxe Phaeton. The 1930 Deluxe Roadster also has a standard fender-well-mounted spare tire, windshield wings, cowl lights, rumble seat, and a trunk rack.

The Deluxe Roadster was offered in 11 basic color combinations, some of which are exclusive to Deluxe models. The main body is trimmed in Washington Blue, black, Brewster Green, Stone Brown, Thorne Brown, Kewanee Green, Chicle Drab, Andalusite Blue, Lombard Blue, Ford Maroon, and Bronson Yellow. Moldings and striping were finished in contrasting and complementary colors. Wheels were painted in colors matching those of the stripe.

The 1930 Deluxe Roadster was offered with only one interior trim scheme. The piped seat, trim welt, and wind cord are made of two-tone tan Bedouin-grain genuine leather. The seat sides, seatback, belt rail, seatback frame, door panels, and cowl are made of two-tone tan Bedouin-grain artificial leather. The floor is covered in brown carpet. The piped rumble seat and compartment is trimmed in two-tone tan Bedouin-grain artificial leather. The rumble seat compartment floor is covered with a black rubber mat.

The Model 45-B Standard Coupe is a two-passenger, two-door closed car with small stationary quarter windows and steel roof quarters. The new 1930 styling lowered the roof 1½ inches over that of the 1928–29 Coupe, greatly modernizing the appearance. The Standard Coupe was offered with either a rumble seat or a trunk with 14 cubic feet of cargo space. The coupe, like all 1930 closed cars, had a swing-out windshield to provide ventilation.

The 1930 Standard Coupe was offered in seven basic color schemes. The main body was finished in Andalusite Blue, Lombard Blue, Kewanee Green, Copra Drab, Chicle Drab, Thorne Brown, and black. The moldings and stripes were finished in contrasting and complementary colors. The single stripe ran on the belt molding from the radiator all the way around the rear lower corner of the body and then followed the lower body molding back to the edge of the cowl band. The top insert was black long-short-grain artificial leather. The 1930 closed-body visors are painted rather than fabric covered, as they were in 1928–29.

An identifying feature of all 1930 Model A closed bodies is that the reveals were usually finished in the lower body color. This gave a lower and longer look to the body styling. For 1931, this scheme was reversed and reveals were generally painted the upper body color.

The 1930 Standard Coupe was offered in two interior trim schemes but only one at a time. The

Original Ford Model A

Front quarter view of a 1930 45-B Standard Coupe. The lower body is finished in Kewanee Green with the upper body and moldings in Elkpoint Green with an Apple Green stripe. The whitewall tires are accessories.

first, offered until April 1930, had a piped seat in brown-checked cloth. The door panels, quarters, seatback, roof rail, and header were trimmed in plain brown cloth. The headlining was brown napped cloth and the cowl was trimmed in two-tone brown dash-grain cardboard. Window curtains were brown cloth and the garnish moldings were painted Molding Gray. The floor was covered in a black rubber mat. The rumble seat was piped and trimmed with black-brown, two-tone Cobra cross-grain artificial leather. The rumble seat compartment was trimmed in matching Cobra cross-grain cardboard and had a rubber floor mat.

New for 1930 was the 45-B Deluxe Coupe. Introduced in February, the Deluxe Coupe used the exact same body shell as the Standard Coupe, but the body colors, fittings, and interior trim were more luxurious than standard models. The Deluxe Coupe also was equipped with an interior dome and plated cowl lights to distinguish it from the Standard Coupe. Like the Standard Coupe, the Deluxe Coupe was optionally available with either a rumble seat or a trunk.

The 1930 Deluxe Coupe was offered in nine basic color schemes. Lower body colors were Andalusite Blue, Lombard Blue, Kewanee Green, Copra Drab, Chicle Drab, Thorne Brown, black, Brewster Green, and Ford Maroon. The reveals, moldings, and stripe were finished in contrasting and complementary colors. The top insert was black long-short-grain artificial leather, as it was in 1928–29. Stripe-color wheels were standard equipment on the Deluxe Coupe.

The stripe on both the Standard and Deluxe Coupes was finished in the same manner with a single stripe running on the center of the belt molding from the radiator shell to the lower rear corner. The stripe turned toward the fender and followed the lower body molding back to the rear edge of the hood. The Deluxe Coupe also had a stripe on the raised areas on each side of the fuel tank dash panel.

The 1930 Deluxe Coupe was offered in three different interior trim schemes, although not all at the same time. Initially, there were two trim combinations for the Deluxe Coupe. One had the piped seat, door panels, quarters, package tray, and header trimmed in brown Bedford cord. The headlining was brown napped cotton and the window curtains were brown silk. The cowl was trimmed in two-tone brown dash-grain cardboard. This trim scheme was dropped in July 1930.

The second original trim combination had the piped seat, door panels, quarters, package tray, and header in brown mohair. The headlining was brown napped cotton and the window curtains were brown silk. The cowl was two-tone brown dash-grain cardboard. This combination was used through July 1931.

All 1930 Deluxe Coupe trim schemes had 10 pleats each on the seat and back cushion while the standard seats had 11 pleats. Deluxe Coupe seats also had a row of buttons about one quarter of the way from the back of the seat and from the top of the rear cushion. This gave a more luxurious appearance to the Deluxe Coupe interior. The Deluxe Coupe rumble seat, when ordered, was trimmed in pleated deep-brown crush-grain artificial leather. The rumble seat compartment floor was covered with a black rubber mat.

1930

Left front quarter view of a 1930 68-B Cabriolet. This lower body is finished in Bronson Yellow with Seal Brown moldings and rear deck. The stripe is orange and the top is tan drab interlined fabric. This same body was used until the slant-windshield 68-C was introduced in March 1931. *Kenneth Keeley*

The original brown Bedford-cord trim combination dropped in July 1930 was replaced with brown broadcloth for the door panels, quarters, package tray, and header. This was a more conventional design, as most other makes did not normally use Bedford cord for side and door panels. Because Bedford cord required directional trim panels, it was also less expensive to use this material only on the seat cushions and backs. The remainder of the brown interior was the same as the first combination.

The Special Coupe and Business Coupe models were dropped for 1930, but the Sport Coupe was carried over into the new designs. The new 50-B Sport Coupe shared many body panels with the Standard Coupe, but its sporty fabric top offered the room of an open car with the comfort of a closed car. The top was still accentuated with painted nonfunctional landau irons. For 1930, exterior and interior trim options were reduced in number. The top was now available in only one material.

The 1930 Sport Coupe was offered in the same seven basic color combinations as the Standard Coupe. The top was trimmed with gray two-tone, diagonal-grain artificial leather. The inside of the top was finished in a brown mock twist cloth until April 1930, when the material was changed to gray mock twist cloth. The landau irons were painted lower body color with the center hinge portion nickel plated.

The 1930 Sport Coupe was offered in two interior trim schemes, although only one at a time. The first had a piped seat in brown-checked cloth with door panels in plain brown cloth. The cowl was trimmed with two-tone brown dash grain cardboard, and the garnish moldings were painted maroon. This trim scheme was dropped in April 1930.

The second trim scheme, adopted in April 1930, had the piped seat in gray-checked cloth and the door panels in plain gray cloth. The cowl was trimmed with two-tone gray dash-grain cardboard, and the garnish moldings were maroon. This trim scheme was used until July 1931.

Another model based on the coupe design was the Cabriolet. The 1930 68-B Cabriolet body was basically a carryover body from 1929 except for the cowl and firewall area. The Cabriolet was a two-door, two-passenger convertible body with roll-up side windows and a fabric-covered folding top that other manufacturers would call a convertible coupe. The outside appearance was similar to the Sport Coupe, but the top and the upper rear door frames folded and the landau irons were functional.

The 68-B Cabriolet was available in seven basic body color schemes. The lower body and reveals were finished in Andalusite Blue, Lombard Blue, Bronson Yellow, Moleskin Brown Light, Kewanee Green, black, and Brewster Green. The moldings, upper body, and rear deck and stripe were finished in contrasting and complementary colors. Like the 1929 Cabriolet, the 1930 model also had the entire rear deck finished in the molding color.

The 1930 Cabriolet initially carried over the gray-check-trim scheme used at the end of 1929. In February 1930, this scheme was dropped and a new tan Bedford cord combination was adopted. The piped seat, door panels, quarter panels, and seatback were trimmed in tan Bedford cord. The inside of the top, package tray, and top bows were trimmed in gray drab cloth. The cowl was drab brown dash-grain cardboard. Garnish moldings were painted mahogany woodgrain. This trim scheme was dropped in July 1930.

The new trim combination adopted in July had a piped seat in brown Bedford cord with the door panels, quarters, and seatback in brown broadcloth. The inside of the top, bows, and package tray were trimmed with the same gray drab cloth used in the first combination. The cowl was finished with two-tone brown dash-grain cardboard. Garnish moldings were painted mahogany woodgrain. The Cabriolet folding top was covered with the same olive-drab rubber interlined fabric used in 1929.

The floor covering for all 68-B Cabriolets was a black rubber spatter-pattern mat. The rumble seat cushion and backrest were piped and trimmed in black-brown Cobra cross-grain artificial leather. The side panels were trimmed in matching black-brown cardboard. The rumble seat compartment floor covering was a black rubber mat.

Original Ford Model A

This 1930 Standard Tudor has accessory stone guard, cowl lights, and whitewalls. The lower body and reveals are Copra Drab while the upper body is Chicle Drab. The stripe and wheels are Straw.

Another model with the totally new lower and longer-appearing styling for 1930 was the 55-B Tudor sedan. The Tudor was the most popular Model A body type with more than twice as many made as the next highest production model. The Tudor had the same type of individual front seats and wide, deep rear seat as the 1928–29 models. It was the ideal car for families. Although the 1928–29 Tudor doors were identical to those on coupes of the same years, in 1930 the Tudor doors were widened 2 inches, making entry to the rear seat easier. These 29½-inch-wide doors were also used on the new 82-B, -A and AA truck closed cab when it was introduced later in the year.

The 55-B Tudor was offered initially in six basic body color schemes. The lower body and reveals were finished in combinations of Andalusite Blue, Kewanee Green, Copra Drab, Chicle Drab, Thorne Brown, and black. In September 1930, the Andalusite Blue combinations were dropped and Lombard Blue was adopted. The moldings, stripe, and upper body were finished in contrasting and complementary colors. The striping was finished in the same pattern as the coupe. The roof center panel was trimmed with black, long-short-grain artificial leather.

The Tudor interior was offered initially in only two trim schemes. The first had piped seats in blue hairline cloth with door panels, seatbacks, quarters, and header in plain blue cloth. The headlining was trimmed in blue napped cloth. Window curtains were blue cloth. The cowl and seat bottoms were blue-gray dash-grain cardboard, and the garnish moldings were painted Molding Gray. The front and rear floors were covered with a black rubber mat.

Rear quarter of a 1930 55-B Standard Tudor with the lower body and reveals in Chicle Drab and the upper body in Copra Drab. The spare tire cover is an accessory.

The second interior trim combination had the piped seats trimmed in brown-checked cloth. The seatbacks, door panels, quarters, and header were finished in plain brown cloth. The headlining was brown napped cotton and the cowl and seat bottoms were trimmed with two-tone brown dash-grain cardboard. Window curtains were brown cloth and garnish moldings were finished in Molding Gray. black rubber mats covered the front and rear floors.

There were six variations of Fordor sedans offered for 1930. They included the standard and Deluxe Fordor and Town Sedans in two-window, three-window, Murray, and Briggs versions. The two-window, steel-back Deluxe Fordor was an entirely new model for 1930.

The 155-C (Murray) and 155-D (Briggs) Town Sedans are identified externally by their small rear

1930

Right: Front compartment of a 1930 Standard Tudor. The seats are trimmed in brown-checked cloth. The seat sides, door panels, and quarters are in plain brown cloth. Note the aluminum door-sill plate.

Far right: The left front door of a 1930 55-B Standard Tudor. The door panels and quarters are trimmed in plain brown cloth. Door interior hardware is bright nickel plated. This late 1930 car has Maroon garnish moldings.

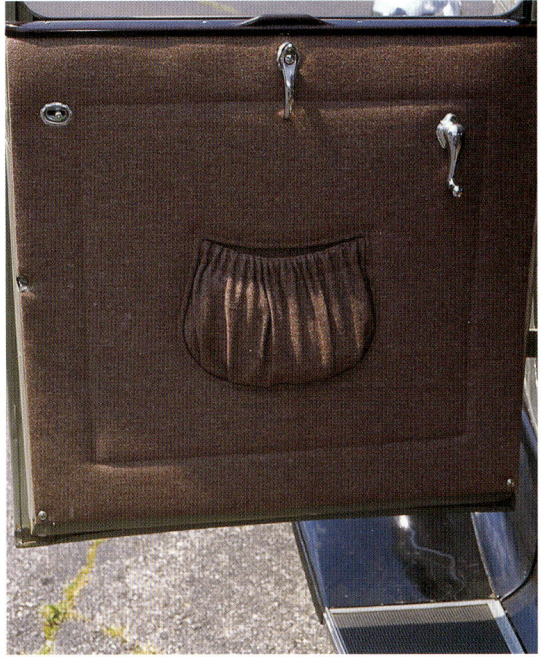

Right: Door handles left to right are A-46205-D (locking for right side) and A-46206-B for right side of 45-B Coupe, 50-B Sport Coupe, 55-B Tudor, 82-B Closed Cab Commercial, and 130-B Deluxe Delivery.

Far right: Another view showing the shank and mounting escutcheons of the 1930–31 closed-body outside door handles. Early 1930 versions were chrome-plated brass, while late 1930 and all 1931 were stainless clad.

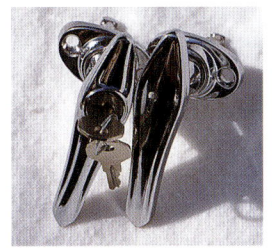
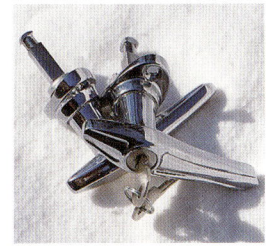

quarter windows and stainless steel cowl lights. The Murray body has a slightly curved upper window reveal, while the Briggs version has straight upper windows. Equipment and trim was otherwise similar on the Town Sedans. Both body designs featured the same military visor and vertical windshield as the Tudor and Coupe. A taxi-cab variation of the Town Sedan was offered in 1930, but records are unclear on whether any of these were actually built. The sales literature described the 1930 Town Sedan for taxicab purposes as having a partition and a meter as standard equipment.

The Town Sedan is a four-door, five-passenger body based on the Standard Fordor bodies, offered as a more luxurious version with more stylish and higher-quality interior fittings and a different choice of exterior colors. The 1930 Town Sedan was offered in six basic body color schemes. The lower body was Copra Drab, Chicle Drab, Kewanee Green, Ford Maroon, black, and Brewster Green. The upper body, reveals, stripes, and moldings were painted contrasting and complementary colors. The top insert was black long-short-grain artificial leather.

The interior trim of the Town Sedan was offered in three combinations, all with a center armrest in the rear seatback. The first had the

The lower body and reveals of this 1930 Murray Town Sedan are finished in Kewanee Green, while the upper body is Elkpoint Green. The wheels are Apple Green. There should also be an Apple Green stripe. The whitewall tires and chrome outside mirror are accessories.

Original Ford Model A

Above: The left cowl light and stainless steel cowl band on a 1930 Murray Town sedan. The lower body color is Kewanee Green with Elkpoint Green moldings. The light stanchion is secured to a wood reinforcement block inside the cowl.

Top left: Notice the rounded top of this 1930 Murray 155-C Town Sedan's side windows, which identify this as a Murray body. The chrome hinge-mounted outside mirrors, trunk rack, and trunk are accessories.

Left: This stamped channel headlight bar was used on some 1930 models. This view also shows the horn and headlight attachment brackets. The license is bolted directly through the channel on this type of bar and does not use separate clamps.

Lower left: The front detail of a 1930 Standard Fordor shows the 1930 stainless radiator and headlight shells. The rare stamped channel headlight support bar did not hold up well and many were replaced with the more common tubular type.

piped seats, seatbacks, quarters, door panels, and header trimmed in brown mohair. The headlining was in brown napped cotton, and the curtains on the rear and quarter windows were brown silk. The cowl was finished in two-tone brown dash-grain cardboard. The floors and lower door panels were covered with brown carpet.

The second interior trim scheme had the piped seats, seatbacks, quarters, door panels, and header trimmed in green mohair. The headlining was green napped cotton, and the curtains on the rear and quarter windows were green silk. The cowl was trimmed with two-tone green dash-grain cardboard, and the front and rear floors and lower door panels were carpeted in brown.

The third interior option had piped seats, seatback, door panels, quarters, and header in brown Bedford cord. In September 1930, all but the seats were changed to brown broadcloth. The headlining was brown napped cotton and the window curtains were brown silk. The cowl was trimmed in brown two-tone dash-grain cardboard, and front and rear floors and the lower door panels were covered in brown carpet.

All versions of the Town Sedan had interior garnish moldings finished in painted mahogany woodgrain. Interior hardware was the same finish as the standard Fordors, but the Town Sedan had an oval A-13776-A, -B, and -C dome light rather than the round type used in standard cars.

The next variation of 1930 Fordor was the 165-C (Murray) and 165-D (Briggs) Standard

1930

Front quarter view of a 1930 165-D Briggs Standard Fordor. The body is black with Apple Green stripe and wheels. The square line to the top of the side windows identify this as a Briggs body. The chrome outside mirrors, trunk rack, and trunk are accessories.

Left front door panel of a 165-D Briggs Standard Fordor. The door panel is trimmed in plain brown cloth. The door hardware is bright nickel. Note the seam in the splash shield identifying this as a 1930.

Fordor. The three-window bodies on these cars were virtually identical to those of the Town Sedan, but the exterior finishes and interior trim were less expensive and luxurious on the standard sedans. The Standard Fordor also did not have the cowl lights, which were standard on the Town Sedan.

The 165-C and 165-D Standard Fordor was initially offered in six basic color schemes. The lower body was finished in Andalusite Blue, Kewanee Green, Copra Drab, Chicle Drab, Thorne Brown, and black. In September 1930, the Andalusite Blue combinations were dropped and replaced with Lombard Blue. The upper body, reveals, stripe, quarter, and moldings were finished in contrasting and complementary colors.

The 1930 Standard Fordor was offered in two interior trim schemes, although only one was available at a time. The first had the piped seats in brown-checked cloth. The seatbacks, quarters, door panels, and header were trimmed in plain brown cloth. The headlining was brown napped cotton and the curtains were brown cloth. The cowl was two-tone brown dash-grain cardboard. The front floor had a black rubber mat, and the rear floor was covered with a brown carpet. This combination was dropped in April 1930.

The second trim scheme, adopted in April 1930, had the piped seat in gray-checked cloth and the seat back, quarters, door panels, and header in plain gray cloth. The headlining was gray napped cotton, and the window curtains were gray cloth. The cowl was two-tone gray dash-grain cardboard. The front floor had a black rubber mat and the rear floor was brown carpet. The garnish moldings in both combinations could have been either Mocha Brown (before April 1930) or maroon.

Original Ford Model A

Far left: The bottom of this 165-D Briggs Standard Fordor door panel is trimmed with the same brown carpet used on the interior floor. The garnish moldings are maroon.

Left: The front compartment on a 1930 165-D Briggs Standard Fordor. The seats are brown-checked cloth with door panels and quarters trimmed in plain brown cloth. The floor is covered with a black rubber mat and garnish moldings are maroon.

Lower left: The round speedometer of this Briggs Standard Fordor instrument panel identifies it as a late 1930 car.

One of the lowest production Model A closed bodies is the 1930 170-B two-window steel-back Standard Fordor Sedan. This design was based on the Briggs steel-back Fordor of 1929 revised to fit the 1930 hood and cowl requirements. The 170-B was made only from the beginning of 1930 until early April, when it was replaced with a new, two-window Deluxe Fordor that was based on the same body shell.

The 1930 170-B Standard Fordor was available in five color combinations. The lower body, reveals, and sill moldings were finished in Kewanee Green, Andalusite Blue, Thorne Brown, black, and Chicle Drab. The upper body, stripe, belt, and quarter moldings were painted contrasting and complementary colors.

The 170-B Standard Fordor was available in only one interior trim scheme. The piped seats were trimmed in brown-checked cloth. The seatback, quarters, door panels, and header were finished in plain brown cloth. Window curtains were brown cloth, and the cowl was finished with a two-tone brown dash-grain cardboard. The front floor had a black rubber mat, and the rear floor was covered with a brown carpet.

Early in 1930, the two-window Standard Fordor was replaced with the two-window Deluxe Fordor, Model 170-B Deluxe. The body was identical to the Standard Fordor, but the Deluxe model had cowl lights and was offered in one additional body color: Ford Maroon.

The interior trim schemes of the new 170-B Deluxe Fordor were offered in two combinations. The first had piped seats, door panels, quarters, seatback, and header of brown mohair. The headlining is brown napped cotton and window curtains are brown silk. The cowl is two-tone brown dash-grain cardboard. The floors and lower door panels are brown carpet. Garnish moldings are painted mahogany woodgrain.

The second combination had piped seats, doors, quarters, seatback, and header of brown Bedford cord until September 1930, when all but the seats were changed to brown broadcloth. The window curtains were brown silk, and the headlining was brown napped cotton. The cowl is two-tone brown dash-grain cardboard. The floors are covered with brown carpet. The garnish moldings are mahogany woodgrain.

One of the most unusual of the new models introduced for 1930 was the 190-A Victoria, or Victoria Coupe as it was originally called. The Victoria is a two-door, four-passenger body style that is distinctively different from anything offered previously. The Victoria has wide doors with folding front seats and a rear seat wide enough for two passengers to ride comfortably. The rear of the body is very different from the Tudor Sedan as it has a rearward slope allowing space inside for storage behind the rear seat.

The Victoria was introduced in November 1930, but it has all the identifying features of a

1930

Right: The rear seat of this 1930 Briggs Standard Fordor is trimmed with brown-checked cloth and the rear quarters in plain brown cloth. The rear floor has a brown carpet with brown-artificial leather binding. The interior hardware is bright nickel plated.

Far right: The trunk rack and bumper mounting on a 1930 Standard Fordor. The trunk rack is an accessory. The fender is insulated from the body with a black fender welting.

Right: Some pre-February 1930 front fenders had an "eyebrow" on the front edge. Some early fenders also did not have a raised area around the front mounting screws.

1931 model, such as the new radiator shell and visorless, slanted windshield. The Victoria was offered only as a Deluxe model and had standard equipment cowl lights and Deluxe colors and interior appointments. The reason for this confusing year identification is that when these cars were being produced, manufacturers did not distinguish new models by year. Thus, Ford did not consider it to be a 1930 model, but only a new model. The Victoria was equipped with the same steering column lowering block as the Deluxe Phaeton.

The Victoria was available in five body color schemes. The lower body and reveals were finished in Brewster Green, Ford Maroon, Kewanee Green, Chicle Drab, and black. The upper body, stripe, belt, sill, and quarter moldings were finished in contrasting and complementary colors.

The Victoria was available in two different upper body configurations. One had a steel back with center fabric top insert like conventional closed cars. The other, now called a leatherback, had a full padded fabric roof that came all the way down to the belt moldings. The roof covering for the leatherback was tan, two-tone, diagonal-grain artificial leather. Both the steel-back and fabric-back Victoria bodies have an underlying wood framework and body sills, which makes repair and restoration more difficult and complicated than is the case with all-steel bodies.

The 190-A Victoria was offered in two interior trim combinations for 1930. The first had piped seats in brown Bedford cord. The seatbacks, quarters, door panels, and header were trimmed in brown broadcloth. The headlining was brown napped cotton and the cowl and seat bottoms were covered with two-tone brown dash-grain cardboard. Window curtains front and rear were brown silk. The floors and lower door panels were brown carpet. The rear floor of the Victoria has a depressed section to allow more legroom in the shortened rear compartment.

The Victoria's second interior trim combination had piped seats of striped tan broadcloth with door panels, seatbacks, quarters, and header of plain tan broadcloth. The headlining was brown napped cotton, and the cowl was two-tone brown dash-grain cardboard. Window curtains were tan silk and the floors and lower door panels were covered in brown carpet. Garnish moldings for both combinations were painted mahogany wood-grain. Like all Deluxe models, Victoria interior hardware was Butler-finished nickel.

Although officially a commercial model, the Station Wagon has a definite passenger car aura to its styling, trim, and color. As with all commercial bodies in 1930, the Station Wagon continued in its 1929 150-A form until June 1930 when the new 150-B styling was adopted. One difference from the other commercial vehicles was that the Station Wagon used the standard stainless steel passenger car cowl band, radiator, and headlight shells, rather than the black-painted steel components of the rest of the commercial line.

The 1930 Station Wagon body showed a number of changes that distinguish it from its predecessor. The roof over the front compartment and the front door window opening had more curve than the 1929 body. The 1930 design eliminated the fabric-covered visor used on the earlier models, giving the Station Wagon a more modern style. Ford also eliminated the curved cutout on the driver's door, which was intended to clear the fender-well-mounted spare tire.

continued on page 83

Original Ford Model A

1930 Interior Trim Combinations

35-B Standard Phaeton & 40-B Standard Roadster
Trim Scheme Black-brown

Seats, Quarters	Doors, Cowl	Floors				Hardware
Piped, black-brown Cobra cross-grain artificial leather	Black-brown Cobra cross-grain cardboard	Black rubber				Bright nickel

40-B Deluxe Roadster & 180-A Deluxe Phaeton
Trim Scheme Tan

Seat faces, Wind cord	Seat sides, Seat back, Doors, Cowl	Floors				Hardware
Piped, two-tone tan Bedouin-grain genuine leather	Two-tone tan Bedouin-grain artificial leather	Brown carpet				Bright nickel (Roadster) Butler nickel (Phaeton)

45-B Standard Coupe (Dropped April 1930)
Trim Scheme Brown check

Seat	Doors, Quarters, Header	Floor	Headlining	Curtain	Cowl	Hardware	Moldings
Piped, brown-checked cloth	Plain brown cloth	Black rubber	Brown napped cotton	Brown cloth	Two-tone brown dash-grain cardboard	Bright nickel	Moulding Gray

45-B Standard Coupe (Adopted April 1930)
Trim Scheme Gray check

Seat	Doors, Quarters, Header	Floor	Headlining	Curtain	Cowl	Hardware	Moldings
Piped, gray-checked cloth	Plain gray cloth	Black rubber	Gray napped cotton	Gray cloth	Two-tone gray dash-grain cardboard	Bright nickel	Moulding Gray

45-B Deluxe Coupe (Dropped July 1930)
Trim Scheme Brown Bedford cord

Seat, Doors, Quarters, Header		Floor	Headlining	Curtain	Cowl	Hardware	Moldings
Piped, brown Bedford cord		Brown carpet	Brown napped cotton	Brown silk	Two-tone brown dash-grain cardboard	Butler nickel	Mahogany woodgrain

45-B Deluxe Coupe (Adopted July 1930)
Trim Scheme Brown Bedford cord

Seat	Doors, Quarters, Header	Floor		Curtain	Cowl	Hardware	Moldings
Piped brown Bedford cord	Brown broadcloth	Brown carpet		Brown silk	Two-tone brown dash grain cardboard	Butler nickel	Mahogany woodgrain

45-B Deluxe Coupe
Trim Scheme Brown mohair

Seat, Doors, Quarters, Header		Floor	Headlining	Curtain	Cowl	Hardware	Moldings
Piped, brown mohair		Brown carpet	Brown napped cotton	Brown silk	Two-tone brown dash-grain cardboard	Butler nickel	Mahogany woodgrain

50-B Sport Coupe (Dropped April 1930)
Trim Scheme Brown check

Seat	Doors	Floor	Headlining, Quarters		Cowl	Hardware	Moldings
Piped, brown-checked cloth	Plain brown cloth	Black rubber	Brown drab mock twist		Two-tone brown dash-grain cardboard	Bright nickel	Moulding Gray

50-B Sport Coupe (Adopted April 1930)
Trim Scheme Gray check

Seat	Doors	Floor	Headlining, Quarters		Cowl	Hardware	Moldings
Piped, gray-checked cloth	Plain gray cloth	Black rubber	Gray mock twist		Two-tone gray dash-grain cardboard	Bright nickel	Moulding Gray

68-B Cabriolet (Dropped February 1930)
Trim Scheme Gray check

Seat	Doors, Quarters	Floor	Headlining package tray		Cowl	Hardware	Moldings
Piped, gray-checked cloth	Plain gray cloth	Brown carpet	Gray drab cloth		Two-tone brown dash-grain cardboard	Bright nickel	Moulding Gray

68-B Cabriolet (Adopted February 1930, dropped July 1930)
Trim Scheme Tan Bedford cord

Seat, Doors, Quarters	Top inside, Package tray	Floor			Cowl	Hardware	Moldings
Piped, tan Bedford cord	Gray drab cloth	Brown carpet			Drab brown dash-grain cardboard	Bright nickel	Moulding Gray

68-B Cabriolet (Adopted July 1930)
Trim Scheme Brown Bedford cord

Seat	Doors, Quarters	Floor	Top inside, Package tray		Cowl	Hardware	Moldings
Brown Bedford cord	Brown broadcloth	Brown carpet	Gray drab cloth		Two-tone brown dash-grain cardboard	Bright nickel	Mahogany woodgrain

55-B Tudor
Trim Scheme Blue hairline stripe

Seats	Doors, Seat backs, Quarters	Floor	Headlining	Curtains	Cowl	Hardware	Moldings
Piped, blue hairline-striped cloth	Plain blue cloth	Black rubber	Blue napped cotton	Blue cloth	Blue-gray dash-grain cardboard	Bright nickel	Moulding Gray (Early) Maroon (Late)

55-B Tudor (Dropped April 1930)
Trim Scheme Brown check

Seats	Doors, Seat backs, Quarters	Floor	Headlining	Curtains	Cowl	Hardware	Moldings
Piped, brown-checked cloth	Plain brown cloth	Black rubber	Brown napped cotton	Brown cloth	Two-tone brown dash-grain cardboard	Bright nickel	Moulding Gray

55-B Tudor (Adopted April 1930)
Trim Scheme Gray check

Seats	Doors, Seat back, Quarters	Floor	Headlining	Curtains	Cowl	Hardware	Moldings
Piped, gray-checked cloth	Plain gray cloth	Black rubber	Gray napped cotton	Gray cloth	Two-tone gray dash grain cardboard	Bright nickel	Moulding Gray (Early) Maroon (Late)

1930 INTERIOR TRIM COMBINATIONS (CONTINUED)

165-C, -D Standard Fordor (Dropped April 1930)
TRIM SCHEME Brown check

SEATS	DOORS, SEAT BACK, QUARTERS	FLOORS	HEADLINING	CURTAINS	COWL	HARDWARE	MOLDINGS
Piped, brown-checked cloth	Plain brown cloth	Black rubber (F) Brown carpet (R)	Brown napped cotton	Brown cloth	Two-tone brown dash-grain cardboard	Bright nickel	Mocha Brown (165-D before April 1930) Maroon

165-C, -D Standard Fordor (Adopted April 1930)
TRIM SCHEME Gray check

SEATS	DOORS, SEAT BACK, QUARTERS	FLOORS	HEADLINING	CURTAINS	COWL	HARDWARE	MOLDINGS
Piped, gray-checked cloth	Plain gray cloth	Black rubber (F) Brown carpet (R)	Gray napped cotton	Gray cloth	Two-tone gray dash-grain cardboard	Bright nickel	Maroon

170-B Fordor Two-window
TRIM SCHEME Brown check

SEATS	DOORS, SEAT BACK, QUARTERS	FLOORS	HEADLINING	CURTAINS	COWL	HARDWARE	MOLDINGS
Piped, brown-checked cloth	Plain brown cloth	Black rubber (F) Brown carpet (R)	Brown napped cotton	Brown cloth	Two-tone brown dash-grain cardboard	Bright nickel	Mocha Brown

170-B Deluxe Fordor
TRIM SCHEME Brown mohair

SEATS, DOORS, QUARTERS, HEADER	FLOORS	HEADLINING	CURTAINS	COWL	HARDWARE	MOLDINGS
Piped, brown mohair	Brown carpet	Brown napped cotton	Brown silk	Two-tone brown dash-grain cardboard	Butler nickel	Mahogany woodgrain

170-B Deluxe Fordor
TRIM SCHEME Brown Bedford cord

SEATS	DOORS, QUARTERS, SEAT BACK, HEADER	FLOORS	CURTAIN	COWL	HARDWARE	MOLDINGS
Piped, brown Bedford cord	Brown Bedford cord (Before September 1930) Brown broadcloth (After September 1930)	Brown carpet	Brown silk	Two-tone brown dash-grain cardboard	Butler nickel	Mahogany woodgrain

155-C, -D Town Sedan
TRIM SCHEME Brown mohair

SEATS, QUARTERS, DOORS, PILLARS	FLOORS	HEADLINING	CURTAINS	COWL	HARDWARE	MOLDINGS
Piped, brown mohair	Brown carpet	Brown napped cotton	Brown silk	Two-tone brown dash-grain cardboard	Butler nickel	Mahogany woodgrain

155-C, -D Town Sedan
TRIM SCHEME Green mohair

SEATS, QUARTERS, DOORS, PILLARS	FLOORS	HEADLINING	CURTAINS	COWL	HARDWARE	MOLDINGS
Piped, green mohair	Brown carpet	Green napped cotton	Green silk	Two-tone green dash grain-cardboard	Butler nickel	Mahogany woodgrain

155-C, -D Town Sedan
TRIM SCHEME Brown Bedford cord

SEATS	DOORS, QUARTERS, SEAT BACK	FLOORS	HEADLINING	CURTAINS	COWL	HARDWARE	MOLDINGS
Piped, brown Bedford cord	Brown Bedford cord Brown broadcloth (After September 1930)	Brown carpet	Brown napped cotton	Brown silk	Two-tone brown dash-grain cardboard	Butler nickel	Mahogany woodgrain

190-A Victoria
TRIM SCHEME Brown mohair

SEATS, SEAT BACKS, QUARTERS, DOORS	FLOORS	HEADLINING	CURTAINS	COWL	HARDWARE	MOLDINGS
Piped, brown mohair	Brown carpet	Brown napped cotton	Brown silk	Two-tone brown dash-grain cardboard	Butler nickel	Mahogany woodgrain

190-A Victoria
TRIM SCHEME Brown Bedford cord

SEATS	SEAT BACKS, QUARTERS, DOORS	FLOORS	HEADLINING	CURTAINS	COWL	HARDWARE	MOLDINGS
Piped, brown Bedford cord	Brown broadcloth	Brown carpet	Brown napped cotton	Brown silk	Two-tone brown dash-grain cardboard	Butler nickel	Mahogany woodgrain

76-B Open Cab Commercial
TRIM SCHEME Black-brown

SEAT	DOORS, COWL, LOCK PILLARS, QUARTERS	FLOOR	HARDWARE
Black-brown Cobra cross-grain artificial leather	Black-brown two-tone Cobra cross-grain cardboard	Black rubber	Bright nickel

79-B, 85-B Panel Delivery
TRIM SCHEME Blue-gray

SEATS	DOORS, COWL, HEADER	FLOOR	ROOF LINING	HARDWARE	MOLDINGS
Blue-gray colonial-grain artificial leather	Blue-gray colonial-grain cardboard	Black rubber	Black duck	Bright nickel	Black

82-B Closed Cab Commercial
TRIM SCHEME Black-brown

SEAT	DOORS, QUARTERS, HEADER, COWL	FLOOR	ROOF LINING	HARDWARE	MOLDINGS
Black-brown two-tone Cobra cross-grain artificial leather	Black-brown two-tone cross-grain cardboard	Black rubber	Cobra Black duck	Bright nickel	Black

130-B Deluxe Delivery
TRIM SCHEME Black-brown

SEATS, HEADLINER, WIND CORD	DOORS, COWL, HEADER	FLOORS	QUARTERS	HARDWARE	MOLDINGS
Black-brown two-tone Cobra cross-grain artificial leather	Black-brown two-tone Cobra cross-grain cardboard	Black rubber	Masonite	Bright nickel	Black

Original Ford Model A

1930 Body Color Schemes

35-B Standard Phaeton & 40-B Standard Roadster

Body	Belt, Quarter & Sill Molding	Stripe
Thorne Brown	Thorne Brown	Orange
Kewanee Green	Elkpoint Green	Apple Green
Copra Drab	Chicle Drab	Straw (Dropped November 1930)
Chicle Drab	Copra Drab	Straw
Andalusite Blue	Andalusite Blue	French Gray (Early 1930 only)
Andalusite Blue	Andalusite Blue	Aurora Red (Dropped August 1930)
Lombard Blue	Lombard Blue	Hessian Blue (Available September 1930)
Black	Black	Vermilion (March to September 1930)
Black	Black	Apple Green (Available October 1930)

40-B Deluxe Roadster & 180-A Deluxe Phaeton

Body	Belt, Quarter & Sill Molding	Stripe
Washington Blue	Riviera Blue	Tacoma Cream
Black	Black	Aurora Red (Dropped September 1930)
Black	Black	Apple Green (Available October 1930)
Brewster Green	Black	Apple Green (Available October 1930)
Stone Brown	Stone Gray, Deep	Tacoma Cream
Thorne Brown	Thorne Brown	Tacoma Cream
Kewanee Green	Elkpoint Green	Apple Green
Chicle Drab	Copra Drab	Tacoma Cream
Andalusite Blue	Andalusite Blue	Aurora Red (Dropped August 1930)
Lombard Blue	Lombard Blue	Hessian Blue (Available September 1930)
Ford Maroon	Black	Aurora Red
Bronson Yellow	Seal Brown	Orange

45-B Coupe, 50-B Sport Coupe

Body, Lower & Reveals	Upper Body, Belt, Quarter & Sill Moldings	Stripe
Andalusite Blue	Black	French Gray (Early 1930 only)
Andalusite Blue	Black	Aurora Red (Dropped August 1930)
Lombard Blue	Black	Hessian Blue (Available September 1930)
Kewanee Green	Elkpoint Green	Apple Green
Copra Drab	Chicle Drab	Straw (Dropped November 1930)
Chicle Drab	Copra Drab	Straw
Thorne Brown	Thorne Brown	Tacoma Cream
Black	Black	Vermilion (Dropped September 1930)
Black	Black	Apple Green (Available October 1930)

45-B Deluxe Coupe

Body, Lower & Reveals	Upper Body, Belt & Quarter Moldings	Stripe
Andalusite Blue	Black	French Gray (Early 1930 only)
Andalusite Blue	Black	Aurora Red (Dropped August 1930)
Lombard Blue	Black	Hessian Blue
Kewanee Green	Elkpoint Green	Apple Green
Copra Drab	Chicle Drab	Straw (Dropped November 1930)
Chicle Drab	Copra Drab	Straw
Thorne Brown	Thorne Brown	Tacoma Cream
Black	Black	Vermilion (Dropped September 1930)
Black	Black	Apple Green (Available October 1930)
Brewster Green	Black	Apple Green (Available October 1930)
Ford Maroon	Black	Vermilion

68-B Cabriolet

Body, Lower & Reveals	Upper Body, Deck, Belt, Quarter & Sill	Stripe
Andalusite Blue	Andalusite Blue	French Gray (Dropped August 1930)
Andalusite Blue	Andalusite Blue	Aurora Red (Available August 1930)
Lombard Blue	Lombard Blue	Hessian Blue (Available September 1930)
Bronson Yellow	Seal Brown	Orange
Moleskin Brown, Light	Moleskin Brown, Light	Tacoma Cream
Kewanee Green	Elkpoint Green	Apple Green
Black	Black	Vermilion (Available March to September 1930)
Black	Black	Apple Green
Brewster Green	Black	Apple Green (Available October 1930)

55-B Tudor

Lower Body & Reveals	Upper Body, Belt, Quarter & Sill Moldings	Stripe
Andalusite Blue	Black	French Gray (Early 1930 only)
Andalusite Blue	Black	Aurora Red (Dropped August 1930)
Lombard Blue	Black	Hessian Blue (Available September 1930)
Kewanee Green	Elkpoint Green	Apple Green
Copra Drab	Chicle Drab	Straw (Dropped November 1930)
Chicle Drab	Copra Drab	Straw
Thorne Brown	Thorne Brown	Tacoma Cream
Black	Black	Vermilion (Dropped September 1930)
Black	Black	Apple Green (Available October 1930)

165-C, -D Standard Fordor

Lower Body	Upper Body, Belt, Quarter, Sill & Reveals	Stripe
Andalusite Blue	Black	French Gray (Early 1930 only)
Andalusite Blue	Black	Aurora Red (Dropped August 1930)
Lombard Blue	Black	Hessian Blue (Available September 1930)
Kewanee Green	Elkpoint Green	Apple Green
Copra Drab	Chicle Drab	Straw (Dropped November 1930)
Chicle Drab	Copra Drab	Straw
Thorne Brown	Thorne Brown	Tacoma Cream
Black	Black	Vermilion (Dropped September 1930)
Black	Black	Apple Green (Available October 1930)

170-B Fordor

Lower Body, Sill & Reveals	Upper Body, Belt & Quarter Molding	Stripe
Kewanee Green	Elkpoint Green	Apple Green
Andalusite Blue	Black	French Gray
Thorne Brown	Black	Straw (Sill molding is black)
Black	Black	Vermilion
Chicle Drab	Copra Drab	Straw

170-B Two-Window Deluxe Fordor

Lower Body, Sill & Reveals	Upper Body, Belt & Quarter Molding	Stripe
Andalusite Blue	Black	French Gray (Early 1930 only)
Andalusite Blue	Black	Aurora Red (Dropped August 1930)
Lombard Blue	Black	Hessian Blue (Available September 1930)
Kewanee Green	Elkpoint Green	Apple Green
Copra Drab	Chicle Drab	Straw (Dropped November 1930)
Chicle Drab	Copra Drab	Straw
Thorne Brown	Thorne Brown	Tacoma Cream
Black	Black	Vermilion (Dropped September 1930)
Black	Black	Apple Green (Available October 1930)
Brewster Green	Black	Apple Green (Available October 1930)
Ford Maroon	Black	Vermilion

155-C, -D Town Sedan

Lower Body, Reveals	Upper Body, Belt, Quarter & Sill Molding	Stripe
Copra Drab	Chicle Drab	Straw (Most Town Sedans have reveals upper body color)
Chicle Drab	Copra Drab	Straw (Most Town Sedans have reveals upper body color)
Kewanee Green	Elkpoint Green	Apple Green
Ford Maroon	Black	Vermilion
Black	Black	Vermilion (Dropped September 1930)
Black	Black	Apple Green (Available October 1930)
Brewster Green	Black	Apple Green (Dropped September 1930)

190-A Victoria

Lower Body & Reveals	Upper Body, Belt, Quarter & Sill Molding	Stripe
Brewster Green	Black	Apple Green
Ford Maroon	Black	Vermilion (Sill molding is Ford Maroon)
Kewanee Green	Elkpoint Green	Apple Green (Reveals are Elkpoint Green)
Chicle Drab	Copra Drab	Straw
Black	Black	Apple Green

130-B Deluxe Delivery

Lower Body	Upper Body & Reveals	Belt & Sill Molding	Stripe
Black	Black	Black	Vermilion (Dropped September 1930)
Lombard Blue	Lombard Blue	Black	Hessian Blue (Available September 1930)
Black	Black	Black	Apple Green (Available October 1930)
Thorne Brown	Thorne Brown	Black	Straw
Kewanee Green	Elkpoint Green	Elkpoint Green	Apple Green
Chicle Drab	Copra Drab	Copra Drab	Straw

Commercial, Open and Closed Cab & Panel Delivery

Body	Stripe (Optional)
Rock Moss Green	Apple Green
Blue Rock Green	Apple Green
Black	Straw
Phoenix Brown	Straw (After September 1930)
Menelas Orange	Straw (After September 1930)
Rubellite Red	Straw (After September 1930)
Pegex Orange	Vermilion (After September 1930)
Copra Drab	Straw (After September 1930)
Thorne Brown	Straw (After September 1930)

1930

Above: This is one of only two 1930 Town Cars known to exist. This car is finished in black with a gold stripe. The last Town Car was delivered in February 1930.

Above right: The front compartment of a 1930 Town Car shows the windshield frame design and outside mount vacuum windshield wiper. The bar on top of the windshield frame is to secure the chauffeur's canopy. Note the 1929-style early 1930 instrument panel.

continued from page 79

Production of the 150-B Station Wagon body was expanded to include the Baker Raulang Body Company of Cleveland, Ohio, in addition to Murray. Since Baker Raulang did not produce metal stampings as did Murray, they only produced the body from the cowl back. These bodies were shipped to the Ford assembly plants where they were joined with the standard closed-car cowl and windshield assembly. Since a windshield was included, the commercial cowl was not used for the 150-B. All Station Wagon sheet-metal body parts were finished in Manila Brown. The roof was covered with black, coarse, long-short-grain artificial leather.

The interior of the Station Wagon was austere and the plain-panel seats were covered in black-brown, two-tone Cobra cross-grain artificial leather. The cowl was trimmed with a dark two-tone Cobra cross-grain cardboard. Black rubber mats covered the floors: the standard style was used up front, while the rear compartment floor featured a special design with straight ribs. The side curtains for 1930 were improved over the previous examples and now had two layers of tan rubberized fabric sandwiched over a cardboard filler. The windows in the side curtains were still clear celluloid.

In June 1930, Ford introduced the new styling on its four Model A commercial bodies: the Open Cab and Closed Cab Pickup, Deluxe Delivery, and Panel Delivery. All models adopted the new, more modern styling used on the Model A passenger car line, eliminating the last vestiges of Model T appearance.

There was still some carryover of 1929 items for the 1930 commercial line. Like all early 1930 Fords, the old-style instrument panel with the oval speedometer was still used, but the cowl tank assembly was new. For commercial vehicles, this carryover was more extensive, as early 1930 commercial models could still have the 1929-style bumpers, gas

A front quarter view of a 1930 82-B Closed Cab Pickup. The body is finished in Blue Rock Green with Apple Green stripe and wheels. Note the black-painted radiator and headlight shells. The whitewalls and wood stakes in the truck bed are accessories.

Original Ford Model A

cap, commercial headlights, and steering wheel. There was actually a special A-9002-BR cowl tank that used the new-style cowl with the old-style fluted cap. The early 1930 78-A open-cab body was continued without outside door handles.

The 76-B Open Cab Pickup body was all new for June 1930 and used the same cowl and windshield as the standard open passenger cars. The rear of the body (A-77310-B) was curved and more modern looking than the 1928–29 versions and offered more interior room. The body also used the same A-35455-D (RH) and A-35456-D (LH) doors and door hardware as the Standard Roadster. One improvement in the new cab was the top, which was now removable although it still did not fold. The lower back of the top covering fastened to the rear belt rail with snaps.

The 82-B Closed Cab Pickup was also a new body style for June 1930. It used the same cowl, tank, windshield frame, visor, doors, and door hardware as the 55-B Tudor sedan, which gave the new pickup a smart, modern appearance. The use of existing passenger-car body panels also served to reduce production costs. The new body, built by Budd Manufacturing, used the A-83700-B back panel and lock-pillar assembly with the upper roof side panels that were slightly different from those of the Tudor. There were three identical A-47232 wood roof ribs in the 1930 82-B cab.

The 82-B cab used a black long-short-grain artificial-leather top material. The inside of the roof was lined with black duck material, which was placed over the wood roof ribs. The ribs were not covered and should be visible inside the cab. The inside of the body shell was generally painted body color, but some may have been finished in black to match the interior garnish moldings. Both the open- and closed-cab trucks used the same narrow 78-A pickup body (bed) as the 1928–29 models. New black-painted steel, diamond-pattern running boards were also adapted for all trucks.

The 76-B and 92-B pickups were available in only three body color schemes upon introduction. The entire body was Rock Moss Green, Blue Rock Green, or black, each with optional contrasting stripes. In September 1930, six additional new color schemes were adopted and the commercial bodies were then also available in Phoenix Brown, Menelas Orange, Rubelite Red, Pegex Orange, Copra Drab, and Thorne Brown. These colors had optional contrasting stripe colors. There were generally no standard trim colors on commercial bodies. Cowl bands were initially painted black but were later changed to body color.

Both the Open and Closed Cab Pickups used the same interior trim materials. The seat and wind cord were trimmed in black-brown, two-tone Cobra cross-grain artificial leather. The door panels, cowl, quarters, and lock pillars were covered in black-brown, two-tone Cobra cross-grain cardboard. The floors had a black rubber spatter-pattern mat. Door and instrument panel garnish moldings and rear window frame in the 82-B cab were painted gloss black.

The 130-B Deluxe Delivery for 1930 was a dramatic change over the Tudor sedan look used in 1928–29. The new body, introduced in August 1930, was longer, wider, and had significantly more interior cargo space than the previous body. The new body used the doors from the 1930 Tudor, but the rest of the body was made up of all new components.

The new body still used individual seats, but the interior of the cargo compartment now used

This is the front of a 1930 pickup truck. All standard commercial vehicles had black-painted radiator and headlight shells. The headlight doors are stainless steel like those on the passenger cars. The Apple Green wheels and whitewall tires are accessories.

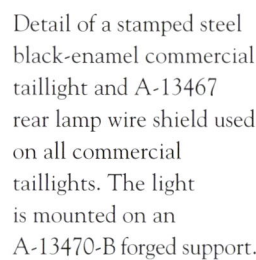

Detail of a stamped steel black-enamel commercial taillight and A-13467 rear lamp wire shield used on all commercial taillights. The light is mounted on an A-13470-B forged support.

Front-quarter view of a 1930 82-B Closed Cab Pickup finished in Cherokee Gray—a 1931 commercial color. The red wheels and cowl lights are accessories. The black cowl band was found on some early 1930 commercial bodies but could have also been body color.

The black enamel rear lamp and forged bracket on a 1930 closed-cab pickup. Commercial vehicles all had the stamped steel wire guard on the rear of the lamp body.

1930

Top right: The rear quarter view of a Cherokee Gray 1930 Closed Cab Pickup shows the 78-A pickup body carried over from the Model T. The AA rear bumper and painted wheels are accessories.

Top far right: Front compartment of a 1930 82-B Closed Cab Pickup. The seat is trimmed with black Cobra cross-grain artificial leather while the door panels and pillars are covered with matching black Cobra cross-grain cardboard. The floor is covered with a black rubber mat.

Right: The view of the rear of a 78-A pickup bed and tailgate shows the artificial leather–covered support chains. The wood and steel strips in the bed were originally finished in body color.

Far right: The driver's door panel on a 1930 82-B Closed Cab Pickup. The trim is black Cobra cross-grain cardboard and the hardware is bright nickel. Garnish moldings are painted black. The door window draft deflector is an accessory.

Lower right: Front compartment detail of a 1930 Closed Cab Pickup. The seat is trimmed with black Cobra cross-grain artificial leather. The floor is covered with a black rubber mat. The 1929-style instrument panel with oval speedometer identifies this as an early 1930 body.

Masonite and steel paneling rather than the cardboard of the earlier version. The seats were trimmed in the same black-brown, two-tone Cobra cross-grain material as the other commercial models.

The 130-B Deluxe Delivery was initially available in four basic body color schemes. The lower body was finished in black, Thorne Brown, Kewanee Green, and Chicle Drab. In September 1930, Lombard Blue was also offered. The upper body, moldings, and stripe were finished in contrasting and complementary colors. The 130-B Deluxe Delivery used the stainless cowl band, radiator, and headlight shells rather than the black-painted steel equipment used on the standard commercial vehicles.

The 79-B Panel Delivery was the largest Model A commercial body in 1930. More truck-like and spacious than the Deluxe Delivery, the Panel Delivery was a more practical choice for the business owner interested in the most cargo capacity for the lowest price. The Murray-built Panel Delivery body was taller than the other commercial bodies and used distinctive A-72760-AR (RH) and A-72761-AR (LH) doors. These doors, which featured unusual belt molding designs, were only used for the 79-B and the 85-B Panel Delivery bodies in 1930.

The Panel Delivery used the same body color schemes as the other standard Model A commercial vehicles, but interior trim materials were unique to this model. The seats and wind cord were trimmed in blue-gray colonial-grain artificial leather identical to that used in 1929 open passenger car bodies. The door panels, cowl, and quarters were finished in blue-gray colonial-grain cardboard. The floors were covered with black rubber mats. The rear compartment was lined with Masonite paneling.

Original Ford Model A

AA Truck Chassis

The frame and chassis components for the 1930 1½-ton AA truck were initially carried over from those of 1929. The first and most significant change was the new AA-4000-K Ford-designed heavy-duty bevel-gear rear axle assembly, which was announced in January 1930. This new axle was a complete departure from previous designs and was much heavier, stronger, and more efficient than the old worm-gear or intermediate bevel-gear designs. The rear axle and driveshaft assembly was finished in black enamel.

The new design featured a straddle-mounted pinion shaft mounted with double taper roller bearings at the front and a heavy special spiral roller bearing at the rear. The axle shafts were much heavier than the old design and incorporated longer AA-1225-C wheel bearings. The new axle was available in gear ratios of 5.14:1 (high speed, adopted in March 1930) and 6.6:1 (standard). The February 1930 Ford Service Bulletin stated that the new rear axle assembly could be adapted to the old chassis on trucks equipped with a center-mounted parking brake lever.

Along with the new rear axle equipment, Ford included a new heavy-duty front axle, larger 14-inch brake drums, and new Budd Wheel Company 20-inch disk wheels. The new brake drums were required for the new wheels. These AA-1015-C wheels were more conventional than the Ford-designed wheels used through 1929. They had five vent holes and were offset, allowing the mounting of dual wheels. There were three variations of these wheels used through the end of Model AA production. Budd truck wheels have their production date stamped on the inside of the mounting area. All truck wheels were painted gloss black.

The Budd 20-inch truck wheels were equipped with a new design double-bent valve stem made either by Schrader or Dill. The stem was still nickel-plated brass, but this new design did not use a dust cover. The exposed valve stem cap was a knurled, heavy-duty type with a valve removal slot in the top. The double-bent design allowed easier access to the valve stem on dual-wheel equipment.

The heavier, stronger AA-3010 front axle used heavier AA-3105-B spindles. The spindle bearing on the AA spindle is mounted below the axle, rather than above it as on the Model A axle unit, for more strength. The new axle also uses the larger AA-3405-B radius rod (wishbone) and heavier tie rod and included the wider AA-5310-C front spring, which at 2½ inches, was the same width as the passenger car rear spring.

In October 1930, the gearshift housing cap on the four-speed transmission was changed from a pin-on design to a screw-on AA-7220-B design. The purpose of this improvement was to lessen the possibility of an oil leak occurring around the cap. This change required a new shift lever, cap, housing, and trunnion.

Ford made a few additional small changes to the AA chassis for 1930. In January 1930, the front cross-member was changed to the AA-5019 design, which was wider to accommodate the wider front spring. The front cross-member also had a riveted-in reinforcement in the spring-rest portion for added strength. The new design also incorporated the lowered radiator mounting pads required for the new 1930 radiator design. In March 1930 the AA-5090-A rear engine supports were changed to the AA-5090-B style, which were similar in appearance to the passenger car supports but were wider.

Front detail of an early-1930 AA 82-A closed-cab truck. The 1929-style 82-A and 76-A bodies were used until June 1930, but the headlights, bumper, fuel filler cap, and sometimes, steering wheel were the later 1930 style.

Front view of an AA truck with a 1929-style 82-A closed-cab body. The bumper, headlights, wheels, and fuel filler cap identify this as an early 1930 truck.

A complete tool set for a 1930 Model A passenger car. This type of case is used to display the tool set for a show, but it is not an original Ford item.

Top: Two types of jacks that were used in the 1930 tool bag. From left they are A-17080-B-1 and A-17080-B1. They were finished in black and used the A-17081-B handle.

Above: Four additional jacks were used during the 1930 model year. They are, from left, A-17080-B2, -B3, -C1, and -C2. The A-17080-B3 used a 35-inch-long A-17081-C handle. They were all painted black.

Another change to the new-style 1930 AA truck introduced in June was the new AA-8005-B radiator and accompanying AA-8200-A black-painted radiator shell. The new radiator has four rows of tubes rather than the three of the passenger car unit. This improvement provided more efficient cooling. The new AA radiator shell eliminated the widow's peak design of the shell opening, giving it a different appearance from the passenger car unit. The same blue background Ford badge was continued. The new radiator and shell caused the spacing from the hood to the radiator shell to increase and required the frame mounting holes to be enlarged to provide fan clearance.

Beginning in September 1930 some AA trucks were equipped with a new A-14582-C nonmetallic horn and headlight wire conduit. This conduit was made from black woven lacquered fabric with black enamel or stainless ferrules. These fabric conduits were used concurrently with the standard stainless conduits, but were not used on the Deluxe AA body types.

Current with the introduction of the new body styling, Ford released an extended length, AA5006-AR, 157-inch wheelbase frame. This extra length allowed the 1930 AA to accommodate 11-foot bodies of various designs with no need to resort to aftermarket frame extensions. The new 157-inch wheelbase frame was equipped with the solid front engine mount ears that were eliminated from passenger frames in late 1928. The 131½- and 157-inch wheelbase lengths were actually industry standards set to accommodate standardized aftermarket body equipment. The 157-inch wheelbase chassis was usually equipped with dual rear wheels.

A new AA-17757-A double-bar chrome bumper was adopted for the AA chassis when the new body styles appeared in June 1930. This bumper is similar in appearance to the passenger car unit, but has wider and thicker bars. In August 1930, a totally new AA-17750-B solid-bar front bumper assembly was adopted for the AA chassis. This bumper bears no resemblance to the passenger car units and is painted gloss black enamel. The new bumper uses new mounting bars, including two BB-17752-A (RH) and AA-17753-A (LH) arms and a BB-17760-A back bar.

All new Ford commercial vehicles incorporated the same cowl, tank, and front body design as the passenger cars except for the commercial radiator shell. The front fenders were exactly the same units as on passenger cars, but there were variations to the rear fenders, running boards, and splash shields used on certain models. Rear fenders were no longer used on the Stake, Platform, and grain bodies as they had been in 1928.

The new design 76-B) open-cab and 82-B closed-cab bodies were used on the AA truck chassis. These were the same bodies used on the Model A chassis. The same colors and trim variations apply to the AA variations. These bodies could be supplied on a bare chassis with no body equipment. They were used on the 88-A Platform, 188-A Stake variation, 89-A Express body, 185-A Platform (157-inch wheelbase), 186-A Stake (157-inch wheelbase), 197-A Large Express (157-inch wheelbase), and 16 variations of dump, coal, and garbage bodies made by various manufacturers.

In addition to the standard open- and closed-cab truck variations there was also a new 85-B AA Panel Delivery. This new body, mounted on the 131½-inch wheelbase chassis, was wider, higher, and nearly 1 foot longer than its 85-A predecessor. The 85-B body was 100.1 inches long, 46.1 inches wide, and 54.6 inches high, holding almost 146 cubic feet of cargo. The body incorporated the new cowl and hood design used on all other 1930 bodies, but the doors and the remainder of the body were entirely new.

The A-79760-AR (RH) and A-79761-AR (LH) doors were significantly higher and longer than the standard 82-B doors. The 85-B used the AA-16438-B (RH) and AA-16439-B (LH) rear fenders and AA-16458-B (RH) and AA16459-B (LH) long running boards and corresponding long splash shields.

The AA Panel Delivery was available in the same body color schemes as the other A and AA standard commercial bodies. The interior trim scheme used in the 1930 85-B was also the same seating configuration and had blue-gray colonial-grain artificial leather as the Model 79-B Panel Delivery.

Tools 1930 A Chassis

Item	Part Number	Finish	Note
Grease gun	A-17125	Dull nickel	Alemite
Tool bag	A-17005	Black top material	11x6½ inches (Closed)
Adjustable wrench			9½ inches
Sparkplug and head nutwrench	A-17017	Black	
Pliers	A-17025	Unfinished/black	
Open-end wrench	A-17015		7/16 x ½
Open-end wrench	A-17016		9/16 x 5/8
Screwdriver		Unfinished/black	8 3/16 inch
Jack	A-17080-B1, -B2, -B3, -C1, -C2	Black	8½ inch
Jack handle	A-17081-B	Black	39 inches
Tire iron	A-17019	Unfinished/black	16 inches
Tire pump		Black	
Crank	A-17036-B	Black	
Owner's manual		Tan	1930

Tools 1930 AA Chassis

Identical to A except for AA starting crank, jack, jack handle, lug nut wrench, lug nut wrench handle, and tire iron.

Starting crank			No lug nut socket
Jack	AA-17080-A	Black	1 3/8 inch square top
Jack handle		Black	24 inches long
Tire iron		Black	16 5/8 inches long
Lug nut wrench		Black	15 inches long, 1½ - 7/8 inch sockets
Lug nut wrench handle		Black	20 inches long

Original Ford Model A

Chapter 4
1931

During the last full year of Model A production Ford Motor Company finally felt the full blow of the Depression, with sales down to 771,444 units. Ford's gross income was $460,000,000 with a net loss of $37,181,000.

Ford advertising for 1931 continued in much the same way as 1930, but because of the deepening Depression and lagging passenger car sales, the company now ardently pursued the fleet and special-duty vehicle market. Ads appearing in newspapers and magazines were geared more toward trucks and commercial vehicles than in past years.

The commercial line grew to such a multitude of body types and chassis configurations that it became impossible for a dealer to display the entire line. In May 1931, Ford created the "Ford Caravans" to show the complete commercial line. This caravan of trucks from the branch factories traveled throughout the countryside and visited Ford dealers in virtually all of the small towns.

One of the most popular and well known of Ford's promotions began on April 14, 1931, when the 20 Millionth Ford came off the assembly line with Henry Ford at the wheel. This car, a slant-windshield Town Sedan, traveled to each and

Front quarter view of a 1931 40-B Deluxe Roadster. The body is Brewster Green with black moldings and Apple Green stripe and wheels. The top is tan drab rubber interlined fabric. The fender-mounted spare tires, mirrors, spotlight, stone guard, quail mascot, and whitewall tires are accessories.

1931

The rear view of a 1931 40-B Deluxe Roadster in Stone Brown and Stone Deep Gray. The stripe and wheels are Tacoma Cream. The fender-mounted spare tire, Motometer, and etched wind wings are accessories.

every dealer in every Ford territory in the nation over a six-month period. The car and its accompanying caravan stopped for 15 minutes at each dealer, and the photos of its exploits appeared in every newspaper where it was displayed.

The only significant styling change for 1931 was the new radiator shell with painted insert panels top and bottom. At the beginning of 1931 production, the upper panel was painted lower body color and the lower panel was painted black, as it had been for 1930. Early in 1931, the Ford badge was changed to a new stainless steel design with black lettering, replacing the blue vitreous enamel used in the past.

A small change in external appearance for the 1931 Model A was the new one-piece running board splash shield, replacing the previous two-piece unit. The two-piece splash shield design was necessarily continued for the AA truck chassis due to the variations in running board and shield lengths.

In April 1931, the A-11805-E instrument panel was adopted for both passenger cars and commercial vehicles. The new panel has a distinct border around the outside of the panel ribs. This design was used concurrently with the old style through the end of production.

Chassis, Axles, and Wheels

By the beginning of 1931, the Model A chassis had been perfected to the point that few changes were made during the last year of production. In August 1931, the rear bumper cross-arm brace was reinforced with a boss where it attaches to the bumper arms. The new brace was given the part number A-17783-E and required longer A-21143-S4 bolts for attachment in the forward holes.

In September 1931, an improved round cross-section A-2503 brake-rod spring was adopted, replacing the old flat springs. The new design was stronger and greatly improved the function of the spring.

Engine Assembly

The Model A engine had also been refined so that it did not require any significant improvements for

The 20 Millionth Ford

The Ford Motor Company has a history of recognizing its achievements and milestones. The 10 millionth Ford was a 1924 Model T Touring that was built on June 15, 1924. It left the plant at Highland Park and led parades in most of the towns and cities along the Lincoln Highway, where several million people saw it. Henry Ford posed with the car at Fairlane alongside his first car, the 1896 Quadricycle. The 11 millionth Ford was produced the same year and was presented to the visiting Prince of Wales in October 1924.

On May 26, 1927, the 15 millionth Ford, a 1927 Model T Touring, came off the Highland Park assembly line. Again, Ford used the event as a promotional opportunity, and with Edsel at the wheel, the car led a motorcade to the Dearborn Engineering Laboratories. The Quadricycle was displayed again and the Fords posed for photographers and reporters. The production of the 15 millionth Ford corresponded with the announcement of the new Model A, which was made official on May 25, 1927.

The most publicized of Ford's production milestones arrived on April 14, 1931, when the 20 millionth Ford was built. Again Henry and Edsel Ford accompanied the car off the assembly line. This time, in addition to the famous Quadricycle, the new Ford was posed with the 1927 Model T 15 millionth car. The 20 millionth Ford was conveniently one of Ford's latest designs, a 1931 160-B slant-windshield Town Sedan. The car was finished in solid black with white lettering on the sides and on the roof identifying it as the 20 millionth Ford. The roof lettering was chosen because of Ford's interest in aviation, allowing the car to be identified from the air.

The 20 millionth Ford soon began an extensive nationwide tour of the United States, extending from east to west, visiting virtually every Ford territory and dealer. In every town and city, the new Ford was given a great deal of publicity. The car was driven by governors, mayors, and celebrities, including Eleanor Roosevelt, Douglas Fairbanks, and Adm. Richard Byrd. It climbed city hall steps, circled the Indianapolis 500 track, and descended to the bottom of Hoover Dam.

After the tour, the car was returned to Detroit, and in December 1931 it was placed on exhibit in the new Henry Ford Museum. The car remained in the museum for many years and was clearly visible in 1935 photographs of the milestone cars. Some time afterward, the car was apparently forgotten until Model A Fords began to become popular in the 1950s and 1960s and questions arose about the disposition of the 20 millionth Ford. No one seemed to know what happened to the car, but the most commonly accepted explanation was that the car was destroyed in a fire.

The mystery of the 20 millionth Ford was solved in September 1999 when Ford Motor Company historian Bob Kreipke followed a lead on the car and traced it to the car's owner in northern Michigan. The car was in the possession of Rod Liimatainen, who had kept it secure and safe for many years. Rod's father, Carl, bought the car for $550 from the Ford Museum in 1940, when they were reducing the size of the collection to create more space. Carl bought the car for his father, Charles, who drove it regularly until 1956, when he gave it back to Carl.

When Carl died in 1958, Rod inherited the car. Although the lettering had been removed before his family bought the car, Rod realized it was a special car. In 1960, he put it on blocks and locked it away in his mother's garage. Rod kept the secret to himself for 40 years.

In December 1999 the 20 millionth Ford was leased to the Ford Motor Company, which planned to restore the car and use it as a part of its 2003 Centennial Celebration. The car will be displayed at Ford's World Headquarters for 10 years. While the car was being restored, its progress was made available on a special 360-degree photo website so that everyone could follow the restoration.

1931. In January, Ford began using new special alloy cast A-6505-A2 engine exhaust valves. The new valve may be identified by the letter "E" and by the Ford script stamped on top of the valve head.

In March, the A-9430 exhaust manifold casting was reinforced with a rib added to the inside curve of the manifold down pipe. This reinforcement rib is readily visible when viewing the manifold on the engine. The exhaust manifold gasket was also changed in May 1931. The new A-9448-A3 gasket provided better sealing and reduced the chance of gasket failure. It mounted with holes for the mounting studs rather than slots as on the previous design.

In August, the engine oil pan was modified by lowering the splash tray ⅛ inch and adding a sheetmetal shield around the oil pump. The new oil pan and shield were designed to be used together so the Ford Service Bulletin advised not to install one without the other. Along with the oil pan changes, piston ring pressure was reduced and oil ring groove clearance was increased. All of the changes were designed to reduce oil consumption.

Also in August 1931, Ford released a high-compression cylinder head as a production option. The improved head was initially intended for police use, but the increase in power and performance was so significant that the option was soon available for public order. The new head increased acceleration by 11 percent and top speed by 5 miles per hour. There was also a noticeable increase in fuel mileage and hill-climbing ability. The demand was such that Ford was soon installing the new heads at the rate of 700 per day.

Transmission and Clutch

There were no significant changes to the Ford transmission and clutch units for 1931. In July, the four-speed AA truck transmission and larger clutch were adapted to the Model A chassis to give more versatility to the light trucks. This involved a change from the A to the AA clutch housing, A-7085-E rear bearing retainer, A-7090-C universal joint, and AA-7095 universal joint knuckle retainer. The four-speed transmission also allowed the use of a power takeoff to operate a variety of equipment on the Model A chassis. Announced July 8, 1931, the four-speed option cost $30.

Cooling System and Radiator

The most obvious change to the radiator and cooling system was the new stainless radiator shell. First used with the late 1930 190-A Victoria, it incorporated a new painted convex insert

Opposite above: The right side view of an early 1931 engine compartment shows the glass fuel sediment bowl and inside fuel shutoff. The carburetor is a Zenith 3.

Opposite below: The left side view of a late 1931 engine compartment. Note the indented firewall with the updated outside A-9189-B fuel shutoff connection. This design was introduced in May 1931.

1931

1930 Model A Engine Numbers

Month	First Number	Last Number
January	4237501	4310300
February	4310301	4393627
March	4393628	4529831
April	4520832	4611921
May	4611922	4695999
June	4696000	4746730
July	4746731	4777282
August	–	–
September	4777283	4824809
October	4824810	4826746
November	4826747	4830806
December	–	–

1930 Model A & AA Engine Numbers

January	4830807	4842983
February	4842984	4846691
March	4846692	4849340

Note:
 Most U.S. Model A passenger car production ceased as of November 1931. The remaining production was a combination of foreign and commercial vehicle chassis. Of the last 2,648 engine numbers produced in March 1, 1932, 1,550 were part of a U.S. Government Mail Truck order. 1,500 of those were AA and 50 were A commercial chassis. There were also a number of extra engines produced for service which may not have had engine numbers.
 In April 1931 Ford produced the 20 millionth Ford. The engine and chassis number on this car were stamped 20,000,000 rather than a number in the normal sequence.

panel in the upper shell, matching the one already used in the lower section. The lower panel was originally painted black, but later in 1931 production it could have been painted lower body color to match the upper insert.

The reasons for this change were economic. The 1930 radiator shell required a deep drawn stamping to achieve the shape. The 1931 style was formed by shaping a single channel into a U shape and then attaching the lower panel to the lower side panels of the shell. This was much less expensive to produce and required less complex stamping operations. In March or April 1931, the new A-8200-C radiator shell stainless steel nameplate with black background recess was adopted.

The 1931 standard commercial vehicles retained the same black-painted steel radiator shell used in 1930, although the new stainless nameplate was added early in 1931. The new 1931 Model A deluxe commercial vehicles used the same radiator shell as the passenger cars.

There were also smaller changes made to the 1931 Ford cooling system. In March the two-bladed fan was changed from a double-thickness to a single-thickness design. Both types were used concurrently after that time. The 7/16-20 castle nut holding the fan to the water pump shaft had been painted black since mid-1930. The fan was still finished in gloss black enamel as it had been throughout production.

Fuel System

A major change was made to the fuel system in May 1931 when a new cowl tank, fuel lines, sediment bulb, and carburetor were adopted. This new system is immediately visible under the hood because of the indented firewall. The new cowl fuel tank assembly A-9002-E moves the previous fuel shutoff valve from under the tank inside the car to outside on the firewall.

On the engine side of the firewall, the new A-9189-B valve assembly is mounted and attached to the carburetor with an A-9240-C fuel line. The sediment bulb is now part of the carburetor and is mounted to the front of the bowl at the fuel inlet. The tops of the Zenith 1, 2, and 3 carburetors were modified to accommodate the new side-bowl fuel inlet assembly.

In conjunction with the new cowl and fuel tank assembly, the steering column support bracket was moved from its permanent attachment on the underside of the tank to a separate bracket bolted to the belt rail and tank. This change eliminated the chance of leaks caused by failure of the welds at the old bracket location. These attachment welds had sometimes leaked

1931 Ford Model A Production

Model	Name	Weight	Price	Number Produced
35-B	Phaeton	2,235	$435	4,076
180-A	Deluxe Phaeton	2,285	$580	2,229
40-B	Roadster	2,155	$430	5,499
40-B Deluxe	Deluxe Roadster	2,230	$475	52,997
45-B	Coupe	2,257	$490	82,894
45-B Deluxe	Deluxe Coupe	2,265	$525	23,696
50-B	Sport Coupe	2,283	$500	21,291
55-B	Tudor	2,462	$490	148,425
55-B Deluxe	Deluxe Tudor	2,488	$525	21,984
68-B	Cabriolet	2,273	$595	4,959
68-C	Cabriolet (SW)	2,273	$595	6,842
150-B	Station Wagon	2,505	$625	2,848
165-C	Std. Fordor (Murray)	2,462	$590	
165-D	Std. Fordor (Briggs)	2,462	$590	18,127 (Combined)
170-B	Deluxe Fordor	2,488	$630	3,251
190-A	Victoria	2,375	$580	36,863
400-A	Convertible Sedan	2,335	$640	4,864
66-A	Deluxe Pickup			293
76-B	Open Cab Pickup			
79-B	Panel Delivery			8,282
82-B	Closed Cab Pickup			
130-B	Deluxe Delivery		$540	9,549
130-B	Drop-Floor DD			100
225-A	Drop-Floor Panel Delivery		$560	
255-A	Special Delivery		$615	900
295-A	Town Car Delivery			196
	A Chassis	1,680	$340	(See Notes)
AA-112	Standrive Chassis			345
	AA-131 Chassis	2,723	$520	(See Notes)
	AA-157 Chassis		$545	
85-B	AA Panel Delivery	3,904		2,781
185-B	AA-157 Platform	4,370	$690	
186-B	AA-157 Large Stake	4,383	$735	
187-A	AA-131 Platform	3,730	$640	
189-A	AA-131 Stake	3,713	$660	
195-A	AA-131 Express	3,590	$670	
197-A	AA-157 Express	3,880	$730	
199-A	AA-131 Ice Wagon	4,160	$735	
201-A	AA Coal Hydraulic	4,563	$850	
201-B	AA Coal Hydraulic	4,801	$905	
201-C	AA Coal Hydraulic	4,801	$905	
203-A	Garbage Hydraulic	4,457	$830	
203-B	Garbage Hydraulic	4,457	$830	
203-C	Garbage Hydraulic	4,575	$865	
204-A	Dump, Light Hydraulic	4,216	$735	
204-B	Dump, Light Hydraulic	4,216	$735	
205-A	Hi-Lift Coal	5,297	$1,165	
207-B	Coal & Coke	4,801	$905	
208-A	Dump, Hydraulic	4,330	$815	
208-B	Dump, Hydraulic	4,330	$815	
210-A	AA-157 Large Panel	4,705	$900	
229-A	AA Service Car	3,575	$715	521
242-A	Heavy Duty Express	4,297	$735	
270-A	Funeral Service Car		$1,550	17
275-A	Funeral Coach	4,170	$1,900	96
280-A	Ambulance	4,823	$1,700	84
285-A	Deluxe Police Patrol		$1,250	45
290-A	Police Patrol		$975	184
300-A	Deluxe Panel Delivery		$950	1,143
315-A	Standrive Delivery		$1,050	

Note:
In June 1931 an order was placed for 500 100-cubic-foot capacity York Hoover Mail bodies to be installed on Model A commercial chassis. An additional 50 Mail bodies were ordered in March 1932 for Model A chassis.

Also in June 1931, 1,000 200-cubic-foot capacity Metropolitan Mail bodies were ordered for AA chassis. In March 1932 an additional 1,500 AA Mail bodies were ordered. These 1,500 vehicles were the last Model A or AA chassis built.

1931

Front quarter view of a 1931 Standard Phaeton. The top is black, fine, long-short-grain artificial leather. The reflectors behind the front bumper are later safety accessories.

The rear quarter view of a 1931 35-B Standard Phaeton. The body is finished in Kewanee Green and the moldings are Elkpoint Green. The stripe is Apple Green. The right taillight and trunk rack are accessories. The back window frame is painted black.

Original Ford Model A

This side view of a 1931 40-B Deluxe Roadster shows the standard side curtains in place. The body is Stone Brown and the moldings are Stone Deep Gray with a Tacoma Cream stripe. The whitewall tires, quail mascot, trunk, and fender-mounted spare tires are accessories.

Far left: The seat of this 1931 Deluxe Roadster is trimmed with piped tan Bedouin-grain genuine leather. The cowl and door panels are covered with matching tan Bedouin-grain artificial leather. Only deluxe cars had a stripe on the dash. The floor is covered with brown carpet.

Left: These 1931 Deluxe Roadster side curtains are made of tan drab rubber interlined fabric with clear celluloid windows and trimmed with tan artificial-leather binding.

due to the stresses of the steering column support. A lowering block was also added for certain deluxe models such as the Deluxe Phaeton, Convertible Sedan, and Victoria.

Electrical System

There were few changes to the Model A electrical system for 1931. The same basic generator, starter, starter switch, and wiring system were carried over from 1930. In May 1930, a new special A-10000-D low-speed generator became available as an option. This unit, intended for police cars, began charging at a speed of about 7½ miles per hour. The output of the generator at 15 miles per hour was about 14 amps.

In September, Ford Motor Company authorized an additional rear lamp to be mounted on the right as a dealer service option. The light improved safety while driving at night, but an important extra benefit was increased accessory sales for the dealer. Instructions in the Ford Service Bulletin detailed the routing of the wiring and mounting of the light and bracket.

Body and Fender Assembly

The most obvious change to the basic Model A body and fender configuration for 1931 was the elimination of the two-piece running board splash shield assembly on the passenger car chassis. The new design featured a one-piece splash shield that

1931

Above: This 1931 Deluxe Roadster seat face is trimmed in piped two-tone tan Bedouin-grain genuine leather. The seat sides, door panels, and cowl are matching tan Bedouin-grain artificial leather. The floor is brown carpet. The etched wind wings are accessories.

Right: The 1931 Deluxe Roadster windshield frame and stanchions. The windshield frame is 1½ inches lower than the standard open-car frame. The spare tire cover and door-top cover are accessories.

no longer had its rear section permanently attached to the running board. The front fender was also changed as it no longer had the front section of the splash shield spot-welded to the inside fender edge. The front inside edge of the splash shield was now bolted to the front fender and sealed with black ³⁄₁₆-inch beaded fender welting. The new design simplified assembly and reduced production costs. Rear fenders were identical to those of equivalent 1930 models. They were sealed from the body with black ³⁄₁₆-inch beaded fender welting.

The 1931 commercial chassis were equipped with the same A-175014-BR front body assembly as the 1930 models. This special cowl section provided a flat vertical surface to allow the attachment of aftermarket commercial bodies such as the Mail Truck. This special body front was used on both the A and AA commercial chassis.

The greatest change for 1931 was the addition of a number of new body styles. There were 22 passenger-body styles and 8 Model A commercial styles available for the 1931 model year. There was also a significant addition to the AA body line. Ford was interested in capturing as much of the market as possible and the goal was to offer a body for every need and every pocketbook.

In May 1931, Ford's Triplex laminated safety glass was made available as special equipment at extra cost on all Ford passenger models. Different glass runs were required as the laminated glass was thicker than the standard plate glass. Dealers were advised that the laminated safety glass and new glass runs could be installed as a service replacement item. Public demands probably had something to do with this change in policy, because by this time other makes, such as Cadillac, had been offering safety glass as standard equipment on all models. Cadillac introduced all standard safety glass in late 1928 with the 1929 model cars.

The Model 35-B Standard Phaeton is the same four-door, four-passenger open car carried over from 1930. It is equipped with snap-on side curtains and a folding fabric top. The 1931 Standard Phaeton has a folding windshield and nickel-plated outside door handles. An electric windshield wiper on the driver's side was standard equipment.

The car was offered in five basic body color combinations. The body was Thorne Brown, Lombard Blue, Chicle Drab, Kewanee Green, and black with contrasting and complementary belt moldings and stripe. As in 1930, striped wheels were an option.

Interior trim for the 1931 Standard Phaeton was identical to that of the 1930 model. The piped seats were trimmed with black-brown two-tone Cobra cross-grain artificial leather. The door panels, cowl, rear lower quarters, and lock pillars were trimmed in black-brown, two-tone Cobra cross-grain cardboard. The floor was covered with a black spatter-pattern rubber mat front and rear. The folding top was made of black, fine, long-short-grain artificial leather with black bow-drill covering the bows. Matching side curtains were stowed in a compartment under the rear floor. A matching top boot was a dealer option.

The Model 40-B Standard Roadster is a two-door, two-passenger open car with a folding top and side curtains. The 1931 Standard Roadster is identical to the 1930 model. It has nickel-plated outside door handles and a folding, nickel-plated windshield with standard equipment electric windshield wiper on the driver's side only.

Original Ford Model A

Front quarter view of a 1931 180-A Deluxe Phaeton. The body is Washington Blue, while the moldings are Riviera Blue with a Tacoma Cream stripe and wheels. The top is a tan drab rubber interlined fabric. The whitewall tires and stone guard are accessories.

The 1931 Standard Roadster was offered in the same five color combinations as the Standard Phaeton. The interior trim was also the same material as the Phaeton with piped seats in black-brown, two-tone Cobra cross-grain artificial leather. The optional rumble seat compartment was finished in the same material. A black rubber floor mat was used in both the front seat compartment and the rumble seat. The side curtains were of the same material as the folding top and were stowed under the front seat.

The 40-B Deluxe Roadster was offered in much the same configuration as its 1930 counterpart. The body was the same two-door, two-passenger type found on the standard model, but it was upgraded with cowl lights; rumble seat; chrome-plated, lowered windshield frame; and chrome outside left mirror. Fender-mounted spare wheels and rear trunk rack were no longer standard as they were on the 1930 model. Wheels were painted in trim colors at the factory for the first time for the 1931 model. As with most other body types, color combinations were reduced in number for 1931.

The 1931 Deluxe Roadster was offered in four body color schemes. The body was finished in Washington Blue, Stone Brown, Brewster Green, and black with moldings and stripe in complementary and contrasting colors.

Interior trim for the Deluxe Roadster was offered in only one scheme, identical to that used in 1930. The piped seat faces were trimmed in two-tone tan Bedouin-grain genuine leather. The seat sides, seatbacks, belt rail, doors, piped rumble seat, and cowl were finished with two-tone tan Bedouin-grain artificial leather. The floor was covered with brown carpet.

Detail of 180-A Deluxe Phaeton top-left rear quarter. The top frame is chrome steel with natural-finish wood bows. Note the chrome top rest in the rear of the body.

The seat faces of this 1931 180-A Deluxe Phaeton are trimmed in piped two-tone tan Bedouin-grain genuine leather with seat sides, door panels, and cowl in matching artificial leather. The floor is brown carpet.

1931

This 1931 Deluxe Phaeton is finished in Washington Blue. The whitewall tires, running board step plates, and right-side taillight are accessories.

Left front quarter view of a 1931 45-B Standard Coupe shows a body finished in Kewanee Green. This car is easily identified as a 1931 by the upper radiator shell and one-piece running board splash shields.
Kenneth Keeley

The Model 180-A Deluxe Phaeton was a direct carryover from 1930 except for the distinctive 1931 changes to the splash shields and radiator shell. As in 1930, the two-door Deluxe Phaeton was an unusual open model and was offered only with Deluxe colors and trim options.

The 1931 Deluxe Phaeton was offered in a greatly reduced number of body color combinations compared to 1930. There were only five basic color schemes, which included Thorne Brown, Lombard Blue, Chicle Drab, Kewanee Green, and black. The moldings and stripe were finished in contrasting and complementary colors.

The interior trim scheme of the 1931 Deluxe Phaeton was identical to that of the 1930 180-A. The piped seats and seatbacks were trimmed in two-tone tan Bedouin-grain genuine leather. The seat sides, door panels, quarters, and cowl were trimmed with two-tone tan Bedouin-grain artificial leather. The front and rear floors were covered with brown carpet. The folding top was made of tan drab interlined fabric with a tan drab cloth interior. A matching top boot was a dealer option. The side curtains were in matching tan drab material and were stowed in a compartment under the rear floor.

The 45-B Standard Coupe for 1931 was unchanged in its basic design except for incorporating the new radiator shell and splash shield designs. Like most other 1931 models, body color scheme options were reduced in number from 1930. This was a move intended to reduce production costs. The lower body was available in Thorne Brown, Lombard Blue, Chicle Drab, Kewanee Green, and black. The upper body, moldings, reveals, and stripe were offered in contrasting and complementary colors. As with other

Original Ford Model A

1931 closed cars, the reveals were finished in the upper body colors rather than the lower body colors as they were in 1930.

The 1931 Standard Coupe was offered in two interior trim combinations. The first, available upon introduction, was a carryover from the 1930 model and had the piped seat trimmed in gray-checked cloth. The door panels, quarters, seatback, package tray, and header were trimmed in plain gray cloth. The headlining was finished with gray napped cotton, and the cowl was two-tone gray dash-grain cardboard. Windows curtains were gray cloth. The floor was covered with a black rubber mat. This combination was dropped in July 1931 when a new metal seat carriage was introduced on the coupe bodies.

The new metal seat frame was accompanied by a new interior trim scheme with the piped seat trimmed in brown small-checked cloth. The door panels, quarters, header, and package tray were trimmed in plain brown cloth. Window curtains were brown cloth. The floor was trimmed with black rubber mat. All Standard Coupes were available with an optional rumble seat trimmed with piped cushions in black-brown Cobra cross-grain artificial leather.

The 45-B Deluxe Coupe for 1931 was distinguished by its cowl lights, dome light, and special body color schemes and interior trim combinations with buttons and pleats. The body was otherwise identical to that of the Sstandard Coupe. The Deluxe Coupe was available in five body color schemes with the lower body finished in Ford Maroon, Brewster Green, Chicle Drab, Kewanee Green, and black. The upper body, moldings, reveals, and stripe were finished in complementary and contrasting colors. Wheels were optionally finished in the stripe colors.

The 1931 Deluxe Coupe was offered in five interior trim combinations. Upon introduction, the Deluxe Coupe had three interior trim schemes, two of them carried over from 1930. The first had the piped seat trimmed in brown Bedford cord. The door panels, quarters, header, and package tray were trimmed in brown broadcloth. The headlining was brown napped cotton, and the cowl was finished with two-tone brown dash-grain cardboard. Window curtains were brown silk. This combination was dropped in April 1931. The floor on all Deluxe Coupes was covered with brown carpet.

The second introductory interior trim scheme for the 1931 Deluxe Coupe had the piped seat, door panels, quarters, package tray, and header trimmed in brown mohair. The headlining was brown napped cotton and the cowl was trimmed with two-tone brown dash-grain cardboard. The curtains were brown silk with brown braided cord. In July 1931, when the new metal

The front compartment of a 1931 50-B Sport Coupe. The seat is trimmed with brown-checked cloth with door panels in plain brown cloth. Note the short aluminum Ford script name plate on the door sill.

The interior of the top on a 1931 50-B Sport Coupe shows the headlining and bows are covered in brown mock twist cloth. The rear window can be folded up inside the top for ventilation.

Far left: The A-70525-B locking rumble seat lid handle on this 1931 68-B Cabriolet was a special scroll-type handle used only on the 68-B.

Left: Original 1931 Model A keys and key ring as provided when the car was delivered. The keys are displayed on a 1931 black pyramid-patterned rubber running board cover.

seat frames were adopted, the number of pleats changed from 10 to 14.

In April 1931, the brown Bedford-cord trim scheme was replaced with one that had the piped seat in tan-striped broadcloth. The seat carriage door panels, quarters, and header were trimmed in plain tan broadcloth. The wind cord was brown artificial leather. The cowl was two-tone brown dash-grain cardboard, and the window curtain was tan silk. The headlining was tan napped cotton. In July 1931, the new metal seat frame was adopted, but the tan broadcloth trim scheme was retained. The only change in the trim design was in the number of pleats, which went from 10 to 14.

1931

Right: The 1931 stainless steel radiator shell was a new design. The upper insert panel was painted body color, and the Ford script badge was stainless steel with a black background and lettering.

Far right: Detail of right rear top iron and spacer on a 1931 68-B Cabriolet. The spacer is long-grain artificial leather and the irons are stainless. The top is trimmed with tan drab rubber interlined fabric.

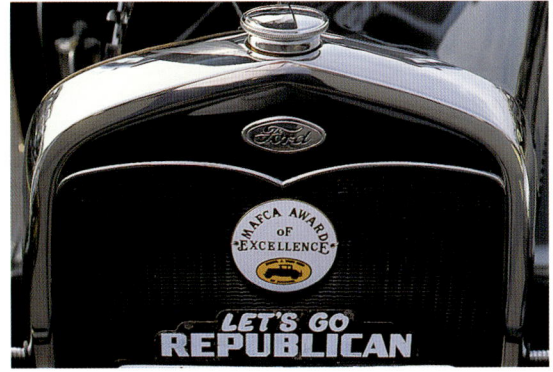

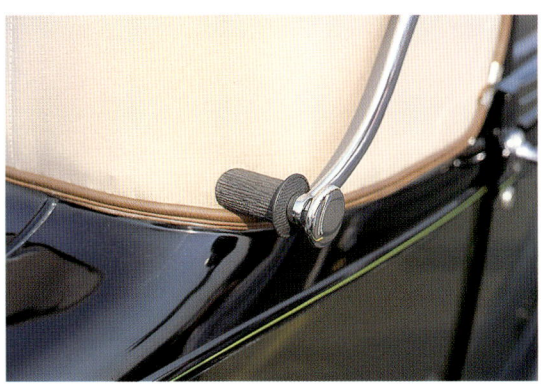

The optional rumble seat compartment on all Deluxe Coupes was trimmed with the same black-brown artificial leather as the 1930 coupes until April 1931, when a new trim scheme was adopted. With this combination, the pleated rumble seat cushions and side panels were trimmed with deep brown crush-grain artificial leather.

In June 1931, a new roll-down rear window was adopted as standard equipment on the Deluxe Coupe. This allowed front seat passengers the opportunity to converse with the rumble seat passengers and also provided for additional interior ventilation. The roll-down rear window was offered as an option on the Standard Coupe at the same time. The window was operated by a T-shaped nickel-plated knob centered just above the package tray below the window.

The 50-B Sport Coupe was essentially a carry-over design from 1930, with only the distinctive 1931 styling features identifying it as a new model. The Sport Coupe body colors are the same as those offered on the Standard Coupe for 1931. The top and exterior trim was also the same two-tone diagonal-grain artificial leather as used on the 1930 Sport Coupe.

The interior trim at the introduction of the 1931 models was still offered in the same gray-check combination used in 1930, but this was dropped in July 1931. The gray-checked interior was replaced with one featuring the piped seat in brown small-checked cloth. The door panels were plain brown cloth and the cowl was trimmed with two-tone brown dash-grain cardboard. The lower quarters and the interior of the top were trimmed with brown mock twist cloth.

At the introduction of the 1931 model year the 68-B Cabriolet was continued as a carryover from the 1930 model. Body color schemes and interior trim were also continued identical to the 1930 model. In March 1931, a new slant-windshield 68-C version of the Cabriolet was introduced. The new slanted windshield offered not only a more modern appearance, but also the angle of the glass helped to reduce the glare from oncoming headlights. The same basic body colors were used on the 68-C Cabriolet, but some of the stripe colors and combinations were changed.

The 68-B Cabriolet continued the same brown Bedford-cord interior trim scheme as the 1930 model but with variations in the number of pleats on the seats. When the 68-C was introduced, three new trim schemes were offered. The first combination had the piped seat in brown Bedford cord, like the earlier design, but the seats now had 14 pleats instead of 10. The door panels and seatback were trimmed with brown broadcloth and the cowl had two-tone brown dash-grain cardboard.

The second trim scheme had the piped seat, door panels, quarters, and seatback in gray drab wool cloth. The cowl was trimmed with two-tone gray dash grain cardboard. In October 1931, a new trim scheme was adopted for the Cabriolet. This

Right: Detail of right door and folding top joint on a 1931 68-B Cabriolet. The body is Brewster Green with black moldings and deck and Apple Green stripe.

Far right: The driver's door interior trim panel on this 1931 68-B Cabriolet is covered in brown broadcloth. The hardware is Butler nickel. Garnish moldings are mahogany woodgrain.

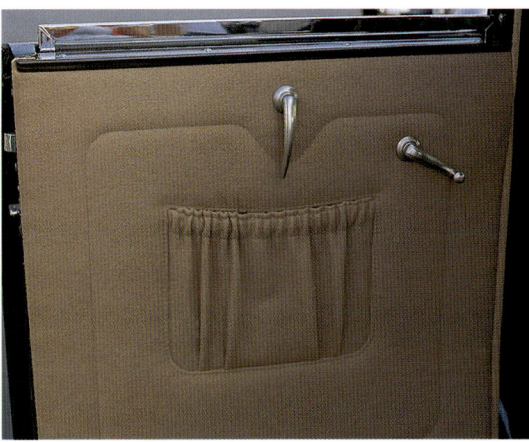

Original Ford Model A

A 1931 68-C slant-windshield Cabriolet. The body is finished in Bronson Yellow with Seal Brown moldings and orange stripe and wheels. The stone guard and quail mascot are accessories.

Far left: The seat of this 1931 68-B Cabriolet is trimmed in brown Bedford cord, while the door panels are brown broadcloth. The floor is covered with brown carpet.

Left: The interior of the top on a 1931 68-C slant-windshield Cabriolet. The lining and package shelf are tan drab cloth.

trim scheme had the piped seat in brown crush grain genuine leather. The door panels, seatback, quarters, and cowl were trimmed with brown crush-grain artificial leather.

All 1931 Cabriolets had brown carpet on the front floor and a black rubber mat in the rumble seat compartment. The piped rumble seat was trimmed with deep brown crush-grain artificial leather. The cushion and back had 11 3-inch pleats.

The most popular model for 1931 was still the 55-B Tudor sedan. The Tudor offered style with comfort and space for families and individual owners. The 55-B body was unchanged for 1931, but body color schemes were reduced to five combinations. The lower body was available in Thorne Brown, Lombard Blue, Chicle Drab, Kewanee Green, and black. The upper body, reveals, moldings, and stripe were finished in contrasting and complementary colors.

Upon introduction, the 1931 standard Tudor was offered in only one interior trim scheme, carried over from 1930. The piped seats were trimmed in gray-checked cloth and the seatbacks, door panels, quarters, and header were trimmed with plain gray cloth. The headlining was gray napped cotton and the window curtains were gray cloth. The cowl and seat bottoms were covered with two-tone gray dash-grain cardboard. Garnish moldings were maroon. This interior combination was dropped in July 1931, when two new interior trim schemes were adopted to replace the gray-checked cloth. One scheme had piped seats in brown small-checked cloth. The door panels,

1931

The 170-B Deluxe Fordor is sometimes known as the "blindback" because of the closed-in steel rear quarters. The body of this 1931 Deluxe is Ford Maroon with black moldings and a vermilion stripe and wheels. The whitewall tires, chrome outside mirror, and trunk are accessories.

Front view of a Ford Maroon 1931 170-B Deluxe Fordor. The frame-mounted toolbox, quail mascot, chrome outside mirror, and whitewall tires are accessories.

The outside door handles on this 1931 170-B Deluxe Fordor are chrome-plated A-61205-CR, rear, and A-61206-CR, front.

quarters, header, and seatbacks were trimmed in plain brown cloth. The curtains were brown cloth and the headlining was brown napped cloth. The seat bottoms and cowl were two-tone brown dash-grain cardboard. Window curtains were brown cloth. Garnish moldings were still painted maroon in all combinations.

The second new interior trim scheme was more unusual and had the piped seats, seatbacks, quarters, headlining, and header finished in deep brown shark-grain artificial leather. The curtains were brown cloth, and the cowl and seat bottoms were finished with two-tone brown dash-grain cardboard.

The 55-B Deluxe Tudor was introduced in June 1931 and added another higher-quality choice for Ford buyers. The Deluxe Tudor shared the Tudor body but was upgraded with a dome light, armrests, carpeting, and deluxe trim combinations and exterior color schemes. The Deluxe Tudor also had cowl lights not found on standard models. All deluxe models also had striping on the inside dash panel area of the fuel tank.

The 1931 Deluxe Tudor was offered in five basic body color schemes. The lower body was finished in Ford Maroon, Brewster Green, Chicle Drab, Kewanee Green, and black. Moldings, upper body, reveals, and the stripe were finished in complementary and contrasting colors. Wheels were optionally available in stripe colors.

The Deluxe Tudor was introduced with three interior trim schemes. The first had the piped seats in brown Bedford cord. The seatbacks, quarters, door panels, and header were in brown broadcloth. The headlining was brown napped cotton, and window curtains were brown silk. The floor, rear seat riser, and lower door panels were trimmed

Original Ford Model A

with brown carpet on all Deluxe Tudors. The cowl and seat bottoms were trimmed with two-tone dash-grain brown cardboard. All Deluxe Tudor garnish moldings were painted with mahogany woodgraining.

The second Deluxe Tudor trim scheme had piped seats, seatbacks, door panels, quarter, and header in green mohair. The headlining was green napped cotton, and window curtains were green silk. The cowl and seat bottoms were trimmed with two-tone green dash-grain cardboard.

The third trim scheme had piped seats, seatbacks, quarters, door panels, and header in brown mohair. The headlining was brown napped cotton and the window curtains were brown silk. The cowl and seat bottoms were trimmed with two-tone brown dash-grain cardboard.

In July 1931, a fourth interior trim scheme was adopted. The piped seats were trimmed with smooth striped tan broadcloth. The door panels, quarters, header, and seatbacks were finished in tan broadcloth. Window curtains were tan silk, and the cowl and seat bottoms were trimmed with two-tone brown dash-grain cardboard. The headlining was brown napped cotton.

At the beginning of 1931, the 155-C (Murray) and 155-D (Briggs) Town Sedans and the 165-C and D Standard Fordors were continued as they were in 1930 without any significant changes other than the identifying 1931 radiator and running board updates. The Standard Fordor and Town Sedan kept the same body color and interior trim schemes until June 1931.

The left front interior door panel on a 1931 170-B Deluxe Fordor is trimmed in brown mohair with mahogany woodgrain garnish moldings and Butler nickel hardware. Note the chrome door pull handle on the door garnish molding.

The front compartment of this 1931 170-B Deluxe Fordor has a brown mohair interior trim scheme. The floor is covered in brown carpet front and rear. Note the deluxe-only stripe on the dash panel.

This 1931 Deluxe Fordor dash panel is body color, while the upper dash rail is finished in mahogany woodgrain. Note the border around the instrument panel ribs. This design was used concurrently with the one without the border.

Left: Close-up view of the rear window, shade, and dome light in a 1931 170-B Deluxe Fordor. The headlining is brown napped cotton.

Far left: Detail of rear passenger compartment of a 1931 Deluxe Fordor. Note the dome light and piped brown mohair trim with brown carpet.

1931

The lower body of this 1931 160-B slant-windshield Town Sedan is Ford Maroon with black moldings and vermilion stripe and wheels. The stone guard, whitewall tires, mirrors, quail mascot, wind wings, and fender-mounted spare tires are accessories.

In July 1931, all Ford four-door sedan bodies were updated to the slanted-windshield design first used on the Victoria. As with the Cabriolet and Victoria, the slanted windshield gave the cars a more modern, streamlined appearance while also reducing glare. The slanted-windshield design also eliminated the visor above the windshield. This change required all new front body pillars, windshield header panel, and front doors on all models. Ford Motor Company specified that the new slant-windshield Fordor bodies would be built to the same design with no visible difference between the Briggs and Murray bodies as there had been.

The 170-B two-window Deluxe Fordor also continued into the 1931 model year identical to the 1930 model with the same interior trim and body color schemes. Phaseout of the two-window Deluxe Fordor began in March 1931 in preparation for the new 160-C slant-windshield Deluxe Fordor. By July 1931, the 165-C and -D Standard Fordors were replaced with the 160-A Standard Fordor. The 155-C and -D Town Sedans were replaced with the 160-B slant-windshield Town Sedan.

The 1931 versions of the Fordors generally had new color schemes available. As with most 1931 models, the number of colors was reduced from 1930. The 160-A slant-windshield Standard Fordor was available in five basic body color schemes. The lower body and reveals were finished in Thorne Brown, Lombard Blue, Chicle Drab, Kewanee Green, and black. The upper body, moldings, and stripe were finished in complementary and contrasting colors. In some cases the reveals were painted upper body color.

The 160-A Standard Fordor was offered in two interior trim schemes. The first had piped seats in brown small-checked cloth. The front seatback, quarters, door panels, and header were trimmed with plain brown cloth. The headlining was brown napped cloth and the curtains were brown cloth. The cowl was trimmed with two-tone crush-grain cardboard. The floor was covered with a black rubber mat.

The second Standard Fordor interior had piped seats, door panels, quarters, headlining, seatback, and header trimmed with deep brown shark-grain artificial leather. Window curtains were brown cloth, and the cowl had two-tone brown crush-grain cardboard. The floor was covered with a black rubber mat.

Original Ford Model A

The 160-B slant-windshield Town Sedan and 160-C two-window Deluxe Fordor were available in five body color combinations. The lower body and reveals were finished in Ford Maroon, Brewster Green, Chicle Drab, Kewanee Green, and black. The moldings, upper body, and stripe were finished in complementary and contrasting colors. Some reveals were painted upper body color.

The new slant-windshield Town Sedan and two-window Deluxe Fordor were initially offered in two interior trim schemes. The first had piped seats, front seatback, quarters, door panels, and header trimmed in brown mohair. The headlining was brown napped cotton and window curtains were brown silk. The cowl was two-tone brown dash-grain cardboard. Floors were covered with brown carpet.

The second interior trim scheme had piped seats in brown Bedford cord. The door panels, quarters, seatback, and header were finished in brown broadcloth. The window curtain was brown silk, and the cowl was two-tone brown dash-grain cardboard. The headlining was brown napped cotton. The floors were covered in brown carpet. This combination was dropped in April 1931, when a new interior trim scheme was adopted to replace the previous brown mohair.

The new scheme had piped seats covered in tan smooth-stripeed broadcloth. The front seat back, quarters, door panels, and header were trimmed in tan broadcloth. The headlining was tan napped cotton and the window curtains were tan silk. The cowl was two-tone brown dash-grain cardboard and floors, and lower door panels were covered with brown carpet.

In June 1931, an additional interior trim scheme was offered for the Town Sedan and Deluxe Fordor. The piped seats, seatback, quarters,

The rear compartment of a 1931 slant-windshield Town Sedan. The seat is piped brown broadcloth with smooth stripes. The quarters and seatback are trimmed in tan broadcloth. The trim welt and wind cord are brown worsted cloth. Note the drop in the carpeted rear floor.

A side view of a 1931 190-A Victoria with steel back. The body is finished in all black with Apple Green stripe and wheels. The whitewall tires, stone guard, Motometer, and turn signals are accessories.

1931

Right: Left front quarter view of a 1931 190-A Victoria finished in Ford Maroon and black with vermilion stripe and wheels. The roof drip rails are special Victoria parts and not used on other body type. The wiper uses a chrome 8½-inch wiper arm and chrome-plated blade.

Below right: The roof of this 1931 190-A leatherback Victoria is covered with two-tone tan diagonal-grain artificial leather. The underlying structure around the rear window is wood and provides support for the fabric roof. The whitewall tires, running board step plates, and right-side taillight are accessories.

Below: The A-161205 right locking outside door handle of the 1931 190-A Victoria was also used on the 68-B Cabriolet and the 400-A Convertible Sedan and 160-B and C Fordor Sedans.

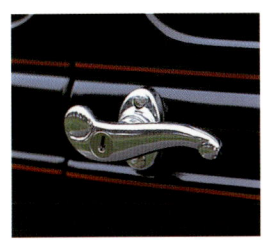

Left rear quarter of a steel-back 1931 190-A Victoria. The sloped area behind the rear seat serves as a small storage compartment. The chrome spare tire cover and whitewall tires are accessories.

headlining, door panels, and header were trimmed with deep brown shark-grain artificial leather. The cowl was two-tone brown dash-grain cardboard, and window curtains were brown silk. The floors and lower door panels were covered with brown carpet.

The 190-A Victoria was carried over almost identical to the late 1930 configuration, but by 1931 the "Coupe" designation had been dropped. The Victoria already had the new design radiator shell as it was actually considered to be a 1931 model. Body color schemes were unchanged from 1930 except for a small change to a Tacoma Cream rather than a Straw stripe in the Chicle Drab color scheme.

Original Ford Model A

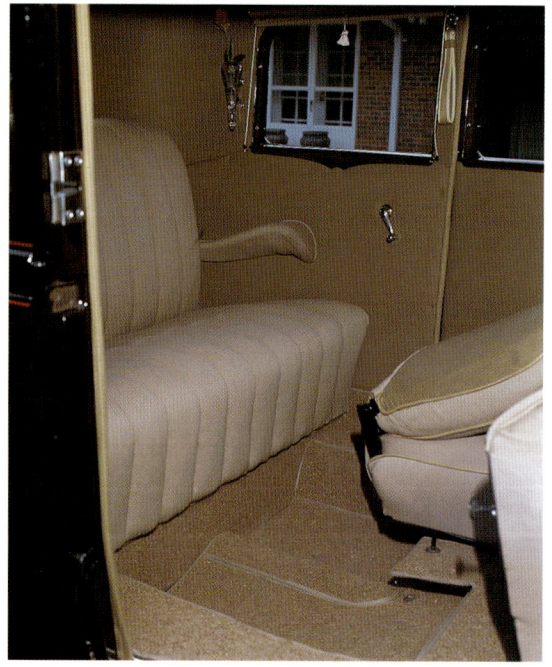

Far left: The door panel of this 1931 Victoria is trimmed with brown broadcloth with brown carpet on the lower portion of the door. Interior hardware is Butler nickel and garnish moldings are mahogany woodgrain.

Left: The front compartment of a 1931 190-A Victoria with brown Bedford cord on the seats and brown broadcloth on the door panels and sidewalls. The floor is covered with brown carpet. Note the rib around the instrument panel and the stripe on the dash panel.

Far left: The folded right front seat of a 1931 Victoria shows the ventilated two-tone brown dash-grain cardboard on the seat bottom. Note the flap covering the back lower portion of the seat. Both Briggs and Murray made Victoria bodies.

Left: The rear passenger compartment of a 1931 Victoria with brown Bedford cord on the seats and brown broadcloth on the quarters and door panels. Note the dropped floor, which only appeared in the Victoria and the 400-A Convertible Sedan.

The Victoria was offered in two interior trim schemes at the beginning of 1931. The first combination had piped seats, seatbacks, door panels, header, and quarters in brown mohair. The headlining was brown napped cotton and curtains were brown silk. The cowl and seat bottoms were trimmed with two-tone brown dash-grain cardboard. Floors and lower door panels were covered with brown carpet.

The second interior trim combination had piped seats in brown Bedford cord. The seatbacks, quarters, door panels, seat sides, and header were in brown broadcloth. The headlining was brown napped cotton and curtains were brown silk. The cowl and seat bottoms were trimmed in two-tone brown dash-grain cardboard. The floor and lower door panels were trimmed in brown carpet. This combination was dropped in April 1931.

The previous trim scheme was replaced in April 1931 with one that had the seats and seat sides in smooth-striped tan broadcloth. The front seatbacks, door panels, header, and quarters were trimmed in plain tan broadcloth. The headlining was tan napped cotton, and curtains were tan silk. Floors and lower door panels were covered with brown carpet.

1931

This 1931 400-A Convertible Sedan has an all-black body with Apple Green stripe and wheels. The original quail mascot on this car is an accessory.

The convertible top is covered with tan drab rubber interlined fabric with deep tan crush-grain artificial-leather binding. The right taillight, right spare tire, and trunk rack are accessories. The full-length rear bumper is standard.

In June 1931, Ford introduced one of the more unusual Model A bodies. The new 400-A Convertible Sedan was an entirely new configuration, not like any body made by any other manufacturer. The basic body design was similar to the Victoria, but the convertible top folded over and was supported by the upper door and window frames. This design gave the sporty open aura of a convertible body combined with the solid body wind and soundproofing of a closed car.

The 400-A Convertible Sedan was available in two levels of body color combinations. The standard list of colors consisted of the upper and

Top: This detail of the left rear of a 400-A Convertible Sedan in tan drab top shows crush-grain artificial-leather binding and a small reinforcement rib. The rear window frame is chrome plated.

Above: The right rear view of a tan drab convertible top on a 1931 400-A Convertible Sedan. The binding is used on the valance and around the edge of top frame. The body color of this car is Aqua Green with gray-green moldings and Tacoma Cream stripe.

Original Ford Model A

lower body in Washington Blue, Brewster Green, Copra Drab, Ford Maroon, black, and Aqua Green. All had complementary and contrasting reveal, molding, and stripe colors. The optional colors were different combinations of three of the standard colors plus Bronson Yellow and Kewanee Green, also with complementary and contrasting reveal, molding, and stripe colors.

The 400-A Convertible Sedan was available in only one Deluxe interior trim scheme. The piped seats, wind cord, and door pockets were trimmed with deep brown crush-grain genuine leather. The door panels, seat backs, seat sides, and cowl panels were in deep brown crush-grain artificial leather. The passenger seat bottom was covered with deep brown crush-grain cardboard. The floors and rear seat riser were trimmed with brown carpet.

The 150-B Station Wagon was a carryover model from 1930, with no significant changes other than the identifying 1931 radiator shell and running board splash shields. As it was from its beginning, the Station Wagon was considered a commercial vehicle but was equipped with the passenger car radiator shell and stainless cowl band. The single standard body color of the Station Wagon was still the exclusive Manila Brown. The wood panels and moldings were finished in clear spar varnish.

The Station Wagon interior consisted of plain-panel seats trimmed in dark two-tone Cobra cross-grain artificial leather. The cowl was covered with dark two-tone Cobra cross-grain cardboard. The side curtains were tan rubber interlined fabric similar to that used on the Deluxe open-car tops.

A variation of the Station Wagon body for 1931 was the 255-A Special Delivery, which was sometimes known as the Natural Wood Special Delivery. It was almost identical to the 150-B Station Wagon, except that the rear side passenger doors were eliminated and the door and quarter window area were replaced with a solid panel of birch plywood. The front doors were equipped with roll-up windows rather than the side curtains of the Station Wagon. The Special Delivery had two side-hinged rear doors for loading. The body was introduced in December 1930 and was built by Baker-Raulang Company of Cleveland, Ohio. Like the Station Wagon, the Special Delivery was finished in Manila Brown and had a passenger car radiator shell, cowl band, and lights. The front seats were also the same as those in the Station Wagon.

The largest addition to the Ford Model A line for 1931 was in the commercial vehicles. Soon after the 1928 introduction of the New Ford, Henry Ford began to turn his attention to the commercial market. Ford realized he was barely scratching the

Above left: Right door interior trim panel on a 1931 400-A Convertible Sedan. The door panel is deep brown crush-grain artificial leather, but the pocket is matching genuine leather like that used on the piped seat faces. Interior hardware is Butler nickel. This is an original interior.

Above: The front compartment and instrument panel of a 1931 400-A Convertible Sedan. The dash panel is body color, while the garnish moldings are walnut woodgrain. Like all Deluxe models, the dash panel is striped.

Left: Rear compartment of a 1931 400-A Convertible Sedan. The piped seat cushions are deep brown crush-grain genuine leather with matching artificial-leather quarters and door panels. The carpet is brown.

1931 Interior Trim Combinations

35-B Standard Phaeton & 40-B Standard Roadster
Trim Scheme Black-brown

Seat, Quarters	Doors, Cowl	Floor	Hardware
Piped, black-brown Cobra cross-grain artificial leather	Black-brown Cobra cross-grain cardboard	Black rubber	Bright nickel

40-B Deluxe Roadster & 180-A Deluxe Phaeton
Trim Scheme Tan

Seat Faces, Wind Cord	Seat Sides, Seat Backs, Doors, Cowl	Floors	Hardware
Piped, two-tone tan Bedouin-grain genuine leather	Two-tone tan Bedouin-grain artificial leather	Brown carpet	Bright nickel (Roadster) Butler nickel (Phaeton)

45-B Standard Coupe (Dropped July 1931)
Trim Scheme Gray check

Seat	Doors, Quarters, Package Tray, Header	Floor	Headlining	Curtain	Cowl	Hardware	Moldings
Piped, gray-checked cloth	Plain gray cloth	Black rubber	Gray napped cotton	Gray cloth	Two-tone gray dash-grain cardboard	Bright nickel	Maroon

45-B Standard Coupe (With metal seat carriage)
Trim Scheme Brown small check

Seat	Doors, Quarters, Package Tray, Header	Floor	Headlining	Curtain	Cowl	Hardware	Moldings
Piped, brown small-checked cloth	Plain brown cloth	Black rubber	Brown napped cotton	Brown cloth	Two-tone brown dash-grain cardboard	Bright nickel	Maroon

45-B Deluxe Coupe (Dropped April 1931)
Trim Scheme Brown Bedford cord

Seat	Doors, Quarters, Package Tray, Header	Floor	Headlining	Curtain	Cowl	Hardware	Moldings
Piped, brown Bedford cord	Brown broadcloth	Brown carpet	Brown napped cotton	Brown silk	Two-tone brown dash-grain cardboard	Butler nickel	Mahogany woodgrain

45-B Deluxe Coupe (10 pipes Dropped July 1931, 14 pipes adopted July 1931)
Trim Scheme Brown mohair

Seat, Doors, Quarters, Header, Package Tray	Floor	Headlining	Curtain	Cowl	Hardware	Moldings
Piped, brown mohair	Brown carpet	Brown napped cotton	Brown silk	Two-tone brown dash-grain-cardboard	Butler nickel	Mahogany woodgrain

45-B Deluxe Coupe (Dropped July 1931)
Trim Scheme Tan broadcloth

Seat	Doors, Quarters, Header	Floor	Headlining	Curtain	Cowl	Hardware	Moldings
Piped, tan broadcloth with smooth stripes	Tan broadcloth	Brown carpet	Brown napped cotton	Brown silk	Two-tone brown dash-grain cardboard	Butler nickel	Mahogany woodgrain

50-B Sport Coupe (Dropped July 1931)
Trim Scheme Gray check

Seat	Doors	Floor	Quarters, Top Quarters	Top Inside	Cowl	Hardware	Moldings
Piped, gray-checked cloth	Plain gray cloth	Black rubber	Gray mock twist	Gray mock twist	Two-tone gray dash-grain cardboard	Bright nickel	Maroon

50-B Sport Coupe (Adopted July 1931)
Trim Scheme Brown small check

Seat	Doors	Floor	Lower Quarters, Top Quarters	Top Inside	Cowl	Hardware	Moldings
Piped, small cloth brown-checked	Plain brown cloth	Black rubber	Brown mock twist	Brown mock twist	Two-tone brown dash-grain cardboard	Bright nickel	Maroon

50-B Sport Coupe
Trim Scheme Black-brown

Seat	Doors	Floor	Lower Quarters, Top Quarters, Top Inside	Cowl	Hardware	Moldings
Piped, black-brown Cobra cross-grain artificial leather	Plain gray cloth	Black rubber	Gray mock twist	Two-tone gray dash-grain cardboard	Bright nickel	Maroon

68-B Cabriolet
Trim Scheme Brown Bedford cord

Seat	Doors, Quarters, Seat Back	Floor	Top Inside	Cowl	Hardware	Moldings
Piped, brown Bedford cord	Brown broad cloth	Brown carpet	Gray drab cloth	Two-tone brown dash-grain cardboard	Bright nickel	Mahogany woodgrain

68-C Cabriolet
Trim Scheme Brown Bedford cord

Seat	Doors, Quarters, Seat Back	Floor	Top Inside	Cowl	Hardware	Moldings
Piped, brown Bedford cord	Brown broad cloth	Brown carpet	Tan drab cloth	Two-tone brown dash-grain cardboard	Bright nickel	Mahogany woodgrain

68-C Cabriolet (Available October 1931)
Trim Scheme Brown leather

Seat	Doors, Quarters, Seat Back, Cowl	Floor	Hardware	Moldings
Piped, brown crush-grain genuine leather	Brown crush-grain artificial leather	Brown carpet	Bright nickel	Mahogany woodgrain

Original Ford Model A

1931 INTERIOR TRIM COMBINATIONS (CONTINUED)

68-C Cabriolet
TRIM SCHEME Gray drab

SEAT, DOORS, QUARTERS,	PACKAGE TRAY, INSIDE TOPSEAT BACK	FLOOR			COWL	HARDWARE	MOLDINGS
Piped, gray drab wool cloth	Tan drab cloth	Brown carpet			Two-tone gray dash-grain cardboard	Bright nickel	Mahogany woodgrain

55-B Tudor (Dropped July 1931)
TRIM SCHEME Gray check

SEATS	SEAT BACKS, DOORS, QUARTERS	FLOORS	HEADLINING	CURTAIN	COWL	HARDWARE	MOLDINGS
Piped, gray-checked cloth	Plain gray cloth	Black rubber	Gray napped cotton	Gray cloth	Two-tone gray dash-grain cardboard	Bright nickel	Maroon

55-B Tudor (Adopted July 1931)
TRIM SCHEME Brown artificial leather

SEATS, SEAT BACKS, DOORS, QUARTERS, HEADLINING		FLOORS		CURTAIN		HARDWARE	MOLDINGS
Piped, deep brown shark-grain artificial leather		Black rubber		Brown cloth		Bright nickel	Maroon

55-B Tudor (Adopted July 1931)
TRIM SCHEME Brown small check

SEATS	SEAT BACK, DOORS, QUARTERS, HEADER	FLOORS	HEADLINING	CURTAIN	COWL	HARDWARE	MOLDINGS
Piped, brown small-checked cloth	Plain brown cloth	Black rubber	Brown napped cotton	Brown cloth	Two-tone brown dash-grain cardboard	Bright nickel	Maroon

55-B Deluxe Tudor (Adopted July 1931)
TRIM SCHEME Tan broadcloth

SEATS, SEAT SIDES	SEAT BACKS, DOORS, QUARTERS, HEADER	FLOORS	HEADLINING	CURTAIN	COWL	HARDWARE	MOLDINGS
Piped, tan broadcloth with smooth stripes	Tan broadcloth	Brown carpet	Tan napped cotton	Tan silk	Two-tone brown dash-grain cardboard	Butler nickel	Mahogany woodgrain

55-B Deluxe Tudor
TRIM SCHEME Brown Bedford cord

SEATS	DOORS, SEAT BACKS, QUARTERS, HEADER	FLOORS	HEADLINING	CURTAIN	COWL	HARDWARE	MOLDINGS
Piped, brown Bedford cord	Brown broadcloth	Brown carpet	Brown napped cotton	Brown silk	Two-tone brown dash-grain cardboard	Butler nickel	Mahogany woodgrain

55-B Deluxe Tudor
TRIM SCHEME Green mohair

SEATS, SEAT BACKS, DOORS, QUARTERS, HEADER		FLOORS	HEADLINING	CURTAIN	COWL	HARDWARE	MOLDINGS
Piped, green mohair		Brown carpet	Green napped cotton	Green silk	Two-tone green dash-grain cardboard	Butler nickel	Mahogany woodgrain

55-B Deluxe Tudor
TRIM SCHEME Brown mohair

SEATS, SEAT BACKS, DOORS, QUARTERS, HEADER		FLOORS	HEADLINING	CURTAIN	COWL	HARDWARE	MOLDINGS
Piped, brown mohair		Brown carpet	Brown napped cotton	Brown silk	Two-tone brown dash-grain cardboard	Butler nickel	Mahogany woodgrain

165-C, -D Fordor (Dropped July 1931)
TRIM SCHEME Gray check

SEATS	SEAT BACK, DOORS, QUARTERS, HEADER	FLOORS	HEADLINING	CURTAINS	COWL	HARDWARE	MOLDING
Piped, gray-checked cloth	Plain gray cloth	Black rubber	Gray napped cotton	Gray cloth	Two-tone gray dash-grain cardboard	Butler nickel	Maroon

160-A Standard Fordor, SW
TRIM SCHEME Brown small check

SEATS	SEAT BACK, DOORS, QUARTERS, HEADER	FLOORS	HEADLINING	CURTAINS	COWL	HARDWARE	MOLDINGS
Piped, brown small-checked cloth	Plain brown cloth	Black rubber	Brown napped cotton	Brown cloth	Two-tone brown dash-grain cardboard	Butler nickel	Maroon

160-A Standard Fordor, SW (Adopted June 1931)
TRIM SCHEME Brown artificial leather

SEATS, DOORS, QUARTERS, SEAT BACK, HEADER		FLOORS	HEADLINING	CURTAINS	COWL	HARDWARE	MOLDINGS
Piped, deep brown shark-grain artificial leather		Black rubber	Deep brown shark-grain artificial leather	Brown cloth	Two-tone brown dash-grain cardboard	Butler nickel	Maroon

170-B Deluxe Fordor, Two-Windows
TRIM SCHEME Brown mohair

SEATS, DOORS, QUARTERS, SEAT BACK		FLOORS	HEADLINING	CURTAINS	COWL	HARDWARE	MOLDINGS
Piped, brown mohair cotton		Brown carpet	Brown napped cotton	Brown silk	Two-tone brown dash-grain cardboard	Butler nickel	Mahogany woodgrain

170-B Deluxe Fordor, Two-Windows
TRIM SCHEME Brown Bedford cord

SEATS	DOORS, QUARTERS, SEAT BACK	FLOORS	HEADLINING	CURTAINS	COWL	HARDWARE	MOLDINGS
Piped, brown Bedford cord	Brown broadcloth	Brown carpet	Brown napped cotton	Brown silk	Two-tone brown dash-grain cardboard	Butler nickel	Mahogany woodgrain

155-C, -D Town Sedan
TRIM SCHEME Brown mohair

SEATS, SEAT BACK, QUARTERS, DOORS, HEADER		FLOORS	HEADLINING	CURTAINS	COWL	HARDWARE	MOLDINGS
Piped, brown mohair		Brown carpet	Brown napped cotton	Brown silk	Two-tone brown dash-grain cardboard	Butler nickel	Mahogany woodgrain

1931 INTERIOR TRIM COMBINATIONS (CONTINUED)

155-C, -D Town Sedan
TRIM SCHEME Green mohair

SEATS, QUARTERS, SEAT BACKS, DOORS, HEADER	FLOORS	HEADLINING	CURTAINS	COWL	HARDWARE	MOLDINGS
Piped, green mohair	Brown carpet	Green napped cotton	Green silk	Two-tone green dash-grain cardboard	Butler nickel	Mahogany wood grain

155-C, -D Town Sedan
TRIM SCHEME Brown Bedford cord

SEATS	DOORS, QUARTERS, BACK, HEADER	FLOORS	HEADLINING		COWL	HARDWARE	MOLDINGS
Piped, brown Bedford cord	Brown broadcloth	Brown carpet	Brown napped cotton		Two-tone brown dash-grain cardboard	Butler nickel	Mahogany woodgrain

160-B, -C Town Sedan & Deluxe Fordor, SW, Two-Widows
TRIM SCHEME Brown mohair

SEATS, SEAT BACK, QUARTERS, DOORS	FLOORS	HEADLINING	CURTAIN	COWL	HARDWARE	MOLDINGS
Piped, brown mohair	Brown carpet	Brown napped cotton	Brown silk	Two-tone brown dash-grain cardboard	Butler nickel	Mahogany woodgrain

160-B, -C Town Sedan & Deluxe Fordor, SW, Two-Windows (Dropped April 1931)
TRIM SCHEME Brown Bedford cord

SEATS	DOORS, QUARTERS, BACK, HEADER	FLOORS	HEADLINING	CURTAINS	COWL	HARDWARE	MOLDINGS
Piped, brown Bedford cord	Brown broadcloth	Brown carpet	Brown napped cotton	Brown silk	Two-tone brown dash-grain cardboard	Butler nickel	Mahogany woodgrain

160-C, -D Town Sedan & Deluxe Fordor, SW, Two-Windows (Adopted April 1931)
TRIM SCHEME Tan broadcloth

SEATS	DOORS, SEAT BACK, QUARTERS	FLOORS	HEADLINING	CURTAINS	COWL	HARDWARE	MOLDINGS
Tan broadcloth with smooth stripes	Tan broadcloth	Brown carpet	Tan napped cotton	Tan silk	Two-tone brown dash-grain cardboard	Butler nickel	Mahogany woodgrain

160-C, -D Town Sedan & Deluxe Fordor, SW, Two-Windows (Adopted June 1931)
TRIM SCHEME Brown artificial leather

SEATS, SEAT BACK, QUARTERS, DOORS HEADLINING, HEADER, SIDES	FLOORS		CURTAINS	COWL	HARDWARE	MOLDINGS
Deep brown shark-grain artificial leather	Brown carpet		Brown silk	Two-tone brown cardboard	Butler nickel	Mahogany woodgrain

190-A Victoria
TRIM SCHEME Brown mohair

SEATS, SEAT BACKS, QUARTERS, DOORS PILLARS, SIDES	FLOORS	HEADLINING	CURTAINS	COWL	HARDWARE	MOLDINGS
Brown mohair	Brown carpet	Brown napped cotton	Brown silk	Two-tone brown dash-grain cardboard	Butler nickel	Mahogany woodgrain

190-A Victoria (Dropped April 1931)
TRIM SCHEME Brown Bedford cord

SEATS	DOORS, SEAT BACKS, QUARTERS	FLOORS	HEADLINING	CURTAINS	COWL	HARDWARE	MOLDINGS
Brown Bedford cord	Brown broadcloth	Brown carpet	Brown napped cotton	Brown silk	Two-tone brown dash-grain cardboard	Butler nickel	Mahogany woodgrain

190-A Victoria (Adopted April 1931)
TRIM SCHEME Tan broadcloth

SEATS, SEAT SIDES	DOORS, QUARTERS, SEAT BACKS	FLOORS	HEADLINING	CURTAINS	COWL	HARDWARE	MOLDINGS
Tan broadcloth with smooth stripes	Tan broadcloth	Brown carpet	Brown napped cotton	Brown silk	Two-tone brown dash-grain cardboard	Butler nickel	Mahogany woodgrain

400-A Convertible Sedan
TRIM SCHEME Brown leather

SEATS, DOOR POCKETS	DOORS, QUARTERS, COWL	FLOORS	WOOD BOWS	PASSENGER SEAT BOTTOM	HARDWARE	MOLDINGS
Deep brown crush-grain genuine leather	Deep brown crush-artificial leather	Brown carpet	Tan drab bow drill	Deep brown crush-grain cardboard	Butler nickel	Mahogany woodgrain

76-B Open Cab Commercial
TRIM SCHEME Black-brown

SEAT	DOORS, COWL, LOCK PILLARS,	FLOORS			HARDWARE	
Black-brown Cobra cross-grain artificial leather	Black-brown two tone Cobra cross-grain cardboard	Black rubber			Bright nickel	

79-B, 85-B, Panel Delivery
TRIM SCHEME Black-brown

SEATS, WIND CORD	DOORS, COWL, HEADER	FLOORS			HARDWARE	MOLDINGS
Black-brown, two-tone Cobracross-grain artificial leather	Black-brown, two-tone Cobra cross-grain cardboard	Black rubber			Bright nickel	Black

82-B Closed Cab Commercial
TRIM SCHEME Black-brown

SEATS	DOORS, COWL, PILLARS	FLOORS			HARDWARE	MOLDINGS
Black-brown, two-tone Cobra cross-grain artificial leather	Black-brown, two-tone Cobra cross-grain cardboard	Black rubber			Bright nickel	Black

130-B Deluxe Delivery
TRIM SCHEME Black-brown

SEATS, HEADLINING, WIND CORD	DOORS, COWL, HEADER REAR DOOR	FLOORS			HARDWARE	MOLDINGS
Black-brown, two-tone Cobra cross-grain artificial leather	Black-brown, two-tone Cobra cross-grain cardboard	Black rubber			Bright nickel	Black

1931 BODY COLOR SCHEMES

35-B Standard Phaeton & 40-B Standard Roadster

Body	Belt, Quarter & Sill Molding	Stripe
Thorne Brown	Thorne Brown	Straw (Tacoma Cream after July 1931)
Lombard Blue	Lombard Blue	Hessian Blue (Tacoma Cream after July 1931)
Chicle Drab	Copra Drab	Straw (Tacoma Cream after July 1931)
Kewanee Green	Elkpoint Green	Apple Green
Black	Black	Apple Green

40-B Deluxe Roadster & 180-A Deluxe Phaeton

Body	Belt, Quarter & Sill Molding	Stripe
Washington Blue	Riviera Blue	Tacoma Cream
Stone Brown	Stone Gray, Deep	Tacoma Cream
Brewster Green	Black	Apple Green
Black	Black	Apple Green

45-B Standard Coupe, 50-B & 50-B Sport Coupe

Lower body	Upper body, belt, quarter, sill molding & reveals	Stripe
Thorne Brown	Thorne Brown	Straw (Tacoma Cream after July 1931)
Lombard Blue	Black	Hessian Blue (Tacoma Cream after July 1931)
Chicle Drab	Copra Drab	Straw (Tacoma Cream after July 1931)
Kewanee Green	Elkpoint Green	Apple Green
Black	Black	Apple Green

45-B Deluxe Coupe

Lower body	Upper body, belt, quarter, sill molding & reveals	Stripe
Ford Maroon	Black	Vermilion
Brewster Green	Black	Apple Green
Chicle Drab	Copra Drab	Straw (Tacoma Cream after July 1931)
Kewanee Green	Elkpoint Green	Apple Green
Black	Black	Apple Green

68-B, -C Cabriolet

Lower body	Upper body, deck, belt, quarter & sill molding	Reveals	Stripe
Brewster Green	Black	Brewster Green	Apple Green
Bronson Yellow	Seal Brown	Bronson Yellow	Orange (Vermilion after July 1931)
Kewanee Green	Elkpoint Green	Kewanee Green	Apple Green
Moleskin Brown, Light	Moleskin Brown, Light	Moleskin Brown, Light	French Gray (Tacoma Cream after July 1931)
Lombard Blue	Lombard Blue	Lombard Blue	Hessian Blue (Tacoma Cream after July 1931)
Black	Black	Black	Apple Green
Ford Maroon	Ford Maroon	Black	Vermilion (Available after July 1931)

55-B Standard Tudor

Lower body	Upper body, belt, quarter, sill moldings & reveals	Stripe
Thorne Brown	Thorne Brown	Straw (Tacoma Cream after July 1931)
Lombard Blue	Black	Hessian Blue (Tacoma Cream after 1931)
Chicle Drab	Copra Drab	Straw (Tacoma Cream after 1931)
Kewanee Green	Elkpoint Green	Apple Green
Black	Black	Apple Green

55-B Deluxe Tudor

Lower body	Upper body, belt, quarter, sill moldings & reveals	Stripe
Ford Maroon	Black	Vermilion
Brewster Green	Black	Apple Green
Chicle Drab	Copra Drab	Straw (Tacoma Cream after July 1931)
Kewanee Green	Elkpoint Green	Apple Green
Black	Black	Apple Green

165-C, -D & 160-A Standard Fordor and SW Standard Fordor

Lower body & reveals	Upper body, belt, quarter & sill moldings	Stripe
Thorne Brown	Thorne Brown	Straw (Tacoma Cream after July 1931)
Lombard Blue	Black	Hessian Blue (Tacoma Cream after July 1931)
Chicle Drab	Copra Drab	Straw (Tacoma Cream after July 1931)
Kewanee Green	Elkpoint Green	Apple Green
Black	Black	Apple Green

(Some reveals are upper body color)

170-B Two-Windows Deluxe Fordor & SW Deluxe Fordor & 160-B, -C Town Sedan'

Lower body & reveals	Upper body, belt, quarter & sill moldings	Stripe
Ford Maroon	Black	Vermilion
Brewster Green	Black	Apple Green
Chicle Drab	Copra Drab	Straw (Tacoma Cream after July 1931)
Kewanee Green	Elkpoint Green	Apple Green
Black	Black	Apple Green

(Some reveals are upper body color)

190-A Victoria

Lower body & reveals	Upper body, belt, quarter & sill moldings	Stripe
Brewster Green	Black	Apple Green
Ford Maroon	Black (Sills Ford Maroon)	Vermilion
Kewanee Green	Elkpoint Green (Reveals Elkpoint Green)	Apple Green
Chicle Drab	Copra Drab	Straw (Tacoma Cream after July 1931)
Black	Black	Apple Green

400-A Convertible Sedan
(Standard combinations)

Upper & Lower body	Belt & sill molding	Reveals	Stripe
Washington Blue	Washington Blue	Riviera Blue	Tacoma Cream
Brewster Green	Brewster Green	Black	Apple Green
Copra Drab	Copra Drab	Chicle Drab	Straw (Tacoma Cream after July 1931)
Ford Maroon	Ford Maroon	Tampa Red	Vermilion (July 1931)
Black	Black	Black	Apple Green
Aqua Green	Gray Green	Gray Green	Tacoma Cream

Optional combinations

Upper & Lower body	Belt & sill molding	Reveals	Stripe
Brewster Green	Black	Black	Apple Green
Ford Maroon	Black	Black	Vermilion
Copra Drab	Chicle Drab	Chicle Drab	Straw (Tacoma Cream after July 1931)
Bronson Yellow	Seal Brown	Bronson Yellow	Orange (Vermilion stripe after July 1931, upper body Seal Brown)
Kewanee Green	Elkpoint Green	Elkpoint Green	Apple Green (Sill molding Kewanee Green)

130-B Deluxe Delivery

Lower body	Upper body & reveals	Belt & sill molding	Stripe
Black	Black	Black	Apple Green
Lombard Blue	Lombard Blue	Black	Hessian Blue
Kewanee Green	Elkpoint Green	Elkpoint Green	Apple Green
Chicle Drab	Copra Drab	Copra Drab	Straw (Tacoma Cream after July 1931)
Thorne Brown	Thorne Brown	Thorne Brown	Straw (Tacoma Cream after July 1931)

1931

1931 Body Color Schemes (continued)

Open Cab, Closed Cab, AA Deluxe Delivery, A & AA Panel Delivery, Deluxe Pickup & Service Car

Body

Rose Beige	Black	Blue Rock Green
Phoenix Brown	Lombard Blue	Rock Moss Green
Thorne Brown	Niagara Blue, Light	Balsam Green
Copra Drab	Niagara Blue, Dark	Vagabond Green
Chicle Drab	Gunmetal Blue	Valley Green
Dawn Gray, Light	Chelsea Blue	Highland Green
Bonnie Gray	Duchess Blue	Kewanee Green
Rubellite Red	Arabian Sand, Light	Elkpoint Green
Vermilion	Commercial Drab	L'anse Green, Dark
Menelas Orange	Pembroke Gray	Lawn Green
Yukon Yellow	Pegex Orange	Cherokee Gray (Deluxe Pickup until July 1931)
Arabian Sand, Dark	Medium Cream	Seagull Gray (Available July 1931)
Dawn Gray, Dark	Cigarette Cream	White (Standard on Deluxe Pickup only)

Note:
 There were no special trim colors as all body colors could be used in any combination.

295-A Town Car Delivery

Body, Belt & Sill Molding	Stripe
Washington Blue	Tacoma Cream
Riviera Blue	Tacoma Cream
Stone Brown	French Gray (Tacoma Cream after July 1931)
Stone Gray, Deep	French Gray (Tacoma Cream after July 1931)
Seal Brown	Orange (Vermilion after July 1931)
Moleskin Brown, Light	French Gray (Tacoma Cream after July 1931)
Bronson Yellow	Orange
Kewanee Green	Apple Green
Elkpoint Green	Apple Green
Brewster Green	Apple Green
Black	Apple Green
Ford Maroon	Vermilion
Ford Maroon, Medium	Vermilion
Chicle Drab	Straw (Tacoma Cream after July 1931)
Copra Drab	Straw (Tacoma Cream after July 1931)
Lombard Blue	Hessian Blue

Note:
 Basic colors could have been used in any combination of one to three colors.

---

the radiator shell nameplate. At the introduction of the 1931 passenger car radiator shell, the radiator nameplate was changed to a stamped stainless steel design with black lettering in the recesses. There is undocumented evidence that the blue vitreous badge was continued on the AA black and Deluxe stainless shell through March 1931.

Although most other Model A options were reduced for 1931, the number of colors available for the commercial line was increased significantly. There were 39 colors available for 1931, and they included all previous commercial and passenger car standard colors and an additional group of special commercial colors only available that year. All of these colors were available on all A and AA body types in any combination. The only change was Seagull Gray, which replaced Cherokee Gray on the Deluxe Pickup in July 1931, and white, which was standard only on the Deluxe Pickup. There were some special combinations available on certain models and these will be discussed in those model descriptions.

The interior trim schemes available for 1931 were also standardized. Most commercial interiors used the black-brown, two-tone Cobra cross-grain artificial leather on plain-panel seats. The only variation was the 85-B Panel Delivery, which continued to use the blue-gray colonial-grain material introduced in 1929. This trim scheme was dropped in February 1931 and was replaced with the black-brown colonial-grain material.

In June 1931, it was announced that passenger cars and commercial vehicles could be ordered in any combination of any present or previous standard color at no extra charge. Other colors, lettering, and painted chassis and fenders were available at extra charge to commercial buyers. The Deluxe colors were still retained for use only on deluxe models unless the commercial buyer had already standardized that color for his business.

The 76-B Open Cab Pickup was basically unchanged from 1930. Other than the increased body color availability and the change in the 1931 identifying features, there were no differences. The Open Cab Pickup still had a nonremovable folding top made of black, fine, long-short-grain artificial leather with matching side curtains.

A significant change was made to both the Open Cab and Closed Cab Pickups in May 1931 when a new Briggs-designed 78-B pickup body (bed) was adopted. This new body had square, straight sides and a full 16-gauge steel floor. It was 59.4 inches long, 46 inches wide, and 16.7 inches high. The new body had a cargo capacity of 22.2 cubic feet, compared to only 16.5 cubic feet in the previous truck body. The new body required the use of narrower A-16168 (RH) and A-16169 (LH) rear fenders and A-16182 bracket. These fenders and bracket were only used on this model.

---

surface of the commercial market with merely 10 percent of the business. Less than 12 percent of the truck chassis left the factory with bodies, leaving the rest to be equipped by outside vendors. This was revenue and profit lost to Ford so the development of new commercial bodies progressed throughout Model A production. By 1931, this increased development had reached its peak.

Another reason Ford increased concentration on the commercial line was that it was feeling the effects of the deepening Depression more strongly on the passenger cars; therefore, strengthening commercial sales was crucial to company profits. The result of this important change in direction was the introduction of 20 new commercial models for 1931. By the end of Model A and AA production, there was virtually a Ford for every purpose to satisfy the desires of any buyer.

Because the commercial vehicles did not use the passenger car radiator shell, the easiest way to tell a 1930 Model A commercial vehicle from a 1931 was the change from the two-piece to the one-piece running board splash shield. Another clue would be

Original Ford Model A

A new 65-A canopy top assembly was made available as an option in March 1931. The canopy extended 46 inches above the floor of the body and was covered with a black, fine, long-short-grain artificial-leather top and side curtains. The design was altered in May to correspond with the introduction of the new wide bed. The canopy top unit was designed to allow large cargo to be carried in the pickup bed but protected from the elements.

The 82-B Closed Cab Pickup was also unchanged at the beginning of 1931 production. The same color schemes and trim materials were available as in all other 1931 commercial vehicles. An important improvement to the closed-cab design came in August 1931 when an all-steel Budd-built 82-B cab was introduced. This was the first all-steel body for any American vehicle and the design replaced the roof ribs and side rails with pressed channel steel.

The old-design black fabric roof covering was replaced with a sheet of steel that included the front visor and was painted body color. One of the reasons this type of roof was not used sooner was the fear that the all-steel construction would create more heat inside the cab and also cause an increase in interior noise. The steel roof had no black-duck interior headlining so only the stamped steel channel cross-rails were visible inside the cab.

The interior of the 82-B cab remained identical to that of the late 1930 model with black-brown colonial-grain artificial leather and matching cardboard door and header panels. The interior of the 82-B cab was generally finished in the same color as the outside of the body. In May 1931, a new shorter A-84330 seatback assembly was adopted as a service item to provide more legroom in the closed truck cab. This new assembly was to be used on any 82-B cab, whether it was for the A or AA chassis.

In August 1931, a new back window screen assembly was made available for the 82-B cab. This unit protected the window from breakage by items that might be thrown around in the back of the truck. The part number for the screen was A-83860 and the installation included accompanying special bolts, nuts, and washers. The window screen was sold and installed through dealer service.

On May 1, 1931, Ford introduced the distinctive 66-A Deluxe Pickup. Its design was based on the 229-A Service Car body offered on the AA chassis. The Service Car was introduced in late 1930 and will be described in the AA section. The Deluxe Pickup was based on the standard 82-B closed cab, but a special rear section extended the lines and molding of the cab and gave a more integrated appearance to the unit. The Deluxe Pickup body was equipped with a tailgate and chrome-plated bed rails.

Left: The late 1931 82-B all-steel closed-cab body has seats trimmed in black-brown Cobra cross-grain artificial leather. Garnish moldings are painted black, and the floor is covered with a black rubber mat.

Above: This is the inside of the roof of a late 1931 82-B closed cab with a Budd all-steel body. The Budd body replaced earlier wood ribs with stamped steel channels. The inside of the roof is painted body color. The interior trim is still black-brown two-tone Cobra cross-grain artificial leather and cardboard.

The Deluxe Pickup was originally intended as a promotional vehicle for General Electric, but its styling soon made it desirable to other businesses. Unlike other pickups, the 66-A was equipped with a stainless cowl band and cowl lights plus a passenger car radiator shell, taillights, and headlights. The Deluxe Pickup also had a fender-mounted spare tire as standard equipment. The running boards were still made of standard commercial steel.

The Deluxe Pickup was the only Model A available with white as a standard color. The original prototype for the 66-A appeared at a General Electric dealer show in St. Louis, Missouri, in March 1931 and was used to publicize the company's new refrigerator. The one-off prototype truck had a slant windshield and genuine leather interior trim.

The 79-B Panel Delivery was carried over unchanged for 1931, but new for 1931 was the 225-A Drop-Floor Panel Delivery. The Murray-built Drop-Floor body was based on the 79-B but added a lower section to the rear floor below the standard inside deck. When the rear doors were opened, the drop-floor design provided additional storage space and an area in which to stand while unloading. The lowered rear section also provided a higher space for dry cleaners to hang garments.

The 1931 Panel Delivery and Drop-Floor variation were the only commercial models to continue the 1929-style blue-gray interior trim scheme. The reason for this was probably that

1931

Right: This 1931 66-A Deluxe Pickup has special side panels that attach to the rear sides of a standard 82-B cab. The 66-A uses the standard passenger car radiator and headlight shells rather than the black-painted parts on the standard truck.

Below: This rear view of a 66-A Deluxe Pickup shows the flat rear tailgate with chrome-plated fittings. The color is Rubellite Red, a 1931 commercial color. The whitewall tires and right-side taillight are accessories.

Bottom: A right front quarter view of a 1931 66-A Deluxe Pickup finished in Lombard Blue with Hessian Blue wheels and stripe.

Ford had ordered more of this material than necessary and it was used until depleted. The newer-style black-brown, colonial-grain interior trim material was adopted, and the blue-gray material was finally dropped in February 1931.

Like the Panel Delivery, the 130-B Deluxe Delivery was carried over from 1930 with no significant changes. The Deluxe Delivery was also offered with a floor variation. The design of the Deluxe Delivery Drop-Floor was executed in much the same way as the Panel Delivery version. The vehicle was directed at the same type of market as the Panel Delivery but with a bit more styling. The Deluxe Delivery had a lower body than the Panel Delivery and was equipped with the same stainless radiator shell, cowl band, and lights as the passenger cars.

Although there was no Town Car in 1931, Ford introduced an unusual variation on the theme in the 295-A Town Car Delivery. The Town Car Delivery was actually introduced in July 1930 as a Briggs-designed straight-windshield version, but only three were built. The 1931 Town Car Delivery was intended for high-visibility businesses such as florist or jewelry shops. It had a slanted windshield and a custom-built aluminum rear body section. The body had solid, rounded quarters with a single rear door for access. Left and right side-mounted spare wheels and tires and also a one-piece rear bumper were standard equipment on the 295-A.

Original Ford Model A

This 1931 76-B Open Cab Pickup has a removable top, but it does not fold. The body color is Duchess Blue with Straw stripe and wheels.

This 76-B Open Cab Pickup is equipped with the early-design 78-A narrow bed. Trucks were not supplied with rear bumpers as standard equipment. The stripe-colored wheels were an option in 1931.

The 295-A was equipped with special floodlights on each side just behind the driver's compartment. These sidelights were intended to light the owner's name printed on the side of the body. The driver's compartment was separated from the cargo area with a sliding division equipped with a ventilator. The driver's compartment of the Town Car Delivery was covered with an artificial-leather canopy that snapped into place at the front edge of the top and the top of the windshield. The doors of the Town Car Delivery were distinctive A-295760 (RH) and A-295761 (LH), which were not used on any other production Model A body. It is believed that these doors were used on the prototype slant-windshield Deluxe Pickup body shown in March 1931.

The interior trim of the Town Car Delivery was of a much higher quality than most other commercial vehicles. The seats were trimmed with black long-grain genuine leather. The front floor was covered with a black rubber mat. The interior of the package compartment was covered with fine-quality birch plywood. There were two dome lights, one in the driver's compartment and the other in the rear cargo area. They were operated by a switch in the lock pillar.

AA Truck Chassis

Ford made several changes to the AA chassis in 1931. The first change was to prepunch the holes for the fender well–mounted spare wheel equipment in the 131.5-inch wheelbase frame. On the 157-inch wheelbase chassis, the holes were not punched, but their location was marked on the frame to expedite drilling by service personnel.

Close-up view of the removable top on a 1931 Open Cab Pickup. The top is black, fine, long-short-grain artificial leather and is mounted on a black-painted steel frame. The outside door handles are the same as those on a Standard Roadster.

1931

This is a 1931 76-B Open Cab Pickup with the top removed. The left-side fender-mounted spare tire is standard on light commercial vehicles.

Right: This is a close-up view of a folding windshield frame and stanchions on a 1931 Open Cab Pickup. The frame and stanchions are painted black. The black-painted wiper motor is a Trico vacuum Model TR-O1C, which is only used on the 76-B. The wiper arm is a black-enamel Trico 6½-inch.

Far right: The front compartment and instrument panel on a Duchess Blue 1931 76-B Open Cab Pickup.

Early in 1931, fender well–mounted spare tire equipment was made available for certain AA chassis. This equipment required the use of the AA-1417 wheel carrier support and accompanying hardware, the AA-16030 splash shield, and the AA-16036 front fender with well (LH). Later, there was similar equipment available for a right side-mounted spare wheel and tire.

In March 1931, a special AA-82766 left-hand door assembly was made available for use with the 82-B cab when a left-side fender well–mounted spare wheel was attached. This door had a depression to clear the spare tire when the door was opened. This door was originally intended for use with the 199-A and 229-B, but was made available for other bodies as needed. There was no indented door available for the right side.

Another change was an increase in the offset of the AA-1015-C wheels to provide more clearance between the tires when dual wheel equipment was installed. This distance was increased from 7¼ inches to 7½ inches because of the industrywide change to balloon-type tires, which had a wider cross-section. All 20-inch Budd wheels continued to use the same double-bent metal valve stem introduced in 1930.

Also in January 1931, a new front crossmember was adopted in the 157-inch wheelbase chassis. The new design eliminated the previous solid front engine mounting on the AA-5017

Original Ford Model A

Above left: This 1931 76-B Open Cab Pickup seat is trimmed with black-brown two-tone Cobra cross-grain artificial leather. The floor is covered with a black rubber mat. By 1931 the parking brake lever is to the right of the gear-shift lever.

Above: Left rear quarter view of a 76-B Open Cab Pickup with the early-style 78-A pickup body. The pickup still uses the frame-mounted forged taillight bracket rather than the fender-mounted units used on passenger cars. The bed-mounted toolbox is an accessory.

front cross-member. The engine support was changed to the normal A-6030 used on the passenger cars and the 131.5-inch wheelbase chassis. Old cross-members could be modified by sawing off the engine support.

A major modification to the 157-inch wheelbase chassis in January 1931 was the change from tapered to parallel frame rails behind the cab. This new AA-5008 frame brought the Ford chassis configuration in line with the rest of the industry and allowed for a larger number of bodies to be mounted without modification. This change required new spring-seat mounting positions.

In April 1931, an improved AA-1015C2 wheel was adopted. This new wheel design added a raised reinforcing bead around the outside of the hub bolt holes. This reinforcement decreased the chance of cracks in the wheel from stress and from improper mounting nut torque. The new wheel eliminated the need for adapter plates previously used to strengthen wheel mountings.

In July 1931, Ford released a new 18-inch AA-1015-F disk wheel and accompanying 32x7 high-pressure tire. The 18-inch wheel used the same nickel-plated double-bent valve stem equipment as the 20-inch Budd disk wheel. This equipment was intended for service where a single rear wheel and tire with the weight-carrying capacity of dual wheels was required. Use of this new tire and wheel increased the rear tread width by 1½ inches

The lower body of this 1931 130-B Deluxe Delivery is finished in Kewanee Green with the upper body in Elkpoint Green. The stripe and wheels are Apple Green. Like the Deluxe Pickup, the Deluxe Delivery has the passenger car radiator and headlight shells.

1931

Above: A left-side fender-mounted spare tire is standard on all commercial vehicles, including this 1931 Deluxe Delivery. The Deluxe Delivery has a single left-hinged rear door. The turn signals are safety accessories.

Above right: Detail of a rear A-132300-B door on a 1931 130-B Deluxe Delivery. The turn signals, center bumper guard, and front door wind wings are accessories.

Above: An interior view of the cargo compartment of a 1931 130-B Deluxe Delivery. The interior sidewalls are trimmed with black-brown Cobra cross-grain cardboard. The headlining is matching artificial leather.

Above right: The individual seats are trimmed with black-brown Cobra cross-grain artificial leather. The floor is covered with a black rubber mat. The turn signal switch is a safety accessory.

Right: Left front driver's door of a 1931 Deluxe Delivery. The interior trim panel is black-brown two-tone Cobra cross-grain cardboard. The garnish moldings are painted black and the hardware is bright nickel.

The detail of a T-shaped A-32550-BR locking handle for the rear door of a 1931 Deluxe Delivery. The large rear door was designed to ease loading of large and bulky cargo.

Original Ford Model A

and required a special spare tire and wheel mounting. When mounted on the left-side running board spare mount, the driver's door could not be used. Collectors and restorers rarely encounter these 18-inch wheels today.

In April 1931, Ford introduced two new AA frames. One was the AA-5005-D long frame, a 10-inch-longer version of the frame used on the 131.5-inch wheelbase chassis. This frame replaced the former AA-5005-B, which was no longer used. In addition to the longer standard frame, Ford produced the AA-5005-D short frame, which was used on the dump truck and the 229-A Service Car.

Also in April 1931, a new AA-16025 reinforced front fender bracket assembly was adopted for the AA chassis, replacing the A-16025-B4 passenger car unit. The reinforcement was added to the frame mounting surface and reduced the chance of stress cracks in this area. This bracket was also available as a service item on the passenger car chassis if customers were complaining of breakage.

In May 1931, a new rear bumper was released for the AA truck chassis. The design was similar to the bumper used on the Deluxe Delivery, Ambulance, and Funeral Coaches but was made in two parts like the passenger car rear bumperettes. The new AA-17814 assembly was

Top: This 1931 Mail Truck is mounted on a standard 103½-inch wheelbase Model A chassis. There were 550 of these 100-cubic-foot capacity bodies made for the U.S. government in 1931 and 1932. The body is constructed of wood with steel bracing.

Above: The 1931 Mail Truck has a body and cowl finished in a special Post Office Department Olive Green. The hood and radiator shell are black.

1931

Above: A detailed view of rear cargo doors on a 1931 Mail Truck body. A similar but larger 200-cubic-foot-capacity body was built on the AA chassis. The rear windows have steel screens and roll-down curtains.

Above right: This 1931 Mail Truck has seats trimmed in standard black-brown Cobra cross-grain artificial leather like that used in other Ford trucks. The front doors are sliding.

available on a variety of models and, of course, for dealer service installation as desired.

In June 1931, the AA rear axle was reinforced with four ribs on the housing. These ribs added even more strength and reliability to the already strong Ford-designed axle.

Ford made another design change to strengthen the AA chassis in August 1931 with new rear hubs. The axle bearing surface in the new AA-1113-F2 and AA-1114-F2 rear hubs was integral with the hub rather than a pressed-in sleeve as in the previous design. This improvement required no changes to the axle or brake drum assemblies.

In August 1931, an entirely new Standrive AA chassis, known as the AA-112, was introduced. With this new chassis, intended for milk and delivery trucks, the driver could operate the truck while standing. The frame was dropped in the center and the wheelbase was reduced to 112.5 inches. The Standrive used different pedal assemblies, engine controls, and starter control. The steel floorpans and driveshaft tunnel were made integral with the chassis. The Standrive was equipped with left- or right-side fender-mounted spare tire and wheel equipment.

The 315-A Standrive Delivery was specifically designed for milk delivery service and was equipped with a Baker-Raulang body. It had a cargo compartment 60.1 inches long by 62.5 inches wide by 63 inches high. These unusual models were so difficult to market that a number of them were still carried over for sale in 1932. Very few Standrive trucks survive today.

The biggest news for the AA chassis for 1931 was the proliferation of bodies available from Ford. The unprecedented number and variety of equipment offered on the 1931 Ford truck chassis was a clear indication of Ford's desire to provide a vehicle and equipment for every buyer's needs. Ford sought to eliminate the need for buyers to go to outside vendors for truck bodies and equipment.

As in 1930, the 76-B open-cab and 82-B closed-cab bodies were used in their standard form on a number of AA units, including the 185-B and 187-A Platform, 186-B and 189-A Stake, 195-A and 197-A Express, 199-A Ice Wagon, and all dump and coal bodies. All bodies for the 157-inch wheelbase chassis were modified to accommodate the new parallel chassis in January 1931. The old bodies could not be used on the new chassis.

The new-design 195-A (short wheelbase) and 197-A Express bodies were introduced in January 1931 and were standard versions for 1931. They were similar in concept to the new wide-bed

Original Ford Model A

Right front quarter view of a 1931 AA dump truck on a 131½-inch wheelbase chassis. There were at least five different types of standard dump bodies offered on the 1931 AA chassis. The body finish is vermilion, which was one of the 39 standard commercial colors available in 1931.

pickup body. The sides were straight and flatter in appearance. The 195-A Express body for the 131.5-inch wheelbase chassis was 102.5 inches long, 54 inches wide, and 16 inches high. There was also a 196-A canopy top offered for the Express body that stood 52 inches above the body floor. The body was known as a Screen-Side Express when equipped with the canopy and optional screens. The canopy top and screens were introduced in January 1931.

The 157-inch wheelbase chassis was offered with a 197-A Express body. The 197-A was the same width and height as the shorter body but was 132 inches long. There was a 198-A canopy top available for the long Express body. Budd built both the short- and long-wheelbase Express bodies. They had full-length running boards, splash shields, and rear fenders.

A new design for 1931 was the 242-A Heavy-Duty Express body. This body was built by Murray and had much higher sides than the standard Express bodies. The 242-A was available only with dual rear wheels. The Heavy Express body was also introduced in January 1931.

There were some entirely new bodies available for 1931. One of the most unusual was the 229-A Service Car. Introduced at the end of 1930, the Service Car, known in some advertising as a Road Service Truck, was the large version of the Deluxe Pickup. Available only on the 131.5-inch wheelbase chassis, the Service Car offered a distinctive style for the operator hoping to enhance the image of his garage, tire, or towing business.

The Briggs-built Service Car used the standard 82-B cab but had body sides that extended to the door openings and followed the molding and lines of the body styling. The body sides were secured to special wood pillars at the cab door opening. The Service Car was equipped with rear fenders and full-length running boards and splash shields.

The rear body was 69.1 inches long, 53.4 inches wide, and 22.5 inches high. Unlike the 66-A, there was no tailgate provided on the 229-A body. Initially, a left-side–mounted spare wheel and indented door were standard equipment for

Detail of left side of 1931 AA dump truck with left-side fender-mounted spare tire and wheel. This truck has the early 1931 AA-1015-C 20-inch Budd wheels. The door is a special AA-82766 with depression to clear the spare tire. This door was only offered as a left-side unit.

1931

A 1931 229-A Service Car on a 131½-inch wheelbase AA chassis. The design of the Service Car was used later on the Deluxe Pickup. The 82-B cab uses the same indented door as the dump truck. This Service Car is finished in vermilion and is equipped with a Weaver crane.

Below: The AA-82766 indented door is used to clear the left-side fender-mounted spare tire and wheel. There is also a rare AA-16035 right-side welled AA fender but no right-side indented door.

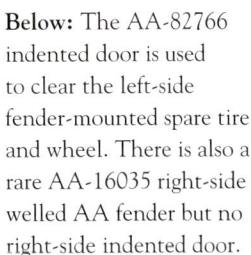

Detail of the left rear AA-16439-B rear fender for use with the 229-A long running board and splash shield. The taillight is mounted on a forged, black-painted A-13470-B lamp bracket.

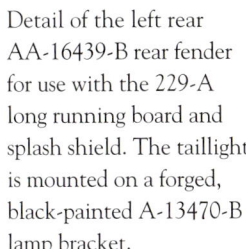

This is a right-side quarter elliptic rear spring mounting and right rear brake assembly on a 131½-inch wheelbase AA chassis.

the Service Car. Later in 1931, the spare was moved to the right-side running board just behind the right door. The 229-A was equipped with a special toolbox mounted in the front of the inside of the body. The inside of the body was finished in Ford Commercial Gray.

On May 8, 1931, Ford also introduced a new 239-A Packer's Express body. This special design body, built by Briggs, was designed for the meat-packing industry and was 96 inches long, 62 inches wide, and 12.5 inches high. The Packer's Express body could be built using either the open or closed cab.

In addition to Ford, many other body builders, such as Wood, Gallion, Square Deal, Omaha, and Wayne, offered truck bodies.

Ford provided a number of new bodies for 1931 that were designed entirely independent of the 76-B or 82-B cab. These included a new AA Deluxe Delivery, Panel Delivery, Ambulance, Funeral Service Car, Funeral Coach, and Large Panel bodies.

The 85-B AA Panel Delivery was built on the standard 131.5-inch wheelbase and was essentially unchanged from its 1930 counterpart. The AA Panel Delivery had a more squared body than

Original Ford Model A

A 1931 school bus mounted on a 131½-inch wheelbase chassis. The body was made by the Wayne Body Company of Richmond, Indiana. This body uses the Ford-supplied commercial cowl strip. The fender-mounted lights are safety accessories.

Front view of a 1931 AA school bus shows the black-enamel AA-8200-A steel radiator shell. Note the straight upper opening, different in design from the passenger car shell. This 1931 truck uses the stainless AA-8212 nameplate. Note the black-enamel AA-17750-B front bumper assembly adopted in November 1930.

the Deluxe Delivery and used the same A-79764-AR (RH) and A-79765-AR (LH) doors as the 225-A and 79-B.

The 210-A Large Panel body, mounted on the 157-inch wheelbase chassis, was introduced late in 1931 and offered a good-looking, fully enclosed panel unit appropriate for furniture dealers and department stores. The interior of the cargo compartment was 136 inches long, 57.5 inches wide, and 60 inches high. The body had a roof vent and rear half-doors with a 20-inch-high-tailgate. Dual rear wheels, wide rear fenders, and full-length running boards were standard equipment.

The 270-A Funeral Service Car was based on the 131.5-inch wheelbase Deluxe Delivery but had single large windows on each side of the body panels. The interior was equipped with casket rollers, window covers, and a flower tray. The seats were trimmed in black, fine, long-short-grain genuine leather. The Funeral Service Car and the Funeral Coach, like the Deluxe Panel Delivery, were equipped with stainless radiator shell, double-bar bumper, cowl band, cowl lights, and stainless head and taillights. The special stainless radiator shell carried part number AA-8200-B.

The 275-A Funeral Coach was also based on the AA Deluxe Delivery with its 131.5-inch

1931

Above: This close-up shows the special cowl molding used on Ford commercial chassis delivered to outside body builders. This cowl strip offered a straight vertical area for attachment of the aftermarket body. It replaces the cowl strip that normally fits under a standard windshield.

Right: Detail of right front AA-1015-C2 Budd 20-inch wheel with reinforcing rib around the center hub. This was the latest design of the Budd wheel, and it was used in similar form through the 1933 model year. The front uses an AA-1131 cadmium-plated hubcap and cadmium-plated snap ring.

Complete tool set for a 1931 Model A chassis. The tools are in a custom-built wooden display box used for car shows. The tools were originally in the black tool bag on the lower left of the display.

wheelbase, but it was equipped with four doors and large side windows. The Funeral Coach and the Funeral Service Car were both equipped with all standard required funeral equipment and used special rear springs, rear shock absorbers, AA-1015-E 20-inch steel spoke wheels, and related AA-1137 hubcaps. The Funeral Coach was trimmed with deluxe interior hardware, carpeting, and green mohair upholstery. Both the Funeral Coach and Funeral Service Car were equipped with left-side fender-mounted spare wheel equipment.

Another derivative of the same body was the 280-A Ambulance. Except for special interior equipment and trim, the 280-A shared its body with the 275-A Funeral Service Car. Like the other derivatives of this body, the Ambulance was equipped with deluxe trim and equipment, such as 20-inch spoke wheels, stainless radiator shell, and lights. The interior trim of the 280-A Ambulance included seats trimmed in black, fine, long-short-grain genuine leather.

The basis for the preceding bodies was the 131.5-inch wheelbase 300-A Deluxe Delivery. This two-door body was intended to be an upgrade to the standard Panel Delivery for the business looking for a more upscale image. The body of the Deluxe Delivery was more rounded and stylish than the standard AA Panel Delivery.

The 300-A was offered with distinctive standard equipment such as a stainless radiator shell, cowl band, cowl lights, stainless headlights and taillights, and chrome AA-1757-A double-bar front bumper. The 300-A used AA-215760-ER (RH) and AA-215761 (LH) doors, which it shared with the Funeral Coach, Funeral Service Car, and Ambulance. The AA Deluxe Delivery also was equipped with the left-side fender-mounted spare wheel and indented door like its derivatives.

The interior of the 300-A Deluxe Delivery had plain-panel seats trimmed in black, fine, long-short-grain genuine leather. The door panels, cowl, header, quarters, and seat base are covered with black, fine, long-short-grain artificial leather. The rear cargo area panels were trimmed with Commercial Gray–painted Masonite. Interior garnish moldings were painted gloss black.

An additional derivative of the AA Deluxe Delivery body was the 285-A Deluxe Police Patrol with two doors. The 285-A was equipped with chrome double-bar AA bumper, AA-8299-B stainless radiator shell, headlights, cowl band, and cowl lights. There was also a 290-A Standard Police Patrol, based on the AA Panel Delivery. The Standard Police Patrol had a black-enamel AA-8200-A radiator shell, black headlight shells, and used the standard single-bar black-enamel front bumper. All of the Police Patrol designs were based on the 131.5-inch wheelbase only.

Original Ford Model A

DEALER OPTIONS AND AUTHORIZED FORD ACCESSORIES

Item	Part Number	Date Adopted	Original Price
Air filter (Air Maze)	A-18500	September 1929	$3.75
Bumper, rear, one piece or two-piece option		July 1931	
Cigar lighter	A-18527	January 1929	$1.75
Clock, header mounted	A-18540	December 1928	$12.00
Colors, special, passenger commercial		June 1931	$14.50
Colors, commercial chassis & fenders		June 1931	$15.00/20.00
Cowl lamps		March 1929	$10.50
Distributor heat baffle	A-12280	December 1929	
Draft deflectors (closed-body wind wings)	A-18275, 76, 77, 78	July 1931	
Fender lamps		March 1929	$5.50
Fender-mounted spare wheel & carrier		May 1928	$12.00
Four-speed transmission in A chassis		July 1931	
Heater, manifold (Ford)		October 1928	$3.50
High-compression head	A-6050-B	April 1931	$7.35
Landau irons on Business Coupe		August 1928	
Lap robe	A-18545	March 1931	$4.50
Low-ratio (4.11:1) rear axle gears		March 1929	
Luggage rack, black enamel	A-18575-A, -B, -C, -D	June 1929	$5.00/11.00
Luggage rack, chrome			$11.50
Package tray & screen for Deluxe Delivery		August 1929	$12.50
Motometer, Boyce	A-18354-AR, -B	July 1929	$5.00
Pedal pads	A-18422	October 1928	$0.35
Quail mascot radiator cap	A-18354-AR, -B	July 1928	$3.00
Rear bumper extension		August 1930	
Rumble seat		December 1927	$35.00
Seat covers	A-18625, 26, 27, 28	May 1929	$11.00/20.00
Spare wheel lock	A-18330-A	July 1928	$2.50
Spare wheel & tire lock	A-18305-AR, -B	July 1928	$3.00
Spare wheel guard		June 1930	$2.25
Sportlight	A-18552	December 1928	$15.00/17.50
Spring covers (gaiters)	A-18400	July 1928	$3.00
Tire cover (fabric)		February 1928	$2.00
Tire cover, metal		June 1930	$6.25/7.50
Tire pressure gauge (US & Schrader)	A-18413-A1, -A2	July 1928	$1.50
Top boot for open bodies		May 1928	
Top rest saddles, standard Phaeton	A-37330		
Trunk		June 1929	
Wheel colors			$10.00 set
Whitewall tires, double sided			
Window screen, rear, for 82-B cab	A-83860	July 1931	
Windshield wings, open body		May 1928 (Standard after 1928)	$8.00

Note:
Some of these items will be removed for final MARC/MAFCA judging, check Judging Standards.
Any additional accessories are either limited or not allowed by the MARC/MAFCA Judging Standards.

TOOLS 1931 A CHASSIS

Item	Part Number	Finish	Note
Grease gun	A-17125	Dull nickel	Alemite
Tool bag	A-17005	Black top material	11x6½ inches (closed)
Adjustable wrench			9½ inches
Sparkplug and head nut wrench	A-17017	Black	
Pliers	A-17025	Unfinished/black	
Open-end wrench	A-17015		⁷⁄₁₆ x ½
Open-end wrench	A-17016		⁹⁄₁₆ x ⅝
Screwdriver		Unfinished/black	8⁹⁄₁₆-inch
Jack	A-17080-C1, -C2, -C3	Black	8½, 8½ inch
Jack handle	A-17081-B	Black	39 inches
Tire iron	A-17019	Unfinished/black	16 inches
Tire pump		Black	
Crank	A-17036-B	Black	
Owner's manual		Tan	1931

TOOLS 1931 AA CHASSIS

Identical to A except for AA starting crank, jack, jack handle, lug nut wrench and tire iron.

Starting crank		Black	No lug nut socket
Jack	A-17080-A, A-17080-B (Sept. 1931)	Black	A-17080-B has a 2-inch square top and larger threaded shaft
Jack handle		Black	24 inches long
Tire iron		Black	16⅝-inches long
Lug nut wrench		Black	15 inches long, 1½ – ⅞-inch sockets
Lug nut wrench handle		Black	20 inches long

Model A and AA Accessories

Although the Model A Ford was clearly intended to satisfy and dominate the low-priced market, Ford offered a great number of factory-authorized, dealer-installed accessories and dress-up items for all Ford cars and trucks. The accessory list, published in June 1931, included more than 50 items that dealers were encouraged to sell to new Ford owners. These items included tire covers, fender lamps, bumper extensions, Motometers, Sportlites, and more. Selling these items gave dealers a significant opportunity for profit. Accessories were sold at a 40 percent discount to the dealer, whereas the discount on the cars themselves was only 22 percent by 1931.

The three jacks used with the 1931 Model A are, from left to right, A-17080-C1, -C2, and -C3. The A-17080-C3 is made by Noblitt Sparks. All jacks are painted black.

The two AA jacks used with the 1928-31 AA truck chassis have a screw-type design. From left to right, they are: AA-17808-A with a 1⅝-inch square top and a AA-17080-B with a 2-inch square top and larger-threaded shaft. The larger jack was introduced in September 1931.

Appendix 1
Related Clubs & Organizations

Related Clubs and Organizations

American Truck Historical Society
P.O. Box 901611
Kansas City, MO 64190-1611
816-891-9900
www.aths.org

Antique Automobile Club of America
501 W. Governor Road P.O. Box 417
Hershey, PA 17033
Phone: 717-534-1910
www.aaca.org

Model A Ford Club of America
250 S. Cypress Street
La Habra, CA 90631-5586
562-697-2712
www.mafca.com

Model A Restorer's Club
24800 Michigan Avenue
Dearborn, MI 48124-1713
313-278-1455
www.modelaford.org

The Society of Automotive Historians
1102 Long Cove Road
Gales Ferry, CT 06335-1812
www.autohistory.org

Related Periodicals and Publications

Hemmings Motor News
P.O. Box 100
Bennington, VT 05201
800-227-4373
www.hemmings.com

Old Cars Weekly News & Marketplace
700 East State Street
Iola, WI 54990-0001
800-258-0929
www.krause.com

Appendix 2
Owners of Featured Cars

Chapter One

Car	Color	Owner
1928 35-A Phaeton	Arabian Sand, Light	Larry Hassel
1928 40-A Roadster	Dawn Gray	Ken Keeley
1928 55-A Tudor	Dawn Gray	Ray Seidel
1928 60-A Fordor	Balsam Green	Walt Gaertner
1928 60-A Fordor	Rose Beige	Kenneth Anderson
1929 140-A Town Car	Black	Timothy Kelly
1928 89-A AA Express	Red	Ray Matthews
1928 AA Railway Express	Green	Bill Henderson

Chapter Two

Car	Color	Owner
1929 140-A Town Car	Black	Carle Garrett
1929 40-A Canadian Roadster	Arabian Sand	Woody Williams
1929 150-A Station Wagon	Manila Brown	Ben Staub
1929 40-A Roadster	Andalusite Blue	Ken Beckwith
1929 45-A Standard Coupe	Vagabond Green	Don Davis
1929 50-A Sport Coupe	Vagabond Green	Lyman Elliot
1929 54-A Business Coupe	Andalusite Blue	Mike and Gail Ross
1929 49-A Special Coupe	Vagabond Green	Les Burton
1929 50-A Sport Coupe	Andalusite Blue	Les Burton
1929 55-A Tudor	Andalusite Blue	Don Temple
1929 135-A Taxi-Cab	Duchess Blue	Carle Garrett
1929 76-A Open Cab Pickup	Rock Moss Green	Kevin Ellway
1929 140-A Town Car	Maroon	Carle Garrett
1929 150-A Station Wagon	Manila Brown	Carle Garrett
1929 155-B Town Sedan	Vagabond Green	Johann Sverdrup
1929 165-B Standard Fordor	Maroon	Roger King
1929 AA 85-A AA Panel Delivery	Maroon	Bill McGeehn

Chapter Three

Car	Color	Owner
C1930 40-B Standard Roadster	Brewster Green	Jim Ruth
1930 55-A Tudor	Chicle Drab	Don Roberts
1930 55-A Tudor	Copra Drab	Craig Rose
1930 45-B Standard Coupe	Kewanee Green	Don Howk
1930 155-C Murray Town Sedan	Kewanee Green	Bob Reale
1930 155-C Murray Town Sedan	Black	Don Mozny
1930 68-B Cabriolet	Bronson Yellow	John and Bonnie Borst
1930 140-B Town Car	Black	Carle Garrett
1930 82-B Closed Cab Pickup	Rock Moss Green	Dean Bittick
1930 165-D Standard Fordor	Black	Bob Austin
1930 82-B Closed Cab Pickup	Cherokee Gray	Jim Ruth
1930 188-A AA Stake	Rock Moss Green	Herb Wuesthoff

Chapter Four

Car	Color	Owner
1931 40-B Deluxe Roadster	Stone Brown	Robert Baker
1931 35-B Standard Phaeton	Kewanee Green	Chuck Shaw
1931 180-A Deluxe Phaeton	Washington Blue	Jerry Pilcher
1931 40-B Deluxe Roadster	Brewster Green	Dean Bittick
1931 40-B Deluxe Roadster	Stone Brown	Val Peistrup
1931 45-B Standard Coupe	Kewanee Green	Jerry and Judy Brown
1931 68-C Cabriolet	Bronson Yellow	Jerry Detomasi
1931 170-B Deluxe Fordor	Ford Maroon	Gene Cogorno
1931 160-B Town Sedan	Ford Maroon	Les Burton
1931 190-A Victoria	Black	Dean Bittick
1931 190-A Victoria	Ford Maroon	Phil Ierardi
1931 400-A Convertible Sedan	Black	Carle Garrett
1931 66-A Deluxe Pickup	Rubellite Red	Chuck Zuidema
1931 130-B Deluxe Delivery	Kewanee Green	Bruce and Bunny Palmer
1931 Mail Truck	Olive Green	Lew Palmer
1931 Dump Truck	Red	Keith Ernst
1931 229-A Service Car	Vermilion	Bruce and Bunny Palmer
1931 School Bus	Wayne Yellow	Bruce and Bunny Palmer
1931 400-A Convertible Sedan	Aqua Green	Lloyd and Ruby Kerr
1931 76-B Open Cab Pickup	Duchess Blue	H. Davie Weston

Index

134-A stock rack body, 61
134-B grain-side option, 61
135-A Taxi-Cab, 48–52
140-A Town Car, 33, 49, 52
150-A Station Wagon, 33, 35, 52, 53
150-B Station Wagon, 108
155-A Town Sedan, 33
155-B Town Sedan, 33
160-A slant-windshield Standard Fordor, 103
160-A Standard Fordor, 103
160-B slant-windshield Town Sedan, 103
160-C slant-windshield Delxe Fordor, 103
170-B Deluxe Fordor, 102
170-B Deluxe Two-Window Fordor, 63-87
180-A Deluxe Phaeton, 63–87, 97
190-A Victorian Coupe, 63–87, 105
1927 Model A Engine Numbers, 12
1928 Model A Engine Numbers, 12
20 Millionth Ford, 90
35-A Phaeton, 8, 9
35-B Standard Phaeton, 93
400-A Convertible Sedan, 107
40-A Roadster, 38
40-A Standard Roadster, 20–22
40-B Deluxe Roadster, 63–88
40-B Standard Roadster, 62–87
45-A Standard Coupe, 21, 22
45-B Deluxe Coupe, 63–87, 98
45-B Standard Coupe, 65–87, 97
49-A Special Coupe, 21, 22
50-B Sport Coupe, 99
54-A Business Coupe, 22, 23, 44, 46
55-A Tudor sedan, 23, 46
55-B Deluxe Tudor, 101
55-B Standard Tudor sedan, 65–87
60-A Fordor, 24, 25
60-A Leatherback Fordor, 24, 25
68-A Cabriolet, 33
68-B Cabriolet, 99
68-C Cabriolet, 99
A-1015-AR, 12
A-11805-AR instrument panel, 16
A-13473 mounting bracket, 9
A-9002 AR, 67

AA 85-A Panel
AA closed-cab Express truck, 30
AA Truck Chassis, 27, 29, 60, 61, 86, 87, 116–126
Accessories, Model A, AA, 126
Allegheny Metal, 62
Arabian Sand Light, 8
Axles, 9–13, 33–35, 64–66, 89
Baker Raulang Body Company, 83
Body assembly, 18–20, 38–60, 69-85, 94–116
Body color schemes, 59, 82, 112, 113
Briggs Manufacturing Company, 49, 50
Canadian Roadster, 32, 33
Chassis, 9–13, 33–35, 64–66, 89
Color Schemes, 27
Cooling system, 15, 37, 66, 90
Copra Drab molding, 8
Depression, 88
DUOLIGHT, 17, 19, 29
Eaton, Welker-Hoops, 67
Electrical System, 16, 17, 37, 68, 94
Engine Assembly, 13, 14, 35, 36, 66, 89, 90
Engine numbers, 35, 64, 91
Fender assembly, 18–20, 38–60, 69-85, 94–116
French Gray, 8
Fuel System, 15, 37, 67, 92
Headlight lenses, 14
Ignition system, 17
Innovations, 62, 63
Interior trim combinations, 28, 57, 58, 80, 81, 109–111
Murray Body Company, 33
Owen-Dyneto electric windshield wiper, 27
Production chart, 9, 34, 64, 92
Radiator shell, 14
Radiator, 15, 37, 66, 90
Stewart Warner, 16
Suspension, 9
Town Sedan, 33, 36
Transmission and Clutch, 14, 15, 36, 66, 90
Trico vacuum windshield wipers, 63
Warner T8-1, 61
Wheels, 9–13, 33–35, 64–66, 89
Zenith 1, 67
Zenith 2, 67